"David Mathis is right that two thousand years later, the biblical qualifications for elders 'continue to pulse with relevancy to the everyday work of Christian leadership.' What a great help this book would have been forty years ago when I was trying to build church-wide consensus around how the local church is to be led. What makes this book unique is the way pastoral joy, patient exposition, and personal application are woven into the fabric of Christian leadership. May God use *Workers for Your Joy* to raise up thousands of leaders who do not lord it over their people's faith, but 'work with you for your joy' (2 Cor. 1:24)."

John Piper, Leader, Teacher, and Founder, desiringGod.org

"As an author who has written two books about leadership in Christ's church, I know of no other book like *Workers for Your Joy*. David Mathis leads you through an examination of the biblical qualifications of an elder in a way that is penetrating, personal, and practical at every point. As I read chapter after chapter, each dedicated to a pastoral qualification, I was both deeply convicted and encouraged. As you read, you cannot help being amazed at the generosity of our Lord in gifting his church with this kind of leadership—all for the joy of his people. And I have to say: I love that joy is the central organizing theme of this book about pastoral ministry! I cannot think of any member or leader in the body of Christ who would not benefit from taking some time to stroll through the garden of practical gospel wisdom that makes up the pages of this book."

Paul David Tripp, Pastor; author, *Lead: 12 Gospel Principles for Leadership in the Church* and *Dangerous Calling: Confronting the Unique Challenges of Pastoral Ministry*

"Our culture is averse to authority, partially because of the sinful abuse of authority. Still, God intended for there to be leaders in our churches, and David Mathis helps us understand in this biblically saturated and pastorally wise book what the Scriptures teach about elders. The duties and responsibilities of elders are unpacked clearly and powerfully chapter by chapter. We desperately need qualified and godly leaders in our churches, and this is the ideal book for church members considering who should lead a church, for leaders as they consider whether they are qualified, and for seminarians and college students as they study what the Scriptures teach about elders."

Thomas R. Schreiner, James Buchanan Harrison Professor of New Testament Interpretation, The Southern Baptist Theological Seminary

T0006438

"The antidote to bad authority is not no authority. It's good authority. And we need a whole lot more good authority—humble, whole, and honorable—in the church today. I commend David Mathis's wonderfully clear and biblical guide to Christian leadership that glorifies God."

Collin Hansen, Vice President for Content and Editor in Chief, The Gospel Coalition; Host, *Gospelbound* podcast; coauthor, *Rediscover Church*

"At a time when Christian reflection on leadership seems to have been hijacked by ideas from the corporate world, it is refreshing to see a book on leadership that derives its material from the Scriptures. The major leadership crisis facing the church today has to do with character, not with method or strategy. The Bible has a lot to say about that. This is the focus of this book. It reflects deeply on what the Scriptures teach in a way that challenges our attitudes and behaviors and encourages change toward Christlikeness."

Ajith Fernando, Teaching Director, Youth for Christ, Sri Lanka; author, *The Family Life of a Christian Leader*

Workers for Your Joy

Workers for Your Joy

The Call of Christ on Christian Leaders

David Mathis

WHEATON, ILLINOIS

Workers for Your Joy: The Call of Christ on Christian Leaders
Copyright © 2022 by David C. Mathis
Published by Crossway
   1300 Crescent Street
   Wheaton, Illinois 60187

All rights reserved. No part of this publication may be reproduced, stored in a retrieval system, or transmitted in any form by any means, electronic, mechanical, photocopy, recording, or otherwise, without the prior permission of the publisher, except as provided for by USA copyright law. Crossway® is a registered trademark in the United States of America.

Cover design: Jordan Singer

First printing 2022

Printed in the United States of America

Unless otherwise indicated, Scripture quotations are from the ESV® Bible (The Holy Bible, English Standard Version®), copyright © 2001 by Crossway, a publishing ministry of Good News Publishers. Used by permission. All rights reserved. The ESV text may not be quoted in any publication made available to the public by a Creative Commons license. The ESV may not be translated into any other language.

Scripture quotations marked KJV are from the King James Version of the Bible. Public domain.

Scripture quotations marked NASB® are taken from the New American Standard Bible®, copyright © 1960, 1971, 1977, 1995, 2020 by The Lockman Foundation. Used by permission. All rights reserved. www.lockman.org.

Scripture quotations marked NIV are taken from the Holy Bible, New International Version®, NIV®. Copyright © 1973, 1978, 1984, 2011 by Biblica, Inc.™ Used by permission of Zondervan. All rights reserved worldwide. www.zondervan.com. The "NIV" and "New International Version" are trademarks registered in the United States Patent and Trademark Office by Biblica, Inc.™

All emphases in Scripture quotations have been added by the author.

Trade paperback ISBN: 978-1-4335-7807-6
epub ISBN: 978-1-4335-7810-6
PDF ISBN: 978-1-4335-7808-3
Mobipocket ISBN: 978-1-4335-7809-0

Library of Congress Cataloging-in-Publication Data

Names: Mathis, David, 1980– author.
Title: Workers for your joy : the call of Christ on Christian leaders / David Mathis.
Description: Wheaton, Illinois : Crossway, 2022. | Includes bibliographical references and index.
Identifiers: LCCN 2021061419 (print) | LCCN 2021061420 (ebook) | ISBN 9781433578076 (trade paperback) | ISBN 9781433578083 (pdf) | ISBN 9781433578090 (mobipocket) | ISBN 9781433578106 (epub)
Subjects: LCSH: Christian leadership—Biblical teaching. | Elders—Biblical teaching. | Prests Biblical teaching. | Clergy—Biblical teaching.
Classification: LCC BS2545.L42 M38 2022 (print) | LCC BS2545.L42 (ebook) | DDC 262/.1—dc23/eng/20220411
LC record available at https://lccn.loc.gov/2021061419
LC ebook record available at https://lccn.loc.gov/2021061420

Crossway is a publishing ministry of Good News Publishers.

To all the saints in Christ Jesus at Cities Church,
with the pastors and deacons

Do not rejoice in this, that the spirits are subject to you,
but rejoice that your names are written in heaven.

LUKE 10:20

Contents

PART 3: HONORABLE: MEN BEFORE
A WATCHING WORLD

Preface

Not that we lord it over your faith,
but we work with you for your joy.

2 CORINTHIANS 1:24

WE LIVE IN AN AGE that has become painfully cynical about leadership—some of it for good reason. Much of it is simply the mood of our times.

Stories of use and abuse abound, and the letdowns make for big headlines. In the Information Age we have more and quicker access than ever before to tales of bad leaders. In our own lives, we all have felt the sting of being let down by some leader in whom we had placed our trust. The pain and confusion are real. The wounds can be deep. We learn to guard ourselves from future disappointment. Cynicism can feel like a worthy shield.

But the high-profile failures can mask the true source of our discontent with being led: we love *self* and come to pine for *self-rule*. Couple with it our generation's distorted sense of what leadership is. When leadership has become a symbol of status, achievement, and privilege—as it has in many modern eyes—we desire to be the leader ourselves, not to bless others but to get our way. And, understandably, we become reluctant to grant anyone else that authority over us.

Led by God through Leaders

Into such confusion the Christian faith speaks a different message. You need leadership. It is for your good. You were designed to be led, first and foremost by God himself—through the God-man, Jesus, who now wields all authority in heaven and on earth at the Father's right hand. God made you to be led. He designed your mind and heart and body not to thrive in autonomy but to flourish under the wisdom and provision and care of worthy leaders and, most of all, under Christ himself. But there is more.

The risen Christ has appointed, even *gifted* his church with, human leaders, in submission to him, on the ground in local congregations. Precious as the priesthood of all believers is—a remarkable truth that was radically countercultural from the first century until the Reformation—today we have need to articulate afresh the nature and goodness of leadership in the local church—an important kind of *gracious inequality* within our equality in Christ.

Christian Vision of Leadership

One of the ways Christ governs his church and blesses her is by giving her the gift of leaders: "He *gave* the apostles, the prophets, the evangelists, the shepherds and teachers, to equip the saints for the work of ministry, for building up the body of Christ" (Eph. 4:11–12).

The mention of shepherds and teachers is of special significance, not only because it is the subject of this book but also because it is intensely personal to you as a Christian. It includes the *pastors* of your particular local church (and note that *pastors* is plural—that's a major theme of this book). You've never met one of Jesus's apostles (even as their writings remain precious to us beyond words!), but chances are you know a pastor. I hope that many readers of this book will themselves be pastors. Faithful pastors are a gift from Christ to guide and keep his church today.

Are pastors flawed? Of course. Sinful? Regrettably. Have some pastors made terrible mistakes, sinned grievously, fleeced their flocks, and harmed the very ones they were commissioned to protect? Sadly, yes, too many have. Such failures do not fulfill the vision of what true Christian leadership is, but fall short of it or depart from it altogether. In fact, such failures show—by contrast—what real leadership in the church *should* be.

That's what this book is about: *what Christ calls leaders in his church to be and do*, especially the lead office or teaching office in the church, that of *pastor* or *elder* or *overseer*—three terms in the New Testament for the same lead office (more on that to come). At times the bar may seem surprisingly low. Other times it may seem almost impossibly high. Sometimes we'll talk in ideals; other times, very practically. My prayer is that these pages will be useful to congregants and leaders alike in considering what Christ expects of, and what vision he himself has cast through his apostles and prophets for, leadership in the local church.

Leaders for Your Joy

The epistle to the Hebrews gives this important glimpse into the dynamic of Christian leadership:

> Obey your leaders and submit to them, for they are keeping watch over your souls, as those who will have to give an account. Let them do this with joy and not with groaning, for that would be of no advantage to you. (Heb. 13:17)

Here is a beautiful, marriage-like vision of the complementary relationship between the church and its leaders. The leaders, for their part, *labor* (they work *hard*; it is costly work) for the advantage—the profit—of the church. And the church, for its part, wants its leaders to work not only hard but *happily*, without groaning, because the pastors' joy in leading will lead to the church's own benefit. The people want their leaders to labor with joy because they know their leaders are working for theirs.

Leaders in the church, then, as Paul says of himself, are to be *workers for the joy of their people.* "Not that we lord it over your faith, but we work with you for your joy" (2 Cor. 1:24). Christ gives leaders to his people for their joy, which turns the world's paradigm and suspicions about leadership upside down.

For Your Advance and Advantage

Paul saw himself as such a *worker for joy* in the lives of the Philippians. Though in prison, he suspected this wasn't yet the end for him but that he would be released: "I will remain and continue with you all, *for your progress and joy in the faith*, so that in me you may have ample cause to glory in Christ Jesus, because of my coming to you again" (Phil. 1:25–26).

The apostle saw his leadership as a laboring for the church's "progress and joy in the faith." Not just progress, but progress *and joy.* How eager, then, would the people have been to submit to such a leader? The prospect of submitting to a leader drastically changes when you know he isn't pursuing his own private advantage but genuinely seeking yours, what is best for you, what will give you the deepest and most enduring joy—when he finds his joy *in yours* rather than *apart from* or *instead of* yours.

For readers who are skeptical of leaders in general (as many people today are—again, sometimes for good reasons), what if you knew that "those who are over you in the Lord" (1 Thess. 5:12) were not in it to stroke their ego, or secure selfish privilege, or indulge their desires to control others, but actively were laying aside their personal rights and private comforts to take inconvenient initiative and expend their limited energy to work for your joy?

For readers who are formal leaders in the church, in the home, or in the marketplace, what if those under your care were convinced—deeply convinced—that your place of relative authority, under Christ, was not for self-aggrandizement or self-promotion but was a sobering call to self-sacrifice, and that you were working for their joy? That your joy in leadership was not a selfish pursuit, but a holy satisfaction you were finding in the joy of those whom you lead?

No Greater Joy

The Christian vision is that leaders taste the greatest joys when they look out for, and give themselves to, the interests of others—when they marshal their power and effort to bring about the advantage and advance (on God's terms) of those in their care. Such leaders know the delight of the apostle John, who says, "I have no greater joy than to hear that my children are walking in the truth" (3 John 4). They can say, with Paul, "What is our hope or joy or crown of boasting before our Lord Jesus at his coming? Is it not you? For you are our glory and joy" (1 Thess. 2:19–20).

When undershepherds in the church show themselves to be *workers for your joy*, they walk in the steps of the great shepherd—the great worker for joy—the one who bore the greatest cost for others' good, and not to the exclusion of his own joy. He found his joy in the joy of those for whom he was Lord. "For the joy that was set before him [he] endured the cross" (Heb. 12:2). He is the one who tells us to pray, "that your joy may be full" (John 16:24) and speaks to us, "that my joy may be in you, and that your joy may be full" (John 15:11; also John 17:13). And he is the one who gives pastors to his church for your joy.

This Book

Christian leadership exists for the joy of the church. Such a vision may turn some of our churches upside down, first for pastors and then for the people. That's the vision I hope to impart, and linger in, in this book.

My hope is that these chapters will be useful for Christians who do not personally aspire to office in the church but hope to get clarity, in confusing times, about what they can and should hope for and pray for and expect in their leaders in the local church. I also hope this book will bless those who aspire to be pastor-elders and deacons (the two offices in the church), to get a fresh sense of what the work is (and is not). The concepts and approach of these chapters originally emerged from teaching seminary students (aspiring pastors) at Bethlehem College & Seminary (BCS), beginning in 2012. With congregants and particularly aspiring pastor-elders in mind, my friend (and instructional designer) Pam Eason lent her expertise to crafting study questions for each chapter, from preface to conclusion. She designed these with both individual and group study in mind. They are located at the back. I'm amazed to see Pam's skill at work, extending the key concepts of these chapters into insightful and enjoyable questions and activities. I pray many will benefit from the study, not just the reading.

If I may be so bold, I also hope that this book might be of some use for those who are already in local-church office, whether newly or for years. This book may not have many new concepts and perspectives to offer you, but perhaps rehearsing them afresh, in this format, could provide some renewed sense of the preciousness of your charge and enrich the joy you find in it—for the good of your people (Heb. 13:17). Perhaps these pages will offer something you've overlooked or neglected. We all are lifelong learners.

In teaching the eldership class for the last decade at BCS, maybe my single biggest discovery has been how much the practical-ministry topics one would want to address with aspiring pastors map onto the elder qualifications in 1 Timothy 3:1–7 and Titus 1:5–9. Imagine that! The apostle Paul, speaking for the risen Christ, really knew what he was talking about. Almost two thousand years later, these qualifications continue to pulse with relevancy to the everyday work of Christian leadership, if we will only slow down enough to really listen and think and learn.

The eldership qualifications are not simply moral hoops to jump through to then be qualified to do the work of pastoring. Rather, Christ, through his apostle, requires these traits because they are *the precise virtues pastor-elders need* for the day-in, day-out work of their calling. These *are* the graces we need to be good pastors. These are not just *pre*requisites but ongoing requisites, because this is *who the elders need to be* to do what they're called to do. Without these fifteen attributes, leaders will not prove, in the long haul, to be genuine workers for the joy of their church. They will devolve, in time, into self-servers. They will not prove to be the kind of pastors we all want. Let me say it once more, so that the particular focus of this book is lost on as few readers as possible. The qualifications are not the main subject of this book. Rather, the pastorate, or eldership, is the subject, and the qualifications are the lens through which we will address the topic.

So, then, if the remarkable ongoing relevance of the elder qualifications is one of the central offerings of the book, why not just keep with Paul's order for the book's structure? Well, lists in a series, in a single sentence, don't necessarily impress themselves upon a reader in the same way that fifteen *chapters* do in the flow of a book. I'm asking you to pause with me over these qualifications and see the pastor's task through them. Intentional as Paul is in his choice of virtues in 1 Timothy 3 and Titus 1, I don't believe he would insist we search them out in a particular order. Just the varying order of his twin lists may make that clear enough.

As for my semi-apologetic for the order of this volume and its parts, I'm taking my cues from the (near) mysterious power of three.[1] Perhaps it's because God is one and three, and our universe, even when we do not perceive it, dances spectacularly to the tune of one and three. Or maybe it's just enduringly helpful for finite creatures like us (prone to see things from a single perspective, or maybe two) to consider three angles. However deep the magic, I often find it illuminating to push myself to ponder three vantage points rather than just one or two. I don't force every sermon into a three-part outline, but I end up there an awful lot—and not just three disparate bullets but three perspectives that illumine and reveal one singular, multidimensional whole. In a previous project, on the so-called spiritual disciplines, a triperspectival approach contributed to the main insights I offered there, considering God's *means of grace* for the Christian life in view of

---

1   See John Frame's article "A Primer on Perspectivalism," The Works of John Frame and Vern Poythress website, June 4, 2012, https://frame-poythress.org/. Also John Frame, *Theology in Three Dimensions: A Guide to Triperspectivalism and Its Significance* (Phillipsburg, NJ: P&R, 2017); and Vern Poythress, *Symphonic Theology: The Validity of Multiple Perspectives in Theology* (Phillipsburg, NJ: P&R, 2001).

three loci: the word of God (normative), prayer (existential), and fellowship (situational).[2]

On the topic of eldership—whether you're a congregant considering your leaders or an aspiring (or current) pastor pondering your call—I find the elder qualifications cleanly cluster to at least one of three axes: (1) the man before his God (the devotional life), (2) the man before those who know him best (his private life), and (3) the man before the watching church and world (public life). In sum, we might say *humbled*, *whole*, and *honorable*. Instead of proceeding through the fifteen qualifications in the order of 1 Timothy 3, I've arranged them according to this paradigm. Sometimes we find insights in simply coming at known concepts in a fresh order.

This book does not mainly offer lessons from my years of pastoral ministry (only fourteen at the time of publication). This book is largely a biblical vision of Christian leadership that takes the elder requirements with utter seriousness. I have not aimed to produce a practical guide. This book is not designed to give you simple answers about many of the perennial questions in eldership—some of them, yes, but this is not mostly lessons and answers.

This book aims to paint a vision, not just in broad brushstrokes but with the fine lines the New Testament gives us and what we discover about those lines as we follow them across the canon of Scripture. Experience is not irrelevant. You probably wouldn't want a book like this to be all theory from a man who has never pastored. But I hope my limited experience (as still a young pastor who recently turned forty) won't be too much of a drawback. Perhaps if I waited another twenty years to write this book, then it would be substantially different. But I doubt it, given its nature.

---

2 *Habits of Grace: Enjoying Jesus through the Spiritual Disciplines* (Wheaton, IL: Crossway, 2016).

Time will tell. For now, I give you what I can offer, informed first by Scripture and tested in about two decades of spiritual leadership, from college ministry to almost fifteen years as a pastor—and sharpened and challenged by a decade in the seminary classroom. Not to mention with many wise, old friends in life and in print.

At the end of the day, I want to point you, like every good Christian teacher should, to the words of the chief shepherd himself in the writings of his apostles and prophets. If readers of this book will simply take the elder qualifications of 1 Timothy 3 and Titus 1 with new seriousness (and fresh enthusiasm to embody them and apply them in the labor of pastoring), I will feel a great satisfaction in this work. I could say, "My joy will increase." Which is another main emphasis and offering of this book.

I take the topic of joy in leadership very seriously. I believe, with John Piper, that "there is a joy without which pastors cannot profit their people."[3] In the Christian life and in spiritual leadership the pursuit of joy is not peripheral. It is not icing on the cake. It is central. Christian leaders, if they are true and faithful, are *workers for your joy*. As are good husbands and fathers and mothers and coaches and bosses and politicians. In one sense, this could be a book for any kind of leader—that is, if he wants to be *Christian* in his leadership. The vision is fundamentally different from the operating assumptions of fallen men in our sin-sick world. But there are Christians today, in business and in politics and elsewhere, who are disillusioned with the world's assumptions about leadership as personal privilege instead of glad self-sacrifice for the collective good. I hope some readers in those spheres will find here—in the elder qualifications of all places!—the fresh vision they are look-

---

3 John Piper, *Desiring God: Meditations of a Christian Hedonist* (Eugene, OR: Multnomah, 2011), 11.

ing for to be a different kind of leader in the world, the kind of leader Jesus would call them to be. But mainly this is a book about Christian leaders in the local church and what the risen Christ calls them to be and do.

So what is the kind of pastor we all want? What does it mean for leaders to be *workers for your joy*? Let's find out.[4]

---

4 Study questions, by chapter, are available at the back of the book, beginning with this preface.

Introduction

The Pastors We All Want

Shepherd the flock of God that is among you,
exercising oversight, not under compulsion,
but willingly, as God would have you.

1 PETER 5:2

SEVERAL NEW TESTAMENT texts give us snapshots of leadership that are plainly different from today's prevailing paradigms.[1] Yet the place I turn most often and most enjoy inviting others into is 1 Peter 5:1–5. I pray that God may be pleased in our day to raise up and sustain pastors like this, the kind of pastors we all want. Here at the outset of this book on Christian leadership in the local church, before we turn to the elder qualifications as a lens into the heart of the call and daily work, consider five glimpses Peter gives of the leading or teaching office in the church, that of pastor or elder.

---

1 Among them would be Mark 10:42–45; Acts 20:18–35; and 2 Tim. 2:22–26, in addition to the qualifications listed in 1 Tim. 3:1–13 and Titus 1:5–9.

Men Who Are Present and Accessible

Peter begins, "I exhort the elders *among you* . . . : shepherd the flock of God that is *among you*" (1 Pet. 5:1–2). He says it twice in just one sentence. The pastor-elders (two terms for the same office in the New Testament, as we will see) are *among the people*, and the people are *among the elders*. Together they are one church, one flock.

Good pastors are first and foremost sheep. They know it and embrace it. Pastors do not comprise a fundamentally different category of Christian. They need not be world-class in their intellect, oratory, and executive skills. They are average, normal, healthy Christians, serving as examples for the flock, *while among the flock*, as they lead and feed the flock through teaching God's word, accompanied with wise collective governance. The hearts of good pastors swell to Jesus's charge in Luke 10:20: "Do not rejoice in this, that the spirits are subject to you, but rejoice that your names are written in heaven." Their first and most fundamental joy is not what God does *through them* as pastors but what Christ has done (and does) *for them* as Christians.

Good pastors, therefore, are secure in soul and not blown left and right by the need to impress or to prove themselves. They are happy to be seen as normal Christians, not a cut above the congregation but reliable models of mature, healthy Christianity.

Another way to say it is that such pastors are humble. After all, Peter charges "all of you"—elders and congregants—"Clothe yourselves, *all of you*, with humility toward one another" (1 Pet. 5:5). Healthy churches are eager to clothe themselves in humility toward their pastors who have led the way in dressing with humility for the church.

Such pastors, humble in practice, not just in theory, are *present* in the life of the church and *accessible*. They invite, welcome, and receive input from the flock. They don't pretend to shepherd God's flock in all the world through the Internet but focus on the flock "that is among you"—those particular names and faces assigned to their charge—and they delight to *be among* those people, not removed, distant, or remote.

Men Who Work Together

One of the most important truths to rehearse about pastoral ministry is that Christ means for it to be *teamwork*. This will be a major theme in this book. As in 1 Peter 5, so in every context in which local-church pastor-elders are mentioned in the New Testament, the title is plural. Christ alone sits atop the church as Lord. He is head of the church (Eph. 1:22; 5:23; Col. 1:18), and he alone. The glory of singular leadership is his. And he means for his undershepherds to labor and thrive *not alone* but as a team.[2]

2   Given the number of churches today with single pastor-elder structures, it may be worth addressing briefly, even this early in the book, how a pastor in such a situation might pray and work toward building a team of fellow pastors. In short, I would counsel him to make a patient plan to get there. Typically it is no fault of his own when a pastor finds himself in such a situation. Don't assume you are in error to be there, but I would think you are mistaken to happily stay there without some intentional effort to raise up other leaders (as Paul charges his protégé in 2 Tim. 2:2). Granted, you cannot raise up leaders overnight. But you may already have some ready-made elders in your congregation. You might start by making a list of Bible teachers. If you were going to have one or two other men in your church, other than you, teach the Bible for the whole church, who would it be? And if you do not already have qualified men at the ready, you can raise up men, God helping you, in a matter of time, whether a few years or perhaps even months, depending on the circumstances and your context. Begin by praying for God to raise up other qualified leaders in your congregation. Pray for particular faces and names. Then, in time, make a plan for regular meetings and opportunities to invest life-on-life in one or a few men in your church who have potential and invite them into the process. You might even pray, as you work, that God would cause a mature brother in Christ to come to your church out of the blue as well. A busy lone-ranger pastor may feel like he simply does not have the time to add personal disciple-making to his full schedule. I would counter that your busyness is precisely the reason to begin making the investment now. The demands on you are likely to increase over time, not recede, and you need more hands on deck to do the work to which

Mature congregations don't want an untouchable leader, perched high atop the church in his pulpit, safely removed from accountability and the rough-and-tumble exchanges of instinct and convictions among leaders that make for real wisdom. The kind of pastors we long for in this age are *good men with good friends*—friends who love them enough to challenge their assumptions, tell them when they're mistaken, hold them to the fire of accountability, and make life both harder and better, both more uncomfortable and more fruitful.

Men Who Are Attentive and Engaged

Pastors also exercise oversight (1 Pet. 5:2). However fragile modern humans have become, deep down we still want leaders who don't just listen and empower but also take initiative, give guidance, and provide genuine leadership. We want leaders who speak to us the word of God (Heb. 13:7) and actually do the hard and costly work of oversight, or governing, which they have been called to do. "Pay careful attention to yourselves and to all the flock, in which the Holy Spirit has made you overseers, to care for the church of God" (Acts 20:28).

However experienced and capable good pastors may be, they are not typically men known for their world-class intellect, extensive experience, or their administrative savvy. Rather, they are known as *men of the book*—men for whom having God's word in Scripture makes all the difference in leadership; men whose leadership style is Bible based. The Bible is not a supplement or assumption for them; the Bible is central and explicit. God has spoken; that changes everything. Such pastors don't just *say* they trust God's

---

Christ calls the church's pastors. I would counsel you not to wait any longer. Begin praying, planning, searching, and taking some small steps now.

word. They trust it enough to know it backward and forward and bring it to bear, in prudent and proper application, on issue after issue in church life.

We want men who steward influence as teachers, not insist on control—"not domineering over those in your charge" (1 Pet. 5:3). Men who manifestly serve others, not self, with their abilities and authority. Men who actually expend the effort it takes to *lead*, not just occupy positions of authority. Men who do not treat the office as a privilege for personal gain but as a call from God to die to private comforts and convenience and to embrace the harder roads. Men who do the hard work to win trust rather than lazily presume it. Men who, as Peter says, "shepherd the flock of God" (1 Pet. 5:2), which not only means leading and feeding, casting vision and communicating truth, but also defending and protecting. This leads to a fourth quality.

Men Who Lean into Hardship

The true colors come out for leaders and congregations when tough times arise. We want the kind of pastors who lean in—not with forcefulness, necessarily, though that may be needed on occasion (yet rarely), but with even greater attentiveness, care, courage, and patient teaching.

In conflict, "the Lord's servant" must not only be kind and patient, and correct opponents with gentleness, but also "able to teach" (2 Tim. 2:24–25), which in this context seems more like an inward temperament than an outward skill (more on that in chapter 3). God's people don't need teaching only in peacetime but just as much when times are tough, and even more. We need pastors who do not mainly see a static world of right and wrong and stand ready to pronounce judgment, but "teachers at heart," ready to take people where they are, in error and ignorance, and patiently present truth in an understandable and persuasive way, seeking to win them. When those who are in error receive such treatment from pastor-teachers, who knows? "God may perhaps grant them repentance leading to a knowledge of the truth, and they may come to their senses and escape from the snare of the devil, after being captured by him to do his will" (2 Tim. 2:25–26).

Good pastors rise to the occasion in hardship. When times get tough, the hired hands flee (John 10:12–13); the true undershepherds abide. Peter's "So" in 1 Peter 5:1 refers to what he just wrote in the previous sentence: "Let those who *suffer* according to God's will entrust their souls to a faithful Creator while doing good" (1 Pet. 4:19). Suffering is the context of Peter's charge to the elders. That's why he turns next in his letter to the elders—when the going gets toughest, the weight falls especially on the elders. As it should.

Good pastors know this and learn to lean in with courage and gentleness. When the situation is fraught, they become more present, not less. When uncertainty emerges, they grow more attentive, not less. Not that they have to be certain, or feign it, about what's next and how the conflict will end. But they lean in and lead together and lean on fellow brothers in the cause. They do not pretend *their way* is best or the only one, but at least, with prayer and counsel, they will propose *a way* forward. When they don't know what to do, they know one thing to do: look to God (2 Chron. 20:12). They initiate. They take a risk and put themselves out there in a world of cynicism and criticism. They overcome their fear of being wrong in the hope of caring for others.

To embrace the calling to the pastoral office in the church is to embrace suffering. Pastors suffer in ways *as pastors* they would not otherwise. But they do so looking to the reward, the selfless gain to be had, the glory commensurate with the work, which is not shameful but pure: "When the chief Shepherd appears, you will receive the unfading crown of glory" (1 Pet. 5:4). Which leads to a final quality.

Men Who Enjoy the Work

Churches want happy pastors. Not dutiful clergy. Not groaning ministers. The kind of pastors we all want are the ones who want to do the work and labor with joy for our joy. We want pastors who serve "not under compulsion, but *willingly*, as God would have you" (1 Pet. 5:2).

God himself wants pastors who labor from the heart. He wants them to aspire to the work (1 Tim. 3:1) and do it with joy (Heb. 13:17). Not dutifully or under obligation but willingly, eagerly, happily. And not just "as God would have you" but "as God himself does"—literally "according to God" (Greek *kata theon*). It says something about our God that he would have it this way. He is the infinitely happy "blessed God" (1 Tim. 1:11) who acts from joy. He wants pastors to work with joy because he is this way. He acts from fullness of joy. He is a God most glorified not by raw duty but by eagerness and enjoyment, and he himself cares for his people willingly, eagerly, happily.

Churches know this deep down—that happy pastors, not groaning elders, make for happy churches. Pastors who enjoy the work and work with joy are a benefit and an advantage to their people (Heb. 13:17).

Our Chief Pastor

Such are the pastors we all want. Of course, no man, and no team of men, will embody these dreams perfectly, but men of God learn to press through their temptations to paralysis and resignation because of their imperfections. They happily lean on Christ as the perfect and great shepherd of the sheep, roll their burdens onto his broad shoulders (1 Pet. 5:7), remember that his Spirit lives and works in them, and then learn to take the next courageous, humble step—ready to repent and retry if it was the wrong one.

As pastors learn to live up to these realistic dreams—albeit not perfectly, but making real progress by the Spirit—some aspects of our wounded leadership culture will find healing. At least our churches, if not our world, will learn to lay down suspicions and enjoy God's gift of good pastor-teachers.

The Church and Its Elders

Now, having lingered in that vision of eldership from 1 Peter 5:1–5, let's establish a few basic, glorious truths about the church before addressing eldership more extensively. The nature of eldership flows from the nature of the church. And 1 Timothy 3:15 may be the best one-verse summary of the essence of the church. If I could give you just one text on the heart of ecclesiology, this would be it. The church, says 1 Timothy 3:15, is "the household of God" and "pillar and buttress of the truth."[3]

Most of us know what pillars are; fewer today may be familiar with buttresses. A pillar lifts the roof up, and a buttress keeps the walls in. A pillar holds up from below so the roof doesn't fall; the buttress holds up from the side so the walls don't come down. What Paul is getting at in 1 Timothy 3:15 with the image of the pillar and the buttress, we might summarize as *presentation* and *protection*. Or advance and defense. Strength and support. A pil-

---

3 Bill Mounce calls this "perhaps the most significant phrase in all the Pastoral Epistles." *Pastoral Epistles*, Word Biblical Commentary (Nashville, TN: Thomas Nelson, 2000), 222.

lar compresses against vertical weight for the sake of lifting an impressive structure high and catching eyes and attention, while a buttress acts against lateral forces to reinforce the defenses and provide security and stability. The church, then, as pillar and buttress holds high the truth (presentation) and holds firm to the truth (protection).

But what is "the truth" in verse 15? Is it truth in general, like the truths of mathematics and chemistry and physics? Is it truth *in general* that the church holds high and holds firm for the sake of maintaining order in society?

Here and throughout 1 and 2 Timothy and Titus, "the truth" doesn't mean truth in general, but specifically *the* truth, the message of the gospel that Jesus saves sinners (as in ten other texts: 1 Tim. 2:4; 4:3; 6:5; 2 Tim. 2:18, 25; 3:7, 8; 4:4; Titus 1:1, 14). And this *truth* contrasts with the *myths* propagated by false teachers. In other words, the truth in view in the Pastoral Epistles is the message of the gospel.[4] So the church, we could say, is the pillar and buttress of *the gospel*. The church exists for the presentation and protection of the gospel of Jesus Christ. For the advance of the gospel and its defense.

Creature of the Word

Another way to say it is that the church is a *creature of the word*— a people ("living stones," 1 Pet. 2:5) created and sustained by the word of the gospel for the advance and defense of the gospel (pillar and buttress), molded and shaped through and through by God and his word and the climactic revelation of himself in Jesus and his work.

---

4 As Mounce summarizes it, "'truth' in the Pastoral Epistles [is] a technical term for the gospel message." *Pastoral Epistles*, 86–87.

The church is the creature of the word, the people of the gospel, created and birthed by the message of Jesus to lift it high and hold it firm. This is why Paul celebrates the way he does in verse 16.

Mystery of Godliness

First Timothy 3:16 expands "the truth" in 3:15. And we have this new enigmatic term "the mystery of godliness":

> . . . the household of God, which is the church of the living God, a pillar and buttress of the truth. Great indeed, we confess, is the mystery of godliness:
>
> > He was manifested in the flesh,
> > > vindicated by the Spirit,
> > > seen by angels,
> > proclaimed among the nations,
> > > believed on in the world,
> > > taken up in glory. (1 Tim. 3:15–16)

Throughout 1 Timothy, *godliness* refers to Christian living. In light of who God is, we are to live together in the church in increasing degrees of likeness to him—godliness. We are to imitate God, imaging him, and live as he would if he were human in the world. And now Paul, in celebrating the church, moves into the very truth that created the church and sustains it and is its organizing principle at its center: the person and message of Jesus. We already saw Jesus's message in "the truth." Now we get his person in the poetic lines of verse 16.

The mystery of godliness, then, is that God himself in the person of his Son did become man and live in our world—true godliness in human form—died for the ungodly, rose again in triumph, and now empowers the spread of his message throughout the world by his Spirit through his church. The mystery of godliness—a mystery no longer hidden but now revealed—is that we are not the source of our own godliness, but Jesus is. We don't *achieve* our own godliness. We begin by receiving God's gift to us in Christ, and his grace goes to work in and through us. As God incarnate, he is godliness incarnate. And only through him and the truth of his gospel and the power of his Spirit can we learn true godliness. The church is not a collection of self-made people. The church is Christ-made, a creature of his word.

Church Hymn

Some call these poetic lines in verse 16 a "Christ hymn," but in this context it's not only about him. It's also a church hymn. This celebration of Christ becomes a celebration of the church. That's how we arrived here, remember. In peeling back the layers to the very heart of the church, we come to the gospel and to the Savior himself. And the poem has something to say not only about Jesus but also his church:

He was manifested in the flesh,
    vindicated by the Spirit,
    seen by angels,
proclaimed among the nations,
    believed on in the world,
    taken up in glory.

The last word of each line forms three pairs: flesh/Spirit, angels/nations, world/glory. The hymn shows the universality and magnitude of Jesus's work. He brings together human flesh and the realm of the Spirit, the angelic hosts and the earthly nations, the physical world and heavenly glory.

What's the connection to the church? The first two descriptions focus on what we might think of as the gospel: "He was manifested in the flesh, vindicated by the Spirit." He came, he lived, he died, he rose, he ascended. But the church—the people created by the gospel—is essential to complete the poem: "proclaimed among the nations, believed on in the world." In union with her groom, the church stands with Jesus in spanning both the realms of flesh and spirit, both the audiences of angels and nations, and both this world and the glory to come.

So we have here a portrait of the glory of Christ and his church in the unrestricted scope of their impact and mission. Two worlds come together: the present world of flesh and nations and the coming world of angels and heavenly glory. And all of this celebrates the grandeur and expansiveness and beauty of Christ—and his church, which is essential in completing his mission in the world.

The church is the people in whom the physical world and spiritual universe come together. Here meets the current age and the age to come. The Lord of heaven kisses the things of earth. And the church is the manifestation, the creature, of Jesus's saving work, and the hands and feet of his ongoing work in the world.

Through the Church

Quite simply, there is no other institution among humans like the church. No other group, no other body, no other coming together in all of creation is more significant. In another memorable place in his letters, Paul celebrates like this the grandeur and centrality of the church in God's plan: Ephesians 3, verses 10 and 20. Let's see them with some context:

Of this gospel I was made a minister according to the gift of God's grace, which was given me by the working of his power. To me, though I am the very least of all the saints, this grace was given, to preach to the Gentiles the unsearchable riches of Christ, and to bring to light for everyone what is the plan of the mystery hidden for ages in God who created all things, so that *through the church the manifold wisdom of God might now be made known to the rulers and authorities in the heavenly places.* (Eph. 3:7–10)

Now to him who is able to do far more abundantly than all that we ask or think, according to the power at work within us, *to him be glory in the church* and in Christ Jesus throughout all generations, forever and ever. Amen. (Eph. 3:20–21)

Through the church—and no other particular institution or instrument—God is making his manifold wisdom known to the spiritual powers in the heavenly places (angels). And his glory— the very glory of God!—is shining from two great sources: "in the church and in Christ Jesus." It is an almost unbelievably awesome calling. Yet we can be so prone to take the church lightly. May God be pleased to work in us wonder, like Paul's, that the church exists and that, in Christ, we get to be a part of the most important body and mission in the world today and in all of history.

Where Pastor-Elders Fit

Now the pastor-elders. If the essence of the church is as a creature of Christ's word, then the essence of eldership, we might say, is that pastor-elders are men of the word, men of the gospel.

I say "pastor-elders" here and throughout the book with the understanding that in the New Testament, elder = pastor = overseer.

These are not three offices in the New Testament but three terms for one office, the teaching or lead office. Three texts, among others, make this unmistakable, from the narrative of Acts, to Paul's letters, to Peter's. Acts 20:17 says Paul gathered the "elders"; 20:28 then says these elders are "overseers" who "care for"—literally the verb "pastor"—"the church of God." Titus 1:5 speaks of appointing elders; 1:7 uses the term "overseer." And like Acts 20, 1 Peter 5 brings all three terms together: Peter exhorts the elders (v. 1) to "shepherd" or "pastor" (same verb as Acts 20:28) God's flock, "exercising oversight" (v. 2).[5]

These pastor-elder-overseers are to be "men of the gospel," just as the church is the creature of the gospel. In chapter 3, we will look at that often underappreciated and very important qualification "able to teach" (Greek *didaktikos*, 1 Tim. 3:2). What is it that the elders teach? They teach the word of God that culminates in the gospel of Christ. Titus 1:9, we might say, expounds the requirement (note well this is for *all elders*, not just teaching elders or a preaching pastor): "He must hold firm to the trustworthy word as taught, so that he may be able to give instruction in sound doctrine and also to rebuke those who contradict it."

Pastor-elders are to be men of the word who know God's word, enjoy it, linger over it, have been shaped by it, live it, and want to teach others about it at every reasonable opportunity they can find. So Paul's charge to Timothy is not only for Timothy but for all pastor-elders: "Do your best to present yourself to God as

---

5 For more on the case that elder = pastor = overseer in the New Testament, see, among others, Benjamin L. Merkle, *40 Questions about Elders and Deacons* (Grand Rapids, MI: Kregel, 2008), 76–83; Gregg Allison, *Sojourners and Strangers: The Doctrine of the Church*, Foundations of Evangelical Theology (Wheaton, IL: Crossway, 2012), 211–12; Dave Harvey, *The Plurality Principle: How to Build and Maintain a Thriving Church Leadership Team* (Wheaton, IL: Crossway, 2021), 26n3.

one approved, a worker who has no need to be ashamed, rightly handling the word of truth" (2 Tim. 2:15).

Christ means for his church—which is a word people, created by his word—to be led by word men. These word men, these teachers, as we'll see, have two main tasks: to lead and to feed. The duly appointed elders, not just men in general, are the ones who "teach" and "exercise authority" (1 Tim. 2:12) in the church. The elders both "rule" (or "lead" or "govern") and "labor in preaching and teaching" (1 Tim. 5:17). The elders are "those who *labor among you* [in teaching] and *are over you* [in governing] in the Lord and admonish you" (1 Thess. 5:12). As we'll see, the New Testament presents no regular category in church life of either "teachers" or "leaders" that are not pastor-elders. Whether the title is elder or overseer or pastor, or the function is teaching or governing, the New Testament consistently refers to one office.[6]

An important clarification to add is that the teaching provided by the elders is not to be thought of as "the ministry" of the church. It's not the pastors who do "the ministry" while the congregation receives it or watches it. Rather, "the ministry" is what the congregation does in the world, in every nook and cranny of the community, in the home, in the neighborhood, at work, at play, in each other's lives, and in the lives of unbelieving friends, neighbors, and coworkers. What the pastor-elders do in their teaching and leading is "equip *the saints* for the work of ministry" (Eph. 4:12).

Receiving the apostles' teaching and freshly proclaiming and applying it to the congregation through preaching and teaching is

---

6   The New Testament presents two offices in the local church: "overseers and deacons" (Phil. 1:1; 1 Tim. 3:1, 8). This book focuses on the lead office, the teaching office, that of overseer/ elder/pastor, though the assisting office, as we might call it, is not irrelevant or unrelated. For more on deacons, see appendix 1.

the central task of the elders, but not the only one. Many today use the title "pastor" because we look to the elders to serve as shepherds in caring for the welfare of the church in its countless facets. The elders do more than simply teach; the elders are not only proactive in teaching and planning but responsive in meeting needs that arise.[7] And every local church faces countless decisions that don't fall out of the Gospels and Epistles like nice exegetical apples. Open Bibles and quoted Scripture at elder meetings are essential, and they rarely provide easy answers to some of thorniest issues facing faithful churches. The elders together must make mind-bending decisions that are not teaching per se; but God, remarkably, appoints that *the teachers*, those who should best know the apostles' word, make these decisions on a regular basis, for the sake of the congregation.[8]

Humbled, Whole, and Honorable

The God of all grace has appointed that a plurality of mature Christian men—who know and love and are able to effectively communicate his word and his gospel—lead and feed his flock in the life of the local church. The God who has spoken—particularly in the Scriptures and his incarnate Word—created and sustains the church, a creature of his word, through the teaching and guidance of its leaders. So who are these men? In part 1, we turn our atten-

---

7 "A substantial part of the ruling/oversight function is discharged through the preaching and teaching of the Word of God. This is where a great deal of the best leadership is exercised. . . . But oversight of the church is more than simply teaching and preaching. . . . Just because a person is an able preacher does not necessarily make him an able pastor/elder/overseer. Indeed, if he shows no propensity for godly oversight, then no matter how good a teacher he may be, he is not qualified to be a pastor/teacher/overseer." D. A. Carson, "Some Reflections on Pastoral Leadership," *Themelios* 40.2 (2015): 197.

8 This is true both in elder-rule churches and in elder-led, congregational-rule churches. For my brief and measured case for elder-led, congregational rule, see "Who Governs the Local Church?" Desiring God, July 30, 2020, https://desiringgod.org.

tion to *humbled*: men before their God, what we might call the Godward or devotional life. Then we will look at *whole*: men in their own homes and private life, among those who know them best. Finally, in part 3, we will conclude with *honorable*: men before the watching eyes of the church and in the world, exemplary in their public life.[9]

---

9 Here is one final reminder about the study questions at the end of the book, designed for individuals or small groups to develop the concepts of these chapters and in particular to move them toward application.

PART 1

———————

HUMBLED

Men before Their God

An overseer, as God's steward, . . . must not be arrogant.

TITUS 1:7

I count fifteen qualifications in 1 Timothy 3:1–7. Some see fourteen. But in a book like this in which we are emphasizing the calling of pastor-elders to be "workers for your joy," we will want to make much of the condition in verse 1: "*If anyone aspires* to the office of overseer, he desires a noble task." As we saw in 1 Peter 5:2, it is no small detail that God wants men who *aspire* to the work, men who *want* to do this labor, men able to *find joy* in what might be joyless work for many others. We need pastor-elders who exercise oversight "not under compulsion, but willingly." Not all who aspire to the work will still do it willingly and joyfully ten or twenty years later. But without an aspiration, we have no good reason to expect the necessary gladness will come.

Here in part 1, we will start where Paul starts in 1 Timothy 3:1, with "aspiration," and consider the perennial question of how God appoints pastors to the work. How does a man know if he is "called" to the lead office in the church? The question is not altogether different from how we might know our calling into any line of labor, though in this one, as we'll see, there is an unusual necessity.

Then we jump to what's second to last in Paul's list—humility—but conceptually so critical that in expanding the qualifications into chapters, it might be wise to address it up front in this book, not wait till the end. The Kings James Version says "not a novice"; the ESV, "not a recent convert"; and then the reason: so that he may not "become *puffed up with conceit* and fall into the condemnation of the devil." In chapter 2 we'll look at both realities: that elders not be new converts, on the one hand; and the deeper reason, and sobering reality, that arrogance in the elders is particularly destructive and spiritually deadly. The church needs pastor-elders who have been humbled and continue to grow in humility as they age.

Next is the single qualification that most sets elders apart from the deacons: able to teach. I'm aware that this is controversial today; it hasn't always been so. Some traditions now lean hard on a distinction between "teaching elders" and "ruling elders." I believe that's a mistake, and instead of just arguing for a particular reading of 1 Timothy 5:17, I'll try to provide a larger vision and framework of the eldership in the New Testament, including the "able to teach" (Greek *didaktikos*) qualification in 1 Timothy 3:2, that leads me to think of pastor-elders as essentially teachers, and that the regular teachers of the whole church are essentially (and ideally) the pastors. Hebrews 13:7 says, "Remember your leaders, those who spoke to you the word of God." He could assume that their leaders were the ones who spoke to them the word of God because the leaders were teachers, not mere governors.

As to why we address *didaktikos* here in chapter 3, so relatively early in the book: in the New Testament, the pastor-elders are so identified with teaching that it would be unwise to proceed at length into this study without tackling this central calling and function. In Paul's list, *didaktikos* is fittingly at the very heart of the list, the eighth of the fifteen. But in this book, I doubt it would be wise to wait until halfway through to consider this one qualification that is perhaps the most distinctive as well as controversial.

Finally, we conclude part 1 with what may well be the most underrated qualification: sober-mindedness. Pastor-leaders are to be men who keep their heads under pressure, in conflict and controversy. And in just the normal, steady-state life of the church, we need level-headed, wise, spiritually and emotionally intelligent leaders rather than those who are impulsive, imbalanced, and reactive because pastor-elders are not just God-appointed teachers but God-appointed governors. I remember on many occasions sitting around the table with fellow elders when a man's name would come up as a candidate. Guys would shake their heads and reach for words. He's not a good fit. Or not yet. I came to learn that often the language we were groping for was right here in the eldership qualifications: sober-minded.

1

How Christ Appoints His Pastors

If anyone aspires to the office of overseer,
he desires a noble task.

1 TIMOTHY 3:1

IS GOD CALLING ME *to be a pastor in a local church?* Many Christian men wrestle with this question at some point in their life of faith. Not just in adolescence or early manhood but sometimes at midlife or even as they approach their golden years.

The New Testament doesn't draw neat and distinct lines between full-time ministry and so-called secular work. In whatever God, by his providence, leads us into for our day job, he calls us to do our work "not by way of eye-service, as people-pleasers, but with sincerity of heart, fearing the Lord" (Col. 3:22). Christ's apostle charges all workers, "Whatever you do, work heartily, as for the Lord and not for men, knowing that from the Lord you will receive the inheritance as your reward. You are serving the Lord Christ" (Col. 3:23–24; also Eph. 6:6–8). Some pastors, unfortunately, may be too quick to overlook the application of these texts to our labors in the church, not just the world.

Discerning His Call

For our purposes in this book, the fundamental divide related to calling is not between full-time ministry and nonministry jobs, but this formal distinction: church office. This book focuses on the lead, or teaching, office of the church. Perhaps the better question to ask, then—or at least where we have some specific texts to give us more clarity—is this: Am I called to the office of *elder*?

Elders in the New Testament are to be spiritually mature men (1 Tim. 3:2; Titus 1:6). Not any Christian and not any man but mature men. Elder, as we rehearsed in the introduction, is the same office often called "pastor" today (based on the noun *pastor* or *shepherd* in Eph. 4:11 and its verb forms in Acts 20:28 and 1 Pet. 5:2). The same office is also called "overseer" in four places (Acts 20:28; Phil. 1:1; 1 Tim. 3:1–2; Titus 1:7). By focusing on the office rather than simply vocational (or nonvocational) ministry, several specific texts give us some bearings.

1. Do I Desire the Work? (Aspiration)

First, God wants pastors to *want* to do the work. He wants elders who happily give of themselves in this emotionally taxing work, "not reluctantly or under compulsion" (2 Cor. 9:7). God loves a cheerful pastor.

When the apostle Paul addresses the qualifications of pastor-elder-overseers, he first mentions aspiration and desire. "The saying is trustworthy: If anyone *aspires* to the office of overseer, he *desires* a noble task" (1 Tim. 3:1). God wants men who want to do this work, not men who do it under obligation. Christ grabs his pastors by the heart; he doesn't twist them by the arm. He wants men with a holy ambition for the office, men with holy dreams about feeding and leading the flock, men willing and eager to stretch themselves to do what the calling requires.

Peter says it even more powerfully. Christ wants elders to pastor his flock "not under compulsion, but willingly, *as God would have you*" (1 Pet. 5:2). Pastoring, eldering, and overseeing the church *from aspiration and desire*, not obligation and mere duty, are "as God would have you." This is the kind of God we have—the desiring (not dutiful) God, who wants pastors who are desiring (not dutiful) pastors. Such a free and happy God means for the leaders of his church to do their work "with joy and not with groaning, for that would be of no advantage" to the people (Heb. 13:17). The good of the church is at stake in the holy desire of its pastors. They will not long work well for her joy if it is not their joy to do such work.

Practically, then, when we hear men, whether young or old, express an aspiration to the pastoral office, why would we not rejoice as a first instinct? How foolish would we be if our first inclination was to be skeptical, to challenge it, squash it, or see if we can disavow them of it? Rather, give them the benefit of the doubt, that God is at work. Such an aspiration is not natural. Let's begin with the assumption that such an ambition is holy and start by encouraging, not interrogating, men who express such an otherwise unusual heart. If the aspiration is not holy, that will become clear in due course.

Desire for the work has a role to play in the calling to church office that it may not in other work. Your day job may be work you're able to do but don't enjoy, and God can be pleased with that. He often calls us to labor that is not our dream job; sometimes Christians may even labor in lines of work for years that, on the whole, they do not enjoy. But a fundamental difference between pastoral work and other callings is the *necessity* of desire for the work.

The presence and persistence (however imperfect) of such desire often marks the beginning of a pastoral calling, but it is never the entirety. *Aspiration* is a great place to start, but desire in and of itself does not amount to a calling. This is a common misunderstanding, at least in the way some speak of their "calling." To complete the calling, God adds two layers of confirmation to pastoral aspirations: the consistent *affirmation* of others and some real-life *opportunity*.

2. Am I a Good Fit for This Work? (Affirmation)

Beyond sensing a subjective desire for pastoral ministry comes a more objective question about our fitness for the work. Have I seen evidence, however small, of fruitfulness in serving others through biblical teaching and counsel? And even more important than my own self-assessment, do others confirm my fit for pastoral ministry?

Here the desires of the heart meet the concrete realities of the real world and the needs of others. Office in the church is not for spiritual self-actualization or simply affirming a man's spiritual maturity; biblical office is for meeting the actual needs of a particular local church. The elder qualifications are, in a sense, pretty unremarkable. Note well: the elders of the church should not be the sum total of all spiritually qualified men in the church. Rather, from among those who are qualified (let's hope the number is great, and ever increasing), the elders are those willing to make extra sacrifices (whether for a season or the long haul) to care for the church and meet her ongoing needs. Aspiration has its vital part to play, but the call to pastoral office is not shaped mainly by the internal desires of our hearts but by external needs of the church.

This creates great tension with the "follow your heart" perspective and "don't settle for anything less than your dreams" counsel we so often hear in society. What's most important in discerning God's call is not bringing the desires of our hearts to bear on the world but letting the actual needs of others meet with and shape our hearts.

Over time, then, an internal dialogue happens between what we *want* to do and what we find ourselves doing fruitfully for the benefit of others. Delight in certain kinds of labor grows as others' real needs are met and as they affirm our abilities and efforts. Often Christians discover a calling to and fitness for ministry first through others' observations and affirmations and only later through their own emerging aspirations.

Before you go looking for opportunities to shepherd in the future, make sure you are able to meet real spiritual needs in front of you today and seek confirmation from your current local church.

3. Has God Opened the Door Yet? (Opportunity)

Third, and perhaps most often overlooked in Christian discussions of calling, is the actual God-given, real-world open door. You may *aspire* and others may *affirm* your general direction, but you are not yet fully called to a specific pastoral ministry until God opens the door.

God in his providence does the decisive work. He started the process by giving you the aspiration. He affirmed the direction as his Spirit produced fruit through your abilities and inclinations and others took notice. Now he confirms that sense of calling by swinging open a real door in real time. It is finally God, not man—and God, not self—who issues the call and appoints to pastoral office:

- God the Spirit is the one who "*made* you overseers" (Acts 20:28).
- God the Son is the one who "*gave* the apostles, the prophets, the evangelists, the shepherds and teachers, to equip the saints for the work of ministry" (Eph. 4:11–12).
- The Lord of the harvest is the one to whom we "pray earnestly . . . to *send out* laborers into his harvest" (Matt. 9:37–38).
- God is the master who "will *set* over his household" faithful and wise managers (Luke 12:42).
- The Lord Jesus Christ is the one from whom we *receive* the ministry we are to fulfill (Col. 4:17).

Excitement about *aspiring* and being *affirmed* can lead to our overlooking the reality check of this final step. Many today might say that a seminary student who aspires to be a pastor and has received affirmation from his home church is "called to ministry." Well, not yet. He *senses* a call to full-time ministry—for which we thank God—and some people have found him to be fit for such work. He is well on his way. But what this aspiring, affirmed brother doesn't yet have—to confirm his *sense* of calling—is a real-world opportunity where some church or Christian ministry presents him with a job description and says, "We are asking you to pastor here. Would you accept?"

Until God, through a specific local church, *makes* a man an overseer (Acts 20:28), *gives* him to the church (Eph. 4:11–12), *sends* him as a laborer (Matt. 9:37–38), and *sets* him over his household (Luke 12:42), he is not yet fully called. Aspiring pastor-elders would do better to speak of their *sense* of calling— and even more precisely, that they *aspire* to the work—rather than declaring, apart from the specific opportunity, that God has indeed called them.

What a marvel and blessing it is when God gives a man a desire for the pastoral office, equips him to meet real needs in the church with the word of God and wisdom, with affirmation from others, and opens a door for him to lead and serve in a specific local church. Then a man knows with conviction that he is indeed called.[1]

———

Aspiration and calling lead naturally to questions about the appointment and disciplining of pastor-elders. Let's address the unpleasant topic first and then end this chapter on the higher note.

1   This chapter is especially mindful of seminary students who feel an initial sense of call (aspiration), receive affirmation from their local church, and then make some major life change, often leaving town and their local church, to pursue a seminary education in preparation for the work. There can be great advantages to a season of such focus and intense study. A downside can be that the aspiring pastor is uprooted from his home church. Options for distance education now abound, which can be good for aspiring pastors to increase their competency without being uprooted from their church and city. But not every aspiring pastor-elder needs to pursue a formal seminary education, whether remote or onsite. What might we say to a man who aspires to the office of pastor-elder in his present church and does not plan to leave town and his church for a season of education elsewhere? First, let me commend patience. Getting a degree and searching for open jobs is often a faster track to a pastoral appointment than growing up organically in one's own church. Again, the needs of the particular church are critical. Does the church need more pastor-elders at present or soon, or not? And what might such an aspiring man do while he waits? Perhaps some readers find themselves in a place like this. I would commend that such a man seek intentionally to grow in the pastor-elder qualifications (one reason this book is structured as it is), and in particular seek to meet teaching needs, modest as they may be, as they become available. Try to get teaching "at bats," I like to say, however insignificant they may seem. Start with the nursery! Teach the Bible to kids. Small steps are vital to get going in the right direction for the long haul. Answer the humble opportunities presented you to teach God's word, prepare well, ask for feedback, and seek to grow. Be faithful where God has placed you, pray that he provide you more opportunities, and steward them well, one at a time.

Disciplining Elders

First, all pastor-elders need to know, and remember, that we have an inspired text for discipline. Paul addresses the disciplining of elders in 1 Timothy 5:19–24.

This is a solemn and weighty topic. As Christians, *we welcome all and affirm none*, as we might broadcast to the world, because all of us are sinners. Including Christian leaders. And sometimes gravely so. Power often corrupts, or at least magnifies the corruption of sin already in us. It is tragic on Capitol Hill and in Hollywood and even more tragic in the church.

We all have heard far too many stories about Christian leaders abusing power and failing egregiously—especially when not held accountable by a plurality of other leaders. And we've heard of leaders covering up the sins of other leaders, across ecclesial traditions and denominations. This is a great evil. And it is expressly what Paul stands against in 1 Timothy 5:21 in one of the most piercing statements in all his letters. He gives a solemn charge to not show partiality or favoritism to guilty leaders:

> In the presence of God and of Christ Jesus and of the elect angels I charge you to keep these rules [which we'll see below] without prejudging, doing nothing from partiality.

The only other place where Paul expresses such a solemn charge is 2 Timothy 4:1–2:

> I charge you in the presence of God and of Christ Jesus, who is to judge the living and the dead, and by his appearing and his kingdom: preach the word.

We've seen that the two main tasks of pastor-elders are preaching/ teaching and leading/governing. So here, right alongside the magnitude of "preach the word," is, *Do not show partiality to leaders to keep them from the just consequences of their sin.*

Perhaps the charge in 1 Timothy 5:21 needs to be so solemn because we often have such great affection for our pastor-teachers, even when they have failed us. It is good when churches deeply love and admire worthy pastors and when fellow pastors have great affection for each other and genuinely are good friends and want to appropriately protect each other from unjust attacks. The danger comes with an inability to be impartial.

Apparently part of the problem (if not the whole) in Ephesus, where Paul had sent Timothy, was that false teaching had arisen among the elders. Paul himself had been part of establishing the church in Ephesus (Acts 19) and had stayed there more than two years teaching. He knew the church well. He knew faces and names and personal histories. And he had prophesied to the Ephesian elders that wolves would rise up from among the Ephesian elders:

> I know that after my departure fierce wolves will come in among you, not sparing the flock; and from among your own selves will arise men speaking twisted things, to draw away the disciples after them. (Acts 20:29–30)

Now Timothy has the task of addressing the trouble Paul had anticipated. I draw comfort from the fact that this conflict didn't take Paul off guard. Nor did it take Christ off guard. Conflicts will arise in the church, even among the elders. There is grace too for this. Choosing elders well goes a long way, but even when such trouble arises, Christ, through his apostle, gives us more direction than simply the qualifications of 1 Timothy 3.

Hold Them Accountable

First Timothy 5:17–18 deals with elders who were leading well. Then because some pastors have not ruled well, Paul broaches the difficult subject of disciplining elders:

> Do not admit a charge against an elder except on the evidence of two or three witnesses. As for those who persist in sin, rebuke them in the presence of all, so that the rest may stand in fear. In the presence of God and of Christ Jesus and of the elect angels I charge you to keep these rules without prejudging, doing nothing from partiality. (1 Tim. 5:19–21)

Perhaps you already sense the tension in these verses: on the one hand is protecting elders from unjust accusations, and on the other is holding them accountable when they've sinned. Because the office of pastor-elder is a public position, much is at stake from both sides. It's not a one-sided affair either way.

On one side, leaders are obvious targets of attack, and especially in a day when society increasingly loves to take out the powerful. The devil is regularly trying to take out the opposing lieutenants. Elders may not deserve special protection, but they should receive at least the kind of protection afforded every individual under the terms of the old covenant—two or three witnesses:

> A single witness shall not suffice against a person for any crime or for any wrong in connection with any offense that he has

committed. Only on the evidence of two witnesses or of three witnesses shall a charge be established. (Deut. 19:15)

Elders deserve the same benefit of the doubt as normal citizens. Timothy should not allow a suspect charge to sideline the ability of a pastor to serve the needs of the church. Leaders can be magnets for maniacal accusations or personal axe-grinding. The principle is *don't let the devil take out pastors with false charges.* "Do not admit a charge against an elder except on the evidence of two or three witnesses."

On the other side, leaders are sinners—and sometimes gravely so, as we've acknowledged. And so Paul gives Timothy the solemn charge in 5:21 not to show partiality or favoritism to leaders.

So verse 19 is in tension with verses 20–21: protect leaders from unjust accusations and treat just accusations seriously and without partiality. What Paul doesn't lay out here is a specific plan for how to proceed with disciplining pastors in every church, or even in Ephesus. That he leaves to the collective wisdom of the elders in good standing. Paul gives principles for disciplining elders, not how-to steps. Each situation has its complexities, which is why we need pluralities of wise leaders, not rule books. So when a charge arises, we proceed carefully and patiently. Pluralities are known for being *inefficient but effective*, while authoritarian structures may seem efficient but are prone to error and partiality.

When elders, who are public servants in the church, are caught in significant sin, their discipline (or removal) needs to be public. Here Paul says, "As for those who persist in sin, rebuke them in the presence of all, so that the rest may stand in fear."[2] This may

2 John Piper, in personal conversation, observed that "rebuke" here (Greek *elegchō*) means "to expose" (as in Matt. 18:15; John 3:20; Eph. 5:11, 13). The persistent sin must be

be another allusion to Deuteronomy 19, where verse 20 says, "*The rest* shall hear and *fear*, and shall never again commit any such evil among you." Paul applies that to the other elders. The public telling of one elder's sin will have a sobering effect on the others, like Paul publicly opposing Peter "before them all" in Galatians 2:14 for the public sin of drawing back from table fellowship with Gentiles. Our leaders should not be untouchable. If not vigilant, they likewise will give in to sin. The discipline of one elder serves as a means of grace not only to him but also to the other elders, and the congregation as well.

So 1 Timothy 5:19 protects innocent elders from false charges, and 5:20 gives guilty elders greater discipline by making it public. The role of the other elders is vital in both counts. This is just one more reason, among many, for churches to have a plurality of elders, not a single pastor. Plurality provides better accountability. It is a plurality of elders that can both protect an elder from unjust charges as well as strive together for impartiality when one of their own has persisted in sin.

Appointing Pastors

Now we turn to the happier topic. In the same passage, Paul also addresses the appointing of pastor-elders:

> Do not be hasty in the laying on of hands, nor take part in the sins of others; keep yourself pure. (No longer drink only water, but use a little wine for the sake of your stomach and your frequent ailments.) The sins of some people are conspicuous, going before them to judgment, but the sins of others appear later. So

---

told or exposed; rebuke does not connote harshness or meanness, but clarity about the sin.

also good works are conspicuous, and even those that are not cannot remain hidden. (1 Tim. 5:22–25)

This is now the second time in the letter that Paul has referenced this ancient ceremony called "the laying on of hands" (previously in 1 Tim. 4:14). In the Old Testament, the laying on of hands has a variety of meanings depending on context. Most often, the phrase is negative, meaning to inflict harm or lay God's curse on someone (as in Gen. 22:12; Lev. 24:14). In Leviticus, the priest is to lay hands on a sacrifice to ceremonially place God's righteous curse on the animal in place of the people. But two Old Testament texts, both in the book of Numbers, anticipate how the laying on of hands would come to be used in the church age. In Numbers 8:10, God's people lay their hands on the priests to officially commission them as their representatives, and in Numbers 27:18, Moses lays his hands on Joshua to formally commission him as his successor.

In the New Testament, we find a noticeable shift in the typical use of *laying on of hands* language. Now, with God himself dwelling as man among his people, Jesus often lays his hands on people to bless and heal. Then in the book of Acts, once Jesus has ascended, his disciples serve as his hands and feet. They heal, as Jesus did, but what's new in Acts is the giving of the Holy Spirit through the laying on of hands—from Jerusalem and Judea, then to Samaria (Acts 8:17), and then beyond, to Ephesus (Acts 19:6) and the ends of the earth (Acts 1:8). But like the two texts from Numbers, we find two mentions in Acts (6:6 and 13:3) of commissioning ceremonies (for the seven and for the first missionaries). These commissionings in Acts then lead to these two references in 1 Timothy 4:14 and 5:22.

When established leaders formally lay their hands on someone for a particular new ministry calling, they both ask for God's blessing on the calling and put their seal of approval on the candidate—and share, in some sense, in the fruit and failures to come. It is both a commissioning to a calling and a commendation of the candidate among the people he will serve.

What Paul stresses here in 1 Timothy 5:22 is how the laying on of hands to ordain a man to the office of elder shares in his work, not just for good but also for ill. Paul charges Timothy and the church to exercise patience: "Do not be hasty in the laying on of hands." Elders are not to be new converts (1 Tim. 3:6), as we will address in chapter 2; they also are not be hastily appointed.[3]

What Is Ordination?

Various traditions in the church have more or less developed practices regarding *ordination*, or formal appointment to office. *Ordination* in the new covenant, if that's the best term for it, is markedly different from ordination of priests in the old covenant. For one, Jesus is our great high priest, and in him the whole church is a priesthood of believers. In this sense, baptism corresponds to old-covenant ordination. This may explain why the language of ordination does not appear in the New Testament. As Benjamin Merkle comments, "The NT never uses the word *ordain* (in the modern, technical sense) in connection with a Christian leader who is installed to an office."[4]

The mention of a laying-on-of-hands *ceremony* in the New Testament is a good warrant for formal acknowledgment in the corporate assembly that a man is officially beginning his calling in the office of pastor (so also a particular moment of appointment for deacons

3 For more on the laying on of hands, see appendix 4.
4 Benjamin L. Merkle, *40 Questions about Elders and Deacons* (Grand Rapids, MI: Kregel, 2008), 211.

would be fitting). These practices vary from church to church and from denomination to denomination. One benefit denominations offer is the process of ordination, as many churches find it beyond their ability to vet well pastoral candidates who come from outside their immediate fellowship. As a wise fellow elder of mine, twice my age, once memorably commented, "Anybody can be Prince Charming for six months." If it's true for six months in premarital dating, how much more for a few days, or even hours, of interviews as a pastoral candidate. Like graduating from a reputable seminary, the practice of denominational ordination provides a credential to help a prospective pastor establish trust and help churches know that others, who have spent more than a few hours with the man, can vouch for his character and abilities.

However wise and helpful such denominational ordinations can be, we do well to realize that these are the result of prudence and development within the tradition, not biblical mandates. As Merkle has captured well in his brief chapter "Should Elders Be Ordained?," the ordination of new elders—or perhaps better, "appointment" or "commission"—so far as the New Testament would lead us, would happen through the church where the man will serve, by "being publicly installed into that office."[5] In this sense, ordination is mainly the public recognition of an office. "The church that elected that elder . . . should be the group to confer the outward recognition at election by installing the person in office or ordaining the pastor."[6]

5 Merkle, *40 Questions*, 212.
6 Merkle, *40 Questions*, 211. Merkle's chapter, in sum, in his words, is this: "Elders should be 'ordained' if by ordination we simply mean the public recognition of someone to a particular office or ministry. Perhaps it would be more appropriate, and biblical, however, to speak of their 'appointment' or 'commission'" (212). This telling of what the Scriptures enjoin, and do not, need not threaten the denominational practice of ordination for what it is in

Hidden Good Revealed

First Timothy 5:24 then continues the thought of 5:22:[7] "The sins of some people are conspicuous, going before them to judgment, but the sins of others appear later." Be careful with your first impressions of people. Hasn't God chosen the weak and foolish (1 Cor. 1:27)? Be patient and give time for testing. Beware candidates who come out of the blue and seem too good to be true. Sometimes they are not true. Paul is calling Timothy and the church to patience in praying for, identifying, observing, and ordaining elders. But even then, after patience and a wise process, we don't know for sure. We hope and pray for their faithfulness and design structures of accountability, and find out in due course. This would be an ominous note to end on: "The sins of others appear later." But Paul doesn't end there.

He concludes with a word of hope in 1 Timothy 5:25: "So also good works are conspicuous, and even those that are not cannot remain hidden." We will not know for sure how every elder candidate will pan out, but God does. And he will care for his church. He sent his own Son to live and die and rise again to create the church. He is more committed to his church than the most faithful

---

providing credentials, but this understanding would caution us from presuming that the denominational practice, prudent as it may be, is mandated in the New Testament.

7   A brief thought on Paul's parenthetical prescription in v. 23, "No longer drink only water, but use a little wine for the sake of your stomach and your frequent ailments." Why give this personal charge here among these instructions for the discipline of elders? Two reasons: (1) Paul knows Timothy well and is aware of the pressure he must be living under in trying to remedy the conflict in Ephesus, and he adds this personal note, to settle his stomach with some wine. Also (2) "drinking only water" may have been just what the false teachers were commending (1 Tim. 4:3), and so Paul aims to unsettle them with this note to Timothy, which clarifies that "keep yourself pure" (at the end of v. 22) does not mean from wine but from sharing in the sins of others. Ironically, the false teachers, while preaching "drink only water" to be pure, were themselves not pure. Paul wants to settle anxious Timothy, and unsettle the false teachers, and a little wine for Timothy might do both.

of elders and most zealous of congregations. And Jesus is building his church. He will protect it. The gates of hell will not prevail against it, no matter what short-term setbacks we seem to suffer with the failures of our leaders.

In the moments when it seems darkest and messiest, God sustains and upholds his church through the hidden good works of its leaders and congregants.[8] Sometimes they are conspicuous. But even when they are not, God will see to it, in his perfect timing, that they do not remain hidden. Your labors in Christ will not be in vain.

---

8 For more on the critical role the elders play when conflict arises—and how conflict is an opportunity for God's grace—see chap. 14, pp. 234–40.

2

Not a Novice—or Arrogant

*He must not be a recent convert, or he may
become puffed up with conceit and fall
into the condemnation of the devil.*

1 TIMOTHY 3:6

FEW EVILS POISON the church and sully her reputation in the world like arrogant pastors. Manifest arrogance in politicians, appalling as it is, we might expect. But arrogance in the pulpit—this is a great blight on the church and in the community where the church is called to shine the light of Christ.

It's not as though the New Testament didn't foresee the danger or that somehow "arrogant pastors" is a recent development. Christians have known from the beginning to keep conceited men from church office. If the Scriptures' pervasive condemnations of pride and arrogance weren't enough, then the express qualifications for pastor-elder make it all the clearer:

He must not be arrogant. (Titus 1:7)

> He must not be a recent convert, or he may become puffed
> up with conceit and fall into the condemnation of the devil.
> (1 Tim. 3:6)

"Recent convert" (Greek *neophytos*) means, literally, "newly planted."
It's an appropriate image for a new convert to Christianity. New
plants haven't yet had time to sink their roots down deep and stretch
them out wide. New plants—whether transplanted or from the
seed—are much easier to uproot than trees that have grown into
the soil over a matter of months and years rather than days and
weeks. "Newly planted" also brings to mind Jesus's parable of the
sower and the seed sown on rocky ground and among thorns. The
first "endures for a while" but falls away when trials come, while
the second is choked out by the cares and deceits of the world
(Matt. 13:20–22).

Elsewhere, when Paul addresses the formal appointing of pastors and elders, he charges Timothy and the churches, "Do not be
hasty in the laying on of hands" (1 Tim. 5:22). This principle of
patience in appointment to office applies not only to pastors but
to deacons as well: "Let them also be tested first; then let them
serve as deacons if they prove themselves blameless" (1 Tim. 3:10).

A cord holds together these warnings: swelling pride in a leader
endangers the whole church, and the longer a man has faithfully
walked with God, the less likely the remaining pride in him is
growing rather than shrinking. So we hope.

Why No New Plants

Pastoral ministry will be emotionally trying—not at every step but
acutely so at times, especially in crisis moments. It's only a matter
of time until pastoral ministry proves more emotionally challenging

than anticipated. Certain kinds of spiritual distress are inevitable because pastors are positioned not only to encounter the depths of human depravity but to do so with frequency.

The surprising pits of indwelling sin in professing Christians, multiplied across a congregation, can be enough to damage, if not uproot, young plants. New plants aren't yet ready to endure such storms on repeat. They need to send roots down and out and strengthen stalks and sprout leaves and learn to bear some initial fruit. Soon enough they will be ready for the hard winds and driving rains of pastoral ministry, but not right away, no matter how mature or gifted in leadership or teaching they seem at conversion.

Added to that, Satan loves to mark the opposing lieutenants, and all the more when one is manifestly young and fragile. A new convert among the pastors is an obvious target, a promising foothold for the devil's efforts (Eph. 4:27). Wise churches arm themselves against such schemes (Eph. 6:11).

These are real dangers with putting new plants in leadership, but the specific danger Paul mentions—and so deserves the most attention—is that the new plant might become "puffed up with conceit" (1 Tim. 3:6). Such *conceit* apparently had become a problem in the Ephesian church (1 Tim. 6:4; 2 Tim. 3:4). The false teachers there may have arisen in precisely this way. Newly converted and manifestly able as teachers, and thus naturally looked to as leaders, perhaps they were hastily appointed as elders, which may have produced two effects at once: (1) these men were not given a sufficient season of testing to see what they were really made of spiritually, and (2) the appointment itself, and serving in office, may have altered the trajectory of what otherwise could have been healthy growth and development.

Has Old Pride Persisted?

In the first case, the roots of the new convert's arrogance may simply remain uncut from his former life of unbelief. Paul lists "swollen with conceit" as characteristic of those outside the church (2 Tim. 3:4). Accordingly, new converts need some time in the faith (with help, divine and human, from the Spirit and disciplers) to reduce the swelling. The caution may be more than simply the concern that being put in leadership may make an immature man arrogant but that, being a new convert, he hasn't yet had as much conceit pounded out of him as he soon will. His life is still being brought under the authority of God in fundamental ways. Not only does the dust need to settle; the new roots need to go down deep.

Pastors must not be arrogant (Titus 1:7), among other reasons, because they are first to be men under authority, stewards of, *and under*, the words of Christ and his apostles. Paul identifies one who is "puffed up with conceit" with one who "teaches a different doctrine and does not agree with the sound words of our Lord Jesus Christ and the teaching that accords with godliness" (1 Tim. 6:3–4). At the heart of the pastoral task, as we will discuss at length in chapter 3, is *teaching*—and not teaching *self* or one's personal *preferences* or *opinions* but teaching "the sound words of our Lord Jesus Christ." In 1 Timothy 3:6 Paul mentions "the condemnation of the devil," who in his pride and swollen conceit would not bow to God's authority.

Will Leadership Provoke New Pride?

Not only does a new convert need time to begin, in earnest, on the shriveling of his old pride, but also we should consider how the appointment to leadership might affect a man who is new to the faith. Will being put forward as a church officer with its title and recognition become an occasion of a new kind of puffing up? This is likely the concern Paul has in mind in 1 Timothy 3:6: not just getting over *former* conceit but being *newly puffed up* by the office itself and thus falling into the same (prideful) condemnation as Satan.

In seeking to fill positions and opportunities for leadership, we often take one of two approaches: "man for the job" or "job for the man." "Man for the job" means the need is such that the candidate should fill the role and its expectations from day one. He is the man for this job. "Job for the man," on the other hand, means the role is one for the developing leader to grow into, an opportunity to rise to a new level of competency and influence and responsibility, having proved himself able in previous testing. While the pastorate is never fully a man-for-the-job scenario (who is sufficient for these things? 2 Cor. 2:16), we should not approach our search with a job-for-the-man mentality when it comes to pride and arrogance.

A man may be able to grow into teaching and aspects of pastoral manner and a host of other abilities while serving, but not so with humility. We are not to think of the pastorate as the crucible that might make an arrogant man humble. The pastorate is indeed a crucible and will make a genuinely humble man all the more humble (2 Cor. 12:7), but it is not a lab for experimenting with arrogant men.

Keeping new converts from the council serves not only the church but also the new convert. For his own spiritual health, he needs to be established for a season as a Christian, to soak at some length in his identity in Christ, not in office. Before attempting, in ministry, to have the spirits subject to us, we first need a good, solid season of rejoicing that our "names are written in heaven" (Luke 10:20). Which is a delight to continue and not ever get beyond.

How Recent?

We might ask, How recent a convert? How new a plant? Here the wisdom of plurality in local-church leadership is critical. The New Testament doesn't give us a particular time frame, whether a year or five or more. As we will see with the other elder qualifications, "not a new convert" is analog, not digital. It's not that a man goes to sleep one night a "new plant" and wakes up the next day ready to weather frequent storms. Rather, such maturity—and in particular, humility—is incremental and grows organically, in small degrees. And Paul leaves such to be determined in particular contexts by the plurality of elders, who already have been duly appointed by the church. Together they will be able to assess the age and maturity of both the candidate and the church and other relevant circumstances, not least of which are the present needs of the church.

Observe the differences between the well-established Ephesian church (in 1 Timothy) and the fledgling Cretan church (in Titus). When writing to Ephesus, Paul specifies "not a new convert." The Ephesian church had aged enough, likely a decade old or more, that relatively new converts would not be needed in leadership. Crete didn't have the same luxury. The whole church was newly planted, and as Titus went to appoint elders, it was inevitable that they all would be, in some sense, new plants. However, the underlying concern remained: conceit. And so Paul specifies for the Cretans, "he must not be arrogant" (Titus 1:7).

An important qualification is that "not a new convert" does not necessarily mean "not young." We know that Timothy himself was relatively young, perhaps in his upper twenties or early thirties. Yet Paul writes to him not to let the church look down on him for his youth but to set an example (1 Tim. 4:12), including fleeing youthful passions (2 Tim. 2:22). As young Elihu spoke truthfully to Job, it is not age that makes a man wise but the Spirit of God (Job 32:8–9). We pray that the passage of time increases the Spirit's work of wisdom in a man, but don't *assume* such merely by the passing of years. In the end, the spiritual youth or maturity of a man, at whatever physical age, is wisely assessed in relation to the particular congregation in question, not any specified universal status.[1] And churches will do well to not assume that gray hair means wisdom, or that youth means spiritual immaturity.

Two Key Questions

To make the pursuit of pastoral humility tangible for churches and councils searching for pastors and for men aspiring to ministry (as well as for current pastors seeking to stay qualified for the work and grow more humble), consider two particular manifestations of humility essential in pastor-elders.

1. Does He Think with Sober Judgment?

Here the question is not only about sober judgment, or wisdom, in general (which is vital, and called sober-mindedness [1 Tim. 3:2], as we'll examine in chapter 4), but in particular about self-assessment. Romans 12:3 says, "By the grace given to me I say to everyone among you *not to think of himself more highly than he ought to think, but to think with sober judgment,* each according to the measure of faith that God has assigned." Is the man self-deprecating? Is he willing and ready to admit faults? Is he regularly angling with his words to build himself up in others' minds? Does

---

1   See appendix 5, "How Old Should Elders Be?"

he give plain evidence of thinking of himself more highly than he ought to think?

2. Does He Count Others More Significant than Himself?

Paul writes to all Christians in Philippians 2:3–4 with a charge that is especially pressing for church leaders: "Do nothing from selfish ambition or conceit, but *in humility count others more significant than yourselves*. Let each of you look not only to his own interests, but also to the interests of others." Counting others more significant than ourselves cuts to the heart of the pastoral calling as workers for the church's joy, and to the heart of the faith as well.

Jesus himself, the great shepherd and overseer of our souls (1 Pet. 2:25), is the paradigmatic *humble leader* who took note of, looked to, and gave himself for the ultimate interests of others (Phil. 2:5–8). Pastoral labor never eclipses or replaces the perfect humility of Christ, who "humbled himself by becoming obedient to the point of death, even death on a cross" (Phil. 2:8), but it does seek to echo his humility, and so point to it, in our daily efforts.

How Do I Humble Myself?

Before concluding this chapter, perhaps it would be helpful—for church members, aspiring pastors, and longtime pastors alike— to ask the question, *How do I humble myself?* I want to be more humble. God's word clearly commends humility and condemns pride. In Christ, we genuinely want to be more humble—so how do we humble ourselves?

With this question in mind a few years ago, I went looking for all the Bible's references to self-humbling, whether "humble yourself" or "he humbled himself" or "they humbled themselves." I remembered reading about self-humbling in particular in the book of 2 Chronicles. Sure enough, the theme is thick there, but it also extends back to Exodus and forward into the New Testament. What I found was humbling to me and my own pretty American instincts: *you can't just up and humble yourself.*

The big surprise to me in studying the texts about self-humbling is how *responsive to God* real self-humbling must be. God is the author of our humility, not we. He takes the first step. The context for the biblical command to "humble yourself" is never bright, sunny, carefree days. It's always conflict, discomfort, suffering, pain, chaos. First, God's humbling hand descends. He takes the initiative. Then the question comes: *Now, will you humble yourself?* Will you welcome and receive his uncomfortable, even painful, work or try to explain it away or even kick back against it? Humbling ourselves is not something we decide to do in our spare time or for self-improvement in a few simple steps. Humility is a work of God. His hand does the humbling. Then he gives us the dignity of acknowledging and welcoming his work, and humbling ourselves.[2]

God, Give Us Humbled Pastors

When God does the double miracle of producing reasonably humbled men and giving them as pastor-teachers to local churches,[3]

---

2 Suspecting others might have the same question I did—How do I humble myself?—led me to write a very short book, which I offer to those with further interest in the topic: *Humbled: Welcoming the Uncomfortable Work of God* (Nashville, TN: B&H, 2021).

3 Some might ask, How much pride does it take to disqualify a pastor? Don't we all have some? Indeed we do. But for the purpose of choosing elders, we can go only on what we can see and discern. Ask yourself, from what you know and can find out from asking perceptive questions, has this man been genuinely humbled? If you immediately cringe or balk, take your hesitation seriously. If everything else in his life seems to check out but he comes off arrogant, then I would suggest moving to address that need first before moving him into office. Give him more time, and let him know what your pause is. But don't give a title and office to a man who seems proud, hoping he'll be humbled over time. Paul says "not

what kind of men might we expect to find teaching and leading our churches? Humbled pastors love the Scriptures and "the sound words of our Lord Jesus Christ" (1 Tim. 6:3). They receive their calling as undershepherds, gladly embracing their role *under* the authority of their chief. Humbled pastors love preaching *not themselves* but Christ Jesus as Lord (2 Cor. 4:5).

Humbled pastors seek to give benefit of the doubt and expect the best (not assume the worst) from members of the flock. They don't let cynicism and bitterness toward their people develop and fester in their hearts. They have a kind of gentleness of spirit, and no less zeal for God's honor, that keeps them from fear of being wrong and, therefore, feeling a constant need to self-protect.

Humbled pastors are transparent rather than evasive; authentic (in the best of senses) rather than superficial. They are not defensive but eager to learn and grow and improve. Humbled pastors learn to listen at times their former selves would have rushed to talk, and they speak up when it takes courage and others would rather stay silent. They are the kind of men not inclined to absorb others' attention; they are more interested in hearing from others than telling others about themselves. If we could sum up in one word what one attribute we need most in the pastorate today, as in every generation, few would come close to *humility*.

God, give us humbled pastors.

---

arrogant." Elders must not be conceited. This is why he says to Timothy, in the Ephesian context, "not a new convert."

3

Pastors Are Teachers

He must hold firm to the trustworthy word as taught,
so that he may be able to give instruction in sound
doctrine and also to rebuke those who contradict it.

TITUS 1:9

ABLE TO TEACH. Ah, that memorable criterion in 1 Timothy 3:2, right in the middle of the list (eighth of fifteen). When we compare the pastor-elder qualifications with those of the deacons (1 Tim. 3:8–13), "able to teach" stands out as distinguishing the former from the latter. In a sense, this qualification for the pastoral office (along with "not a new convert") also sets the elders apart from what the New Testament expects of all Christians.[1]

All church officers should be above reproach, one-woman men, good household managers, not drunkards, not greedy, not without

---

1 Though all should pursue and grow into maturity, which will include teaching others in some form (Heb. 5:12–14)—whether parents to children (Eph. 6:4), older women to younger (Titus 2:3–4), or all Christians one to another as we teach and admonish each other, including in our songs of worship (Col. 3:16)—the New Testament nowhere expects *skill* in teaching of all Christians.

provenness through a season of testing. The respective lists for pastor-elders (1 Tim. 3:1–7) and deacons (1 Tim. 3:8–13) read so similarly in their substance but for this one: "able to teach."

Authority through Teaching

It is *teaching*, after all, given the nature of the New Testament church, and the nature of God's dealing with his people going back to the garden, that is at the heart of the pastoral office. What Christian pastors offer, most fundamentally, is not their cosmopolitan and interdisciplinary brilliance, ability to entertain masses, or executive facility. They are stewards and publicists of God's very words. God has given his church "the pastor-teachers" (Eph. 4:11) as those with the ability to receive, understand, integrate, index, access, illustrate, winsomely defend, and effectively communicate his word to his people, and through them to the world.[2]

The New Testament does not vest pastor-elders with authority apart from their function as teachers of God's word. Rather, pastoral influence (and indeed their formal authority, rightly understood) is bound to the very source of authority in the church: Christ himself, expressed in the words of his first-century apostles and Old Testament prophets, stewarded and taught by the pastor-elders

---

2   Pastor-elders are among Christ's gifts to his church for its good, and they are gifts first and foremost associated with teaching, not mere decision-making or oversight: "He gave the apostles, the prophets, the evangelists, *the shepherds and teachers*, to equip the saints for the work of ministry, for building up the body of Christ" (Eph. 4:11–12). A literal rendering of "the shepherds and teachers" here is "the pastors and teachers." Grammatically, "shepherds" and "teachers" are not two groups but one. Throughout the New Testament, the office of pastor-elder overlaps significantly, when not totally, with those who provide formal teaching in the church. It's not as if one group in the church is the pastors or elders, and then some other group is the teachers. The pastors are teachers, and those who are skilled in teaching God's word, while meeting the other qualifications of the office, are those who, in time and in view of the church's needs, become pastors.

to the whole church. As we have seen, Christ is the lone head of his church. He has the unique glory of ruling singularly. He has the first and final say in his church. And he appointed *apostles* to speak authoritatively on his behalf in the church's first generation. The church's enduring objective source of authority today, under Christ, is the apostles' written word, which is why *teaching that word* is so centrally important in the Christian church.

Faithful pastors in faithful churches are instruments of Christ's life-giving authority to the degree that the pastors faithfully teach the word of the apostles and the prophets, which is the very word of God.

Centrality of Teaching

Inevitably, our churches lose their way over time if we lose touch with the central importance of teaching for God's people from the very beginning, and particularly in the New Testament. In the Bible, learning is far more like getting our next meal than getting a degree. Teaching from God, through his spokesmen, is daily bread we receive to stay alive, not a course of study we endure for a while and then graduate. So, for the Christian, sitting under able teaching is not a season of life, but a lifestyle.

We could begin with God's instructions to Adam in the garden and rehearse God's teaching Abraham and Jacob, and teaching his people paradigmatically through Moses (*torah* means "instruction" or "teaching"), and through Joshua and righteous judges and Samuel, and even through the psalms and proverbs of poets and sages and through the old-covenant prophets, one after another, even as the nation plugged its ears and downward-spiraled in decline. Then when God himself came and dwelt among us in the person of Christ, he taught. Oh, did he teach. Jesus never self-identified as a healer, but he did embrace the title of teacher. His healings and miracles were "signs," serving his teaching. They pointed to his words of instruction—his parables, his Sermon on the Mount, his Olivet Discourse. Jesus is the single greatest teacher the world has ever known. Then the great teacher died and rose for his *disciples* (which means "learners," implying teaching) and left his apostles to lead his church *through teaching*. The Gospels teach. Acts teaches. The Epistles teach. The Apocalypse teaches.

Teaching serves a far more central role in the life and health of the church than many today are prone to think. I'll leave the full biblical theology of teaching, from Genesis to Revelation, to elsewhere, but here, for our purposes in approaching the importance and meaning of this qualification "able to teach," consider seven observations, among others, from just the Pastoral Epistles (1–2 Tim. and Titus).

1. *God's reputation relates to what the church teaches.* What more could be at stake? The very honor and name of God himself in the world he made, and in our particular towns and cities, are at stake in what our churches teach. "The name of God and the teaching" go together, according to 1 Timothy 6:1, either in being revered or reviled: "Let all who are under a yoke as bondservants regard their own masters as worthy of all honor, *so that the name of God and the teaching may not be reviled.*" This alone could be enough to awaken us to the importance of Christian teaching. But there is more.

2. *It was essential for the apostles to be teachers.* The nature of the Christian faith—with ongoing teaching at its heart—means that it was essential for the apostles to be teachers, not just decision makers (ruling or governing apart from teaching). There were no administrators among the apostles who did not become *spokesmen,*

teachers, on behalf of the risen Christ. There was no "teaching apostles" and "ruling apostles" bifurcation. Interestingly enough, Paul twice mentions that he is not just an apostle but also a teacher (1 Tim. 2:7; 2 Tim. 1:11). So critical, and not marginal, was the practice of teaching in the early church that Paul himself, as an apostle, would not feel it beneath him to note his calling as *teacher*.

3. *The church's mission requires teaching.* Christian disciple-making, the lead charge in the Great Commission (Matt. 28:18–20), requires teaching. Disciple-making is essentially holistic teaching. Again, the word *disciple* means "learner." To be *discipled* is to be taught, to follow another's teaching (2 Tim. 3:10), not just in theory but in life. Also, vital to the disciple-making process is not simply training up new Christians but raising up "faithful men, who will be able to *teach others* also" (2 Tim. 2:2).[3] Christ's commission makes it explicit: "Make disciples . . . *teaching* them to observe all that I have commanded you."

4. *God means for his word to be taught.* The word of God, spoken through old-covenant prophets and new-covenant apostles, is not simply to be heard, but taught. It is profitable or useful for something. He means for us to do something with it—and first and foremost, that is teaching. "All Scripture is . . . profitable *for teaching*" (2 Tim. 3:16). Paul charges church leaders, like Timothy, to "preach the word; be ready in season and out of season; reprove, rebuke, and exhort, with complete patience and *teaching*" (2 Tim. 4:2). Teaching, as we have seen, goes hand in hand with Christ's authority in and through the church. "To teach" and "to exercise authority" (1 Tim. 2:12) are not two separate activities but a unified whole, centered in the plurality of pastor-elders.

---

3 For the specific call to disciple-making as it relates to the pastor-elders, see chapter 12.

5. *Error spreads though false teachers*. Error in the church spreads through *teaching* (1 Tim. 1:3–7; 4:1; Titus 1:11). What do false teachers do? They *teach*. The fact that those who spread error are called false *teachers* alerts us to the importance of teaching, for good or for bad, in the church, which leads to the next observation.

6. *Elders address error through teaching*. The battle lines between truth and error are drawn between true and false teachers and their teaching, not any other proficiency or skill. Faithful leaders propagate "the sound words of our Lord Jesus Christ and the teaching that accords with godliness," while those who infect the church with error "teach a different doctrine" (1 Tim. 6:3). When the time comes that wandering souls no longer "endure sound teaching," they "accumulate for themselves *teachers* to suit their own passions" (2 Tim. 4:3). The question for all of us is not whether we will have teachers but who they will be, and whether they will lead us toward the real Jesus or subtly, stealthily away from him.

7. *Pastor-elders in the church are teachers*. Leaders in the local church devote themselves to teaching (1 Tim. 4:13). False teaching must be answered with faithful teaching, and genuine faith in God's people remains genuine through ongoing faithful teaching. And this faithful teaching must be compelling and appropriately clear and forceful—and prove fruitful—for the church to endure and flourish. Teaching is not optional in the church; it's essential—not as a course of study to complete but as daily bread. So Paul instructs Timothy to "teach these things" (1 Tim. 4:11; 6:2), and to keep a close watch not only on himself but also on the teaching (1 Tim. 4:16). Titus must "teach what accords with sound doctrine" (Titus 2:1), and "*in your teaching* show integrity, dignity, and sound speech that cannot be condemned" (Titus 2:7–8).

Leaders in the local church are not expected to be savvy decision makers or experienced businessmen but "those who labor in preaching and teaching" (1 Tim. 5:17). Hebrews 13:7 is a powerful and often overlooked statement on church leaders as teachers, and teachers as church leaders: "Remember your leaders, those who spoke to you the word of God. Consider the outcome of their way of life, and imitate their faith." When we remember our leaders, Hebrews assumes, we remember them *as teachers*: "those who spoke to you the word of God." Christ appoints teachers to be pastor-elders and not only teach but also lead the church. However idealistic and inefficient we might fear that teachers as a group might be, Christ appoints them to *both teach and lead* rather than appointing efficient administrators and executives who themselves do not teach.

Daily Bread for Hungry Souls

Simply put, the idea of pastor-elders being gifted executives but not teachers is foreign to the New Testament. Also foreign is the concept of ministry-specialized pastors who mainly administrate programs and jettison the regular practice of pastoring through teaching. Such men who are gifted servants, worthy recipients of title and office, but not teachers aren't barred from formal service in the church. They too are a great blessing, useful for many forms of ministry leadership and service. But they are not pastor-elders. This is why God has given us a second office called "deacon."[4]

The societal pressure today is extraordinary for pastor-elders to practice and be proficient at just about anything else other than teaching. But if we are to be faithful to the teaching of the Bible,

---

4 For more on deacons, see appendix 1.

to God's own word and teaching to us, we will lean against this pressure to reduce, minimize, and go thin on teaching in the life of the church. We're not handing out degrees but feeding souls. And that doesn't happen well without skilled, dedicated teachers working together to shepherd the flock with open Bibles.

Must Elders Be Skilled in Teaching?

Having rehearsed just a few reasons why teaching is central and critical in the Christian church, and why the New Testament assumes that pastors teach (and that formal, regular teachers in local churches will be largely the pastor-elders), now we're ready to return to our original question: What is meant by the qualification that pastor-elders be "able to teach" (1 Tim. 3:2)? We could ask, Is this a more minimalist or maximalist criterion? In other words, does it mean something like *willing and able to teach when necessary* or more like *skilled at teaching*?

In the New Testament, as we've seen, *pastor*, *elder*, and *overseer* are three names for the same teaching office (Acts 20:17, 28; Titus 1:5–7; 1 Pet. 5:1–2). Pastors are elders are overseers. And the pastors are the chief teachers (Eph. 4:11; Heb. 13:7). Pastoral authority, in the New Testament, is tied to the teaching of God's word. Faithful leaders exercise oversight first and foremost through teaching, even as that oversight includes more than just teaching. Ongoing teaching is centrally important in the church and is the central work (though not the only work) of its lead officers.

But how central? *Able* is an ambiguous word in our English. How high or low a bar is "able to teach"? Is this a minimal standard or more maximal? Does this teaching *ability* point to elders being simply *willing to teach* as needed, or *skilled and eager teachers* relative to their particular context? More to the point: are pastor-elders the kind of men who *can* teach if they have a gun to their head, or are they the kind who *won't stop* teaching even at gunpoint?

Possibility or Ability?

"Able to teach" translates a single word in the original (Greek *didaktikos*), which appears only twice in the New Testament: in the elder qualifications in 1 Timothy 3:2 and in Paul's calling "the Lord's servant," in the midst of church conflict, to "not be quarrelsome but kind to everyone, *able to teach*, patiently enduring evil, correcting his opponents with gentleness" (2 Tim. 2:24–25).

What we glean from 1 Timothy 3:2 (with *didaktikos* appearing as it does in the list of fifteen) is minimal, though not insignificant. The fact that this is a requirement of pastor-elders, and no less the distinguishing requirement when compared to the deacon qualifications, signals its importance (so also may its placement in the middle of the list). We need to locate "able to teach" within the larger biblical portrait (above) of the centrality of teaching in God's dealing with his people, old and new, as well as in light of Christ's calling on the pastor-elders in particular to *lead and feed* (or teach and govern) the church. This larger picture clearly points us in the maximalist direction, that "able to teach" is not marginal or negotiable. Something far more akin to skill, or we might say "ability," in terms of effectiveness, is required for the pastor-elders. Skilled teaching protects a church from error, and if false teaching does arise and take root, the church will stand or fall on whether the pastors, under God, can adequately and compellingly answer with their own teaching.

Kind, Gentle, Patient, *Didaktikos*

The New Testament leader or "Lord's servant," as Paul puts it in 2 Timothy 2:24–26, then adds an important piece to our composite of "able to teach." Considering the context of this passage, as instructions to a leader in the midst of church conflict, we can say that one who is *didaktikos* is not merely externally skillful at teaching but also has a particular temperament or internal demeanor. We might say such a man is not only an effective or gifted teacher but also a "teacher at heart." He approaches life and the world and disagreement and conflict with the proclivities of a teacher. He teaches not only willingly (whatever his level of skill) but eagerly. *Didaktikos* here is a kind of virtue that shines in conflict alongside kindness, gentleness, and patience.

It's one thing to be a teacher in practice and another to be a teacher at heart. Good teachers see possibilities in people, perhaps especially in times of conflict and when there are suspicions to the contrary. Good teachers are hopeful that others can learn and grow. They don't assume people are who they are and will never change. Rather, teachers want to influence, to shape, to guide. They want to inform and present new facts and provide fresh perspective and motivation. They are *inclined to teach*—they seek *through words* to change people, not simply judge them as they are. Good teachers don't give the final exam on the first day of class. The time for judging will come, but their first instinct is to teach. Not only do they expose and correct error. They also encourage and envision, with complete patience and teaching (2 Tim. 4:2).

Equipped, Eager, and Effective

However, critical as this internal teacher-at-heart dimension is— we want men who see the world as teachers do—the proclivities and temperament of a teacher are not enough. For the church to be healthy and stay healthy, the elders must, first, have sound doctrine themselves and, second, get the job done in teaching the church. The elders must be *equipped* with the content of the Christian faith and *effective* in teaching it. Their teaching must be true and bear fruit; they must be skilled *for* teaching by knowing the Scriptures and Christian theology and skillful *at* teaching—not necessarily on the world's stage, compared with the most gifted communicators and preachers alive (and now accessible online) but relative to the particular congregation they are called to serve.

Titus 1:9 is critical in shedding light on *didaktikos*, even though the word doesn't appear here. In fact, given the correspondence between the elder-overseer qualifications in 1 Timothy 3 and Titus 1, we might say we have far more here on *skillful at teaching* because now Paul fleshes out the concept as it relates to what it means to be able to teach in the local church:

[An elder] must hold firm to the trustworthy word as taught, so that he may be *able to give instruction* in sound doctrine and *also to rebuke* those who contradict it. (Titus 1:9)

What the eldership requires is no mere willingness, but capability and proclivity. The elders must be effective in both the offensive and defensive needs of their calling to teach. First, they will have accurately received the deposit of the faith. They will know the Scriptures and true doctrine and be competent in Christian theology. This is no trifle. And it doesn't happen casually. It typically requires some intentional course of study or season of preparation. Good churches naturally prepare their people in Christian theology, but additional study and focus in some form is usually required to become an able teacher. So being biblically and theologically *equipped* is one aspect.

Another aspect here in Titus 1:9 is the need to be *effective*. Pastor-elders will go on the offensive and teach God's word and his gospel and Christian doctrine to the church. Again, not as a one-time course of study but as daily bread. The pastors feed the flock with Christian truth. And as needed, they go on the defensive—not just providing food but protecting faith. They expose and correct false teachers who undermine or contradict Christian teaching. And they must be effective when they take aim at false teachers and false doctrines. In a very basic sense, this is why the elders must not just be willing to teach, if forced, but *good teachers*—teachers at heart and in skill. They must be effective at their calling, in their particular context, to provide ongoing spiritual nourishment for the church through teaching and possessing enough skill to wage word-to-word combat with false teachers in their church and emerge, with the elder team and the Spirit's help, victorious.[5]

Teaching with Ability

Bill Mounce makes this important observation about the civic context of the elder qualifications in 1 Timothy:

The problem in Ephesus was false teaching, and it is difficult to see Paul allowing for only the passive possession of the gift [of

---

5   On the elders' calling to protect the church's doctrine, Greg Beale observes, "The office of elder is not a response to occasional or temporarily unique conditions but rather owes its existence to the ongoing, uninterrupted eschatological tribulation [throughout the church age] of false teaching and deception. . . . The office was also created to protect the church's doctrine so that it will remain healthy as it conducts its mission to the world to expand the invisible boundaries of the new creation. Such an office is needed until the time when the new creation is consummated" (G. K. Beale, *A New Testament Biblical Theology: The Unfolding of the Old Testament in the New* [Grand Rapids, MI: Baker, 2011], 822). Thanks to my fellow pastor, and "first among equals" of our plurality at Cities Church, Jonathan Parnell, for pointing me to this observation.

teaching] and not active participation. [Second Timothy 2:24 and Titus 1:9] confirm that those who could teach did teach.[6]

Those who could teach did teach. In other words, elders are practicing teachers, not just able and willing upon request. Capable teachers become elders, and elders continue to exercise their proclivity and ability for the sake of building up the church. Philip Towner agrees that "able to teach" is no mere willingness but "skill in teaching" or "ministry skill or gift." "Church leaders," he writes, are to be "chosen from among those who display this gift."[7]

In other words, "able to teach" is not a minimal criterion but maximal. The question is not whether elders can teach if necessary, but are they *equipped, eager, and effective* teachers for this particular local church?

What about 1 Timothy 5:17?

The often-cited text against all pastor-elders being teachers is 1 Timothy 5:17: "Let the elders who rule well be considered worthy of double honor, especially those who labor in preaching and teaching." If we're not reading carefully, and in light of the canonical context, we might assume a larger council of elders who only "rule,"

---

6 Bill Mounce, *Pastoral Epistles*, Word Biblical Commentary (Nashville, TN: Thomas Nelson, 2000), 174.

7 Philip Towner, *The Letters to Timothy and Titus*, New International Commentary on the New Testament (Grand Rapids, MI: Eerdmans, 2006), n.p. David Platt also agrees. Elders, he writes, "can't just know the Word extensively; it is imperative that elders communicate the Word effectively. . . . An elder must know the Word and spread the Word throughout the church and from the church throughout the world. He must be able to persuade people with the Word, plead with people from the Word, comfort people with the Word, encourage people from the Word, instruct people in the Word, and lead the church according to the Word. This is nonnegotiable." David Platt, *Exalting Jesus in 1 & 2 Timothy and Titus*, Christ-Centered Exposition Commentary (Nashville, TN: Holman Reference, 2013), 56.

and then, within that council, a subgroup who preach and teach. Some even go so far as to name two kinds of elders: ruling elders and teaching elders.[8] But does 1 Timothy 5:17 teach—as no other text does—two classifications of elder, those who teach (teaching elders) and those who (typically) do not (ruling elders)?

Much discussion has focused on the word *especially* (". . . especially those who labor in preaching and teaching"). For instance, David Platt comments:

That word "especially" might be better translated as "that is," so that the verse might also be translated, "The elders who are good leaders should be considered worthy of double honor, *that is*, those who work hard at preaching and teaching." In other words, good leaders in the church *are* those who labor in preaching and teaching.[9]

Similarly George Knight comments, "Paul is giving here [in 1 Timothy 5:17] a further description of those he has already mentioned."[10] In other words, the "elders who rule well" *are* "those who labor in preaching and teaching." Elders "rule well" by laboring first and foremost as teachers. So, then, all elders are teachers in an important sense, not just a subgroup of a larger council. Mounce agrees: "A straightforward reading of the text would infer that all overseers were supposed to be skilled teachers."[11]

However, I do not think it all falls on a minority reading of the Greek word (*malista*) as "especially" or "that is." I think it's impor-

---

8   For instance, Robert Rayburn, "Ministers, Elders, and Deacons," in *Order in the Offices*, ed. Mark Brown, Classic Presbyterian Government Resources (1993).

9   Platt, *Exalting Jesus*, 90.

10   George Knight, *The Pastoral Epistles*, New International Greek Testament Commentary (Grand Rapids, MI: Eerdmans, 1999), 232.

11   Mounce, *Pastoral Epistles*, 174.

tant to see that, in context, an even more important word, and often overlooked, is "labor." All elders are teachers, but some *labor* at preaching and teaching. The "especially" is not about ability or proclivity but about *labor*, and in particular *labor* as vocation that pays the bills. The next verse says the *laborer* deserves his wages. All good pastor-teachers are worthy of double honor—and especially those who *labor*, that is, as their bread-winning vocation, at pastoral work. All elders teach but not all *labor* full-time at pastoral ministry. In short, my understanding of 1 Timothy 5:17 is this: *all taught; some labored at pastoral work as their profession.* The point is the amount of labor (and thus necessity of remuneration), not a division among elders. The distinction here is along the lines of full-time and volunteer, not teaching and nonteaching. All the pastor-elders teach. Some *labor* at the work as their day job, and are thusly more deserving of the "double honor" of respect and remuneration. As this works out practically in the life of the church, it is often those who labor as a profession in pastoral work who are most equipped and often carry more of the teaching and especially preaching. But this does not mean that nonvocational pastors are not teachers.

Preaching and teaching remain at the heart of the pastoral calling. The pastors are called to more than teaching—also to leading, overseeing, governing. But the heart of the calling is teaching. Teaching is the nonnegotiable. A healthy church might limp along with inadequate administration, but we dare not compromise on the quality of our teaching.[12]

---

12 Preaching/teaching is the priority, and yet elders/pastors are not only teachers but also *overseers*, as D. A. Carson argues well. Pastor-elders must do more than teach, and yet not let teaching take a back seat. Such are the tensions we live in for this age. Should we expect it to be different? On the one hand, pastors should not give in to the pressure to do a thousand other things than preaching and teaching. And on the other hand, it is naïve to

Two Offices or Three?

During my college days in Greenville, South Carolina, I was involved briefly with a church plant of the Presbyterian Church in America (PCA) and later attended, and for two years was deeply involved with, a long-established PCA church in town. Through these two rich experiences, and through many dear PCA friends to this day, as well as the skilled teachers I had as professors at Reformed Theological Seminary in Orlando, I am not unaware of the two- and three- (and 2.5-) office debate in Presbyterian circles. Robert Rayburn's article "Ministers, Elders, and Deacons" claims that "the elders" in Acts "evokes the Old Testament image of a senate of rulers and counselors, *not of teachers*."[13] Where does he get this assumption?

Rather than locking horns on 1 Timothy 5:17 with those, like Rayburn, who argue for three offices (teaching elder, ruling elder, and deacon), my approach is to take a step back, as I've tried to do in this chapter, and first ask about the place of ongoing teaching in the life of the New Testament church. How pervasive or limited is it? Is it, say, half an hour per week from the pulpit, or does the church feed on teaching in classes, small groups, one-on-one conversations, personal study and reading, seminars, church newsletters, and more? Nature abhors a vacuum. If the pastors leave their people void of Christian teaching for all but half an hour each week, the sheep will fill their stomachs and souls with other food.

---

think they can only preach and teach. Pastors are called neither to a thousand things nor to one thing alone. The three-office view, as we'll see below, admirably aims to protect the "teaching elders" from shouldering too much oversight, but by introducing the category of "ruling elder" creates two classes of elder and in effect removes "skilled at teaching" from the qualifications of one class. D. A. Carson, "Some Reflections on Pastoral Leadership," *Themelios* 40.2 (2015): 195–97.

13 Rayburn, "Ministers, Elders, and Deacons."

Then, with that larger picture in view, let's ask whether minimally willing teachers will rise to what the church really needs.

For those who argue for two types of elders (teaching and ruling), I would agree that we distinguish *teaching* from *rule* in terms of these being the two main *tasks* of the elders, but what's remarkable in the New Testament is that they are not separated into *types* of elders. And when we do try to separate them, it's just a matter of time until the separation breeds conflict. The elders are to be men "able to give instruction in sound doctrine and also to rebuke those who contradict it" (Titus 1:9). Under Christ, sound doctrine is the locus of authority in the local church. Christ is head, with his authority expressed in his word, through his apostles, taught with patience and persuasion by the elders to the church.

I suspect that what may limit the thinking of some three-office advocates is that it is imponderable that all pastors would be teachers. They have known so many good men who were not good teachers, but they were good pastors, so it seems, or good "ruling elders." In all likelihood, such men were indeed good officers, but would it have been demeaning to call them what they perhaps really functioned as—deacons?

I appreciate Rayburn's (and John Murray's[14]) desire to exalt the ministry of the word. Yes and amen. But to do so, we need not separate the elders into types and raise the profile for the "teaching elders." I am arguing in this chapter for (in a sense) a lower view of the ministry, and with it, a higher view of the place of teaching God's word in the life of the local church by maintaining, as I believe the New Testament does, that all pastors be able to teach as (1) adequately equipped, (2) with internal eagerness, and (3) with external effectiveness relative to the particular church context at hand.

---

14 See John Murray, *Collected Writings of John Murray*, vol. 2 (Edinburgh, UK: Banner of Truth, 1977), 357–65.

Skilled in Context

Some might ask, might "skilled at teaching" prove to be too high a standard in practice? Does a small, rural church stand much chance of finding skilled teachers? Wouldn't such a maximalist qualification leave thousands of good churches not only without the *plurality* of pastor-teachers the New Testament prescribes but even without a *single* qualified pastor-teacher?

One brilliant attribute of the elder qualifications, as we will see, is that they are *relative* in the best sense. They are not simple boxes to check, but criteria for sober-minded evaluation by a local church and its leaders prior to the appointment of new leaders. The qualifications are meant to be suitably flexible and therefore apply to and serve specific local churches throughout the ages, around the world, in vastly different contexts.

One way to say it (again) is that the qualifications are analog, not digital. They are not meant to be either true or false of any given man's life *whatever the context*. Rather, these are qualifications to consider at a particular time by a particular church *relative to a particular call and context*. And so it is with "able to teach." Note well, a seminary degree or certificate of ordination doesn't make a man able to teach. It just makes him a seminary graduate or ordained minister. But whether this man is, in fact, able to teach relative to a certain congregation is to be determined by that congregation as it (or its leaders) assesses him for their specific flock.

Whether a man is skilled at teaching in a rural church plant may be quite different from whether he is sufficiently skilled at teaching in a long-established, bustling, city church. Again, what individual churches are to look for in their pastor-elders is not men who are skilled at teaching relative to the best preachers online or even to the church across town, but whether they are skilled at teaching relative to this specific congregation, whether urban or rural, fledgling or mature, long-established or newly planted. In assessing a new pastor-elder, or evaluating the ongoing effectiveness of a longtime pastor, a congregation and its current leaders might ask questions such as:

- Will this man be able to teach *our people* (not just any people) in a true and compelling way?
- Is he skilled enough to feed *us* regularly by teaching us God's word?
- Will *our hearts* soar regularly under *his teaching God's word to us*?
- Will he not just be *willing* but *eager* to rise to the occasion to persuade our people toward the truth and away from error?
- Is he skilled enough as a teacher to lead and engage and inspire the people of *our particular church* to love God and his word and fulfill the mission Christ calls us to in this locale?

Such questions will help us keep our standards both appropriately high and reasonably attainable, guard the indispensable place of teaching, and ensure we have the right men in the right offices for the long-term health of the church.

Making sure that our elders really are *didaktikos*—not just able to get by, but equipped and eager to teach and able to do so with effectiveness—will not only keep our churches well-fed, but have them ready to face the challenges that are coming and are already here, when we need both faithfulness and fruitfulness in combating false teaching.

For Current and Aspiring Teachers

As we close this important chapter, let's do so with two lessons for those who are current teachers or who aspire to be regular teachers of God's word. And these two lessons are relevant to all of us, since, as we've said, we all are recipients of true teaching in Christ and come to teach others in some measure (Eph. 6:4; Col. 3:16; Heb. 5:12; Titus 2:3).

First, in the divisive and conflicted times in which we are living, most of us, if not all, have room to grow in learning to be *didaktikos* with others, in the sense we saw in 2 Timothy 2:24–26. Christianity is a teaching movement. We are people of a book—and what's in the book? Teaching. Content to be welcomed and taught. This means that as we're called to teach in some form, we're called together to a kind of pedagogical patience, the patience that doesn't hear someone say one wrong or suspect word and write him off. Rather, we take a deep breath, ask God for patience, and set about the hard work of teaching. Without being patronizing, we teach. We keep teaching. The time for judging will come, but we need not snap to it.

Our generation effuses the opposite of James 1:19: "Be quick to hear, slow to speak, slow to anger." We are quick to speak, slow to hear, quick to anger. And perhaps like never before, social media provides well-meaning brothers and sisters the opportunity to make all manner of verbal missteps in public.[15] Let's take a deep breath and ask God for the patience we need for these days—patience not

---

15 Here I mainly have in mind our local church contexts—not, say, teaching published online. Though note that even for Apollos, the newly celebrated public teacher, Aquila and Priscilla patiently took him aside and taught him "the way of God more accurately" instead of first taking aim in public (Acts 18:26). It would not have been unjust for them to confront him in public. His error had been public, and they could have corrected him in public, if that seemed necessary. However, even when Apollos erred publicly, they showed him the mercy

to write people off prematurely because they used a certain phrase or quoted someone we're fearful of—or didn't disavow the latest boogeyman term we want everyone to renounce to be orthodox.

Let's cultivate the heart and approach of a teacher. Let's give the space and provide the teaching that patience requires. Let's hope for change and pray for change. And under God, let's seek to change people.

Teacher's Heart of Our God

In closing this chapter, perhaps the most important truth about teaching skill, and both its external ability and internal temperament, is how God has been such a skilled and patient teacher with us. Aren't you glad that God has handled you like this? Oh, the patience of our God! We have the Book we do because he is inclined to teach. Over centuries. What patience. We have the lives we do, the faith we do, and the shared calling we do because our God is patient, with such a divine proclivity to teach. Our God loves to teach. He is indeed a teacher at heart.

Make no mistake; the final exam is coming. Christ will return as judge. But in the meantime, he continues to teach. Through the teachings of his apostles—and the faithful, heartfelt, skilled teaching of his word by pastor-teachers in local churches—he teaches.[16]

---

and patience of taking him aside privately. Teachers at heart, they did not presume he was set in his ways, but they were hopeful he could be persuaded. In this instance, he was.

16 One last topic that relates to this chapter that I did not have space to cover here is team preaching. For those interested, I have written about what our team has learned so far, in seven years, in "Team Preaching: Why Our Pastors Share the Pulpit," Desiring God, August 15, 2021, https://www.desiringgod.org/.

4

Pastors Keep Their Head
in a Conflicted World

As for you, always be sober-minded.

2 TIMOTHY 4:5

WE ARE IN GREAT NEED today of Christians with sober minds.

As the swirling winds of religious pluralism and progressive "tolerance" meet with the gales of globalization, a parade of new gadgets and brain-highjacking software, and the constant drip of round-the-clock news creation and politics driven by unbelieving assumptions, we may be more prone than ever to diversion and distraction—and with it, muddle-headedness and outright confusion. Are we learning to just drown our clouded and anxious minds in social media, electronic games, television series, and football on the tube five nights a week?

Level heads have long been in high demand, but is the supply now at a record low? The Information Age gives us access like never before to data to feed the highest IQs, but raw intellect is prone to extremes and debilitating imbalances when wielded without the great stabilizer of emotional intelligence (EQ). Call it wisdom, level-headedness, or just sanctified common sense—the biblical attribute of sober-mindedness is at a premium. This should get our attention when such a virtue is central to both a healthy Christian church and a healthy Christian walk.

Fortunately, sober-mindedness is something for which God holds out great promise for development and growth. He does this kind of work, and we have good reason for great hope.

Importance of a Sober Mind

"Sober-minded" is one of the first traits given for the church's leaders (1 Tim. 3:2) as well as the women of 1 Timothy 3:11. It's the first encouragement to the congregation's aging men (Titus 2:2) and one of Paul's most pronounced charges to his protégé Timothy: "As for you, always be sober-minded" (2 Tim. 4:5). The NIV translates it memorably: "Keep your head in all situations." Oh, do we need leaders like this—who keep their heads whatever the circumstance.

As much as ever, as we grope our way forward in the complexities and conflicts of modern society, we need our pastor-elders—and as many in the congregation as possible—to be balanced and clear-headed. In such a confused milieu, we need models who will not be suckers for extremes or "wander off into myths" (2 Tim. 4:4) or "devote themselves to myths . . . which promote speculations rather than the stewardship from God that is by faith" (1 Tim. 1:4). At the helm, give us stewards of the faith who sacrificially love, not speculators who are easily diverted into the vain peripheral discussions that come along incessantly.

In a day when clarity and level-headedness can be sorely lacking, it is deeply encouraging that balanced thinking and sober-mindedness can be taught. It can be developed and learned over time, as Paul instructs Timothy, and us, toward sober judgment when he writes:

Have nothing to do with irreverent, silly myths. (1 Tim. 4:7)

Avoid the irreverent babble and contradictions of what is falsely called "knowledge," for by professing it some have swerved from the faith. (1 Tim. 6:20–21)

Charge them before God not to quarrel about words, which does no good, but only ruins the hearers. Do your best to present yourself to God as one approved, a worker who has no need to be ashamed, rightly handling the word of truth. But avoid irreverent babble, for it will lead people into more and more ungodliness, and their talk will spread like gangrene. (2 Tim. 2:14–17)

Have nothing to do with foolish, ignorant controversies; you know that they breed quarrels. (2 Tim. 2:23)

Silly myths. Irreverent babble. Quarreling about words. Foolish, ignorant controversies. Sober-mindedness means keeping your head when others are running around with theirs on fire. Sober-mindedness means not being detoured from the central things, from the gospel "of first importance" (1 Cor. 15:3), by diversions at the margins. And in our environment of extremisms, it means fresh focus on and excitement about the heart of the faith. With our proliferation of idiosyncrasies and endless hobbyhorses, we need preoccupation with "the faith that was once for all delivered to the saints" (Jude 3)—not speculative theories and newfangled hypotheses, but "what you have heard from me in the presence of many witnesses" (2 Tim. 2:2). Not preoccupation with *fighting* but with *the faith*, even if that takes some occasional combat.

Helmet of Salvation

Then how do we get help? Where do we go to clear our clouded heads? First Thessalonians 5:4–8 gets us pointed in the right direction:

> You are not in darkness, brothers, for that day [of Christ's return] to surprise you like a thief. For you are all children of light, children of the day. We are not of the night or of the darkness. So then let us not sleep, as others do, but *let us keep awake and be sober*. For those who sleep, sleep at night, and those who get drunk, are drunk at night. But since we belong to the day, *let us be sober*, having put on the breastplate of faith and love, and for a helmet the hope of salvation.

In particular, verse 8 gives us this important path to cultivating a sober mind: "the hope of salvation." Here we find a helmet to protect our heads. Gospel hope—which is not a thin wish but a well-grounded surety about the future—guards our minds in the battle swirling around us and lifts our gaze beyond our present confusion to the certainty of the coming victory. The most sober thinkers in the world are those who have drunk most deeply of the gospel, and it has filled them with solid, secure, substantiated hope.

Right at the heart of the good work God has begun in us (Phil. 1:6) is developing our discernment—our sober-mindedness—"so that [we] may approve what is excellent" (Phil. 1:9–10). As we walk the path of increasing holiness, we get our heads back little by little. Our minds get clearer as we breathe in gospel air and feast at the table of the Scriptures in the context of the church; our heads become more level under the gravitational sway of Jesus's person, work, promises, and people.

In Christ, we are increasingly "renewed in the spirit of [our] minds" (Eph. 4:23) and "transformed by the renewal of [our minds], that by testing [we] may discern what is the will of God" (Rom. 12:2). And in that growing clear-headedness, the Christian learns "not to think of himself more highly than he ought to think, but to *think with sober judgment*" (Rom. 12:3)—and not only about self, but all the world and life as well.

Master of Every Situation

Not only is growth in sober-mindedness part of Christian sanctification, but we have a particular focal point and source in the God-man himself. "Beholding the glory of the Lord, [we] are being transformed into the same image from one degree of glory to another" (2 Cor. 3:18). When we have the Spirit of God, we have the mind of Christ (1 Cor. 2:15–16), and our being conformed to his image (Rom. 8:29) includes our minds.

Never has the world witnessed a human mind more sober, thought more lucid, assessment more balanced, and a head more level than that of Jesus. Solomon was known in his day, far and wide, for the greatness of his wisdom, but when Jesus is on the scene, "something greater than Solomon is here" (Matt. 12:42).

In Jesus "are hidden all the treasures of wisdom and knowledge" (Col. 2:3). His wisdom and sober-mindedness make him "master of every situation," writes John Piper. "One reason we admire and trust Jesus above all persons is that his knowledge and wisdom are unsurpassed."[1] Oh, do we need pastor-elders like this—men whose minds are becoming conformed to the sober mind of Christ.

No Greater Remedy

Not only is Jesus's wisdom peerless, but he shares it liberally. "I will give you a mouth and wisdom, which none of your adversaries will be able to withstand or contradict" (Luke 21:15). "If any of you lacks wisdom, let him ask God, who gives generously to all without reproach, and it will be given him" (James 1:5).

In a day of endless distraction and diversion, there is no greater remedy for our clouded heads and hectic lives than the sober mind of Christ put on display in church life, and pressed into the service of godly wisdom and teaching, by sober-minded men who lead through good teaching and wise governance and know how to keep their heads in the most imbalanced and bewildering of times.

―――――

Most Underrated Trait?

Sober-minded may be the most underrated of the elder qualifications. A level head and a balanced mind affect essentially everything the elders do, from their teaching (what they teach on and when and for how long, and how they approach and present the teaching and draw lines of application) to their leading, oversight, and decision-making. One particularly important application of collective sober-mindedness for the council is how the pastor-elders bring the congregation along in various seasons in the life of the church. Do the elders merely consult with themselves, make a significant

1   John Piper, *Seeing and Savoring Jesus Christ*, rev. ed. (Wheaton, IL: Crossway, 2004), 52.

decision, and spring it on the church? Or do they carefully and patiently plan how to introduce a new direction, in an unpressured moment? Do they do their homework (put in the extra labor) to prepare the presentation and documents well and give plenty of notice on when Q&A sessions might be and how to contact the elders to ask questions and when votes might be taken? Do they give the church time to receive and make peace with new directions, steering the ship gently rather than sending people rolling on the deck and tumbling overboard?

On Generational Dynamics

One particular area in church life that can be thorny but is cushioned by sober-minded leaders is generational tension, which is an age-old, though not constant, conflict in ministry.[2] This can come and go in seasons, especially as a senior pastor or the gravitational center of the elders or congregation nears retirement age. In the last decade, and continuing at the publication of this book, many churches have felt this tension as one massive generation tries to make what can be an awkward handoff to another.

The so-called baby boomers were born in the post–World War II birthrate "boom" from 1946 to about 1964. After this significant two-decade spike, there was a kind of birthrate recession from about 1965 to 1980—referred to as Generation X. Then followed from about 1980 through the end of the century a kind of "echo boom," as the boomers produced offspring en masse and the birthrate again rose. These boomers' kids have been called Generation Y, among other

2 I also would encourage pastor-elders to consider "church-size dynamics" and the need for sober-mindedness in considering what we might expect, and plan in light of, at various congregation sizes. See Tim Keller, "Leadership and Church Size Dynamics: How Strategy Changes with Growth," Senior Pastor Central, accessed January 13, 2022, https://seniorpastorcentral.com/.

names, but the label that gained most traction has been millennials. But whatever the big-picture timing in society, individual churches find themselves from time to time with forms of generational tension and the potential for misunderstanding and clashes. Sober-minded pastor-elders will want to lean into such conflicts, not passively wait for the conflicts to resolve without leadership. Not to oversimplify, but essential will be the younger and older generations viewing each other with Christian eyes and loving with Christian hearts.

Consider, first, what it might look like for the younger generation to make a plea to the older: "We desperately need you."

Better Country for Old Men

Dear aging Christian, please don't phone it in just when the King's about to call. Don't retire on the world's terms and abandon your longtime local church. As your generation begins to flood the shores of retirement, please don't leave us to fend for ourselves and make the same mistakes all over again. For your joy and for our good, we need you in this family called "the church." You are our fathers (1 Tim. 5:1). The apostle wrote not only to young men but to you—not just to the younger generation, but to the "fathers" (1 John 2:12–14). Don't leave us as orphans.

We need your wisdom. We need your experience. You have made the long journey, watched fads come and go, rejoiced with those who have rejoiced, wept with those who have wept, endured the dark night of the soul. As the young men see visions, we need you still to dream dreams (Acts 2:17) and lean in, not out. Help us be courageous when we should, and gently direct us to a different course when we should back off.

Your Example

We need your example. The young bucks need your discipling and your encouragement to be self-controlled (Titus 2:6), to "flee youthful passions and pursue righteousness, faith, love, and peace" (2 Tim. 2:22). We need you to model for us how "not [to] be quarrelsome but kind to everyone, able to teach, patiently enduring evil" (2 Tim. 2:24).

We need you to be "sober-minded, dignified, self-controlled, sound in faith, in love, and in steadfastness" (Titus 2:2), to temper the energy of our youth with your patience, to complement the young man's ambition with the perspective of the happy old man who's already been around the block a few times.

Your Grace

We may need your forgiveness. In our fervor to create the future, we may have seen things out of focus. At times, we may have been so naïve as to think our lives would be better if your generation would just get out of the way. It might be easier, but it emphatically would not be better. How deadly it is when spiritual ardor ferments into arrogance. Some of us have been foolish and sinned against you. We need your mercy.

We need your patience. We need your grace. The mature leaders of tomorrow are not always easy to deal with today. We ask you to remember what it was like to be younger, even as we try to keep in mind that one day soon we will be older. We ask you to listen and give those of us who manifestly love Jesus some benefit of the doubt. We're not trying to ruin your church, but to prepare the way for greater things yet to come. We're not trying to kill your gospel legacy, but to keep it alive.

And we need you to do all this, not in your own strength, but in the strength that God supplies so that in everything he gets the glory through Jesus (1 Pet. 4:11). He has promised explicitly not to forsake you (Ps. 71:18) but to carry you, even to old age and gray hairs (Isa. 43:4). He will empower you and preserve you to hear his voice: "Well done, good and faithful servant" (Matt. 25:21, 23).

More than Ever

For decades, you have walked as "strangers and exiles on the earth" (Heb. 11:13). And now, as you slow down and grow weaker and feel yourself closer than ever to heaven, more than ever "seeking a homeland" (Heb. 11:14)—as you "desire a better country, that is, a heavenly one," a city prepared for you by God himself (Heb. 11:15)—please don't settle for a little Sabbath evening of rest on this side.

We need you—ordinary, average, imperfect you. Not only do we long for the likes of Raymond Lull (martyred among Muslims at age eighty), and Polycarp (bishop of Smyrna, burned alive at age eighty-six), and J. Oswald Sanders (who wrote one book a year beginning at age seventy and died a week after he turned one hundred). But we also earnestly need the unknown senior sages, laboring without renown in out-of-the-way local churches, participating without occupying the positions of privilege, engaged without making the final calls, on the bus without having to be in the driver's seat.

"Most men don't die of old age," said Ralph Winter, "they die of retirement."[3] Please don't retire from the local church. We need you more than ever.

———

3 Ralph Winter, "The Retirement Booby Trap," *Mission Frontiers* 7 (July 1985): 25.

Church, Make Room for Young Leaders

What some aging Christians need from the younger generation is an invitation to lean into the local church, and not retreat or retire. But others from the older generation may need a different challenge—a summons to lay aside suspicion of those young enough to be their offspring, a charge to dispose of a derogatory view of the real-live specimen of the next generation. Consider, next, a plea for some older leaders not to get off the bus but to aggressively make room for young leaders at the front.

Do Not Despise the Young

It was a two-part charge the aging apostle gave to his younger-generation protégé in 1 Timothy 4:12: "Let no one despise you for your youth, but set the believers an example in speech, in conduct, in love, in faith, in purity." One part goes to the younger generation: by exhibiting model Christian posture in word and deed, give the older generation no good cause for despising your youth.

But the second part is for the aging generation that overhears the directive, like the Ephesian church reading Paul's letter over Timothy's shoulder: by exuding a model Christian disposition toward brothers and sisters in Christ, give the younger generation the benefit of the doubt. Don't expect the worst of fellow believers, regardless of their age. Let the gospel go to work on your subtle age prejudice.

Create Space for New Leadership

In this generation, Larry Osborne has been one pastor and author helping the massive leadership transition between boomers and their millennial progeny. Whether in business, government, or the church, many have felt the tensions, as what was America's largest generation has been giving way to its more numerous offspring.

Osborne makes the observation that on the high school and college campus, it seems "the freshmen always get smaller." As we age, each year's crop of incoming students seems less impressive than the class before. If that's true of just four years on the campus, what about the long arc of adult life? In the church, says Osborne:

> The seniors never graduate (at least not until they've become literal seniors and start dying off). They hog the leadership table, shutting out the next generation. It's one of the main reasons that most churches stop growing and lose their evangelistic touch (and cultural relevance) around the twenty-year mark.[4]

Let Young Eagles Fly

The Christian vision for leadership is not a tenure model in which whoever's been around longest occupies the seats of privilege and prominence as long as they want. Rather, the force goes the other way: laboring proactively and assertively to raise up younger leaders to fill our shoes and do our job better than we did. This gets at the Great Commission essence of making disciples (Matt. 28:19) and applies it to church leadership. But such a vision of leadership is costly. There's a price to pay, says Osborne:

> Leadership is a zero-sum game. One person's emerging influence is always another person's waning influence. That's why making

---

4 Larry Osborne, *Sticky Teams: Keeping Your Leadership Team and Staff on the Same Page* (Grand Rapids, MI: Zondervan, 2010), 114.

room for the young eagles is a hard sell, especially to those who already have a seat at the table.[5]

Such a deferential and self-humbling dream for raising up new leaders may seem far-fetched in government and business, but shouldn't it have its best chance in the church, where we follow one who came not to be served but to serve (Mark 10:45)? Do we not believe that true greatness is in service, not in lording it over and exercising authority (Mark 10:42)? We aim "in humility [to] count others more significant" and "look not only to [our] own interests, but also to the interests of others" (Phil. 2:3–4).

But are we not, then, compromising wisdom in church leadership by replacing some qualified members of the older generation with those from the younger?

Let the Young Speak

On Sunday morning, August 29, 1982—with the first of the millennials still in diapers—a thirty-six-year-old baby boomer took up Job 32:7–11 and preached on the young man Elihu. The sermon was titled "Let the Young Speak." That night, the church would be ordaining twenty-seven-year-old Tom Steller, and John Piper wanted to prepare his congregation of gray heads for laying hands on such a youth. The key verses were Job 32:8–9: "It is the spirit in man, the breath of the Almighty, that makes him understand. It is not the old who are wise, nor the aged who understand what is right." Said Piper:

The lesson Elihu teaches us here is that it is not age that brings wisdom but the Spirit of God. There is no necessary correlation

5 Osborne, *Sticky Teams*, 114.

between gray hair and good theology. There is no necessary connection between a wizened face and a wise heart. . . .

Of course, there is, then, no necessary connection between youth and wisdom, either. What Elihu has done is remove age as the dominant consideration in deciding who is wise and understanding. He teaches us that there may be folly in the old and folly in the young; wisdom in the young and wisdom in the old. When we search for a source of wisdom, we do not end our search with the question, "How old is he?" We end it with the question, "Who has the Spirit of wisdom and understanding?"[6]

Make Room at the Table

Alongside the plea above to the older generation to not abandon the younger for retirement is also this request:

> Don't frown on us young adults and think we're fools simply because we're young. In Christ, and by his Spirit, be on the lookout for the best, and let us have a chance to show you that not all of us are as bad as you might expect. For the advance of the gospel and the good of the church tomorrow and today, don't keep us locked out of leadership. Take the extra initiative to make room at the table for younger voices, and please put in the energy to hear us out. Before long, the younger generation will be driving the ship. Better to begin handing over the wheel sooner than later and make the transition a tribute to the age-defying wisdom of God.

6 John Piper, "Let the Young Speak," Desiring God, August 29, 1982, https://www.desiringgod.org/. See appendix 5, "How Old Should Elders Be?"

PART 2

WHOLE

Men Where They Are Known Best

In an important sense, the pastor-elder qualifications are largely public. In part 2 we will focus on the five that may seem most private, or at least may provide the most revealing glimpses into a man's private life. These five relate especially to what we might call "integrity" or "wholeness"—a private life that matches the one on display in public. Yet none of these are strictly private. Self-control, or lack thereof, will soon enough be manifested publicly. So also, "one-woman man," while nothing less than private, will in time strike public notes. What was whispered in quiet rooms will come to be proclaimed from the rooftops. So, also, those who love drink and money will, in time, give public evidence to it, as will good management of the home.

While formal leadership in the local church, as depicted in the New Testament, is irreducibly public (as we'll see even more clearly in part 3), the men who serve in the office are not to be performers or dramatists. They are not just public teachers and public examples. The church needs leaders who, in a sense, do not clock in and out. They are men "ready in season and out of season" (2 Tim. 4:2), men who stay immersed in the Scriptures, and so in time, their progress becomes plain to all (1 Tim. 4:15). They are whole, which means that for those with eyes to see, such men are even more impressive in everyday life than they are behind a pulpit.

5

Self-Control and the Power of Christ

Urge the younger men to be self-controlled.

TITUS 2:6

IT SOUNDS so simple and straightforward, perhaps even commonplace.

It's not a flashy concept or an especially attractive idea on its own. It doesn't turn heads or grab headlines. It can be as seemingly small as saying no to another Oreo—or another twenty minutes streaming shows or scrolling social media—or it can feel as significant as living out a resounding yes to sobriety and sexual purity. It is at the height of Christian virtue in a fallen world, and its exercise is quite simply one of the most difficult things sinful humans can learn to do.

Self-control—our hyphenated English is frank and functional. There's no cloak of imagery or euphemistic pretense. No punches pulled, no poetic twist, no endearing irony. Self-control is simply that important, impressive, and nearly impossible practice of learning to maintain control of the beast of one's own passions and behaviors. It means remaining master of your own domain not only on sunny days, but also when faced with trial or temptation. Self-control may be the epitome of "easier said than done."

It Can Be Taught

"Marshmallow man" Walter Mischel is an Ivy League professor known for his experiments in self-control. In the late 1960s he created a test to see how various five-year-olds would respond to being left alone with a marshmallow for fifteen minutes with instructions not to eat it—and with the promise that if they didn't, they would be given another marshmallow. In a 2014 opinion piece, the *New York Times* reported:

> Famously, preschoolers who waited longest for the marshmallow went on to have higher SAT scores than the ones who couldn't wait. In later years they were thinner, earned more advanced degrees, used less cocaine, and coped better with stress. As these first marshmallow kids now enter their 50s, Mr. Mischel and colleagues are investigating whether the good delayers are richer, too.[1]

At the time of the 2014 interview, Mischel, an octogenarian, freshly wanted to make sure that the nervous parents of self-indulgent children didn't miss his key finding: "Whether you eat the marshmallow at age 5 isn't your destiny. Self-control can be taught."

If It's Christian

Along with love and godliness, self-control serves as a major summary term for Christian conduct in full flower (2 Tim. 1:7; Titus 2:6, 12; 1 Pet. 4:7; 2 Pet. 1:6). It is the culminating "fruit of the

---

1 Pamela Druckerman, "Learning How to Exert Self-Control," *New York Times*, September 14, 2014, http://www.nytimes.com/.

Spirit" in the apostle's famous list (Gal. 5:22–23) and one of the first traits required of leaders in the church (1 Tim. 3:2; Titus 1:8). Acts summarizes the apostle's reasoning about the Christian gospel and worldview as "righteousness and *self-control* and the coming judgment" (Acts 24:25). Proverbs 25:28 likens "a man without self-control" to "a city broken into and left without walls." So remarkable is this virtue that as Paul gives various instructions to older men, older women, younger women, and younger men in Titus 2, he need give only one directive to the last group: "Urge the younger men to be self-controlled" (Titus 2:6).

For starters, the idea of controlling one's own self presumes at least two realities: (1) the presence of something within us that needs to be bridled, and (2) the possibility in us, or outside of us, for some source of power to restrain it. For the born-again, our hearts are new, but the poison of indwelling sin still courses through our veins. Not only do we have evil desires to renounce altogether but also good desires to keep in check so they don't become sinful through inappropriate expression or overdesire.

Christian self-control is multifaceted. It involves both "control over one's behavior and the impulses and emotions beneath it."[2] It includes our minds and our emotions—not just our outward actions, but our inner person.

Heart, Mind, Body, Drink, and Sex

Biblically, self-control, or lack thereof, goes to the deepest part of us: the heart. It begins with control of our emotions and then includes our thoughts as well. Self-control is often paired with "sober-mindedness" (not just in 1 Tim. 3:2; Titus 1:8; but also in

---

2 Philip Towner, *The Letters to Timothy and Titus*, New International Commentary on the New Testament (Grand Rapids, MI: Eerdmans, 2006), 252.

Titus 2:2; 1 Pet. 4:7), and in several places the language of self-control applies especially to the mind. Mark 5:15 and Luke 8:35 characterize the healed demoniac as "clothed and *in his right mind.*" Paul uses similar language to speak of being in his right mind (2 Cor. 5:13), as well as not being out of his mind (Acts 26:25). Romans 12:3 exhorts every Christian "not to think of himself more highly than he ought to think," but to exercise a form of self-control: thinking "with sober judgment."

Self-control is bodily and external as well. The apostle disciplines his body to "keep it under control" (1 Cor. 9:25–27).[3] It can mean not being "slaves to much wine" (Titus 2:3–5), and in particular, the language of self-control often has sexual overtones. Paul instructs Christians to "abstain from sexual immorality; that each one of you know how to *control his own body* in holiness and honor, not in the passion of lust" (1 Thess. 4:3–5). In a charge to women in 1 Timothy 2:9, self-control relates to modesty, and 1 Corinthians 7 presumes some lack of self-control in married adults that might give Satan a foothold were they to unnecessarily deprive each other for an extended time (1 Cor. 7:5). God has

---

3   Mark Jones writes, "Of all the people in the church who should be most conscious about exercise and healthy eating, should it not be ministers of the gospel? God calls pastors to be examples in our conduct—that is, in our overall lifestyle (1 Tim. 4:12; 1 Peter 5:1–3)." To this we could add that countless recent studies have confirmed that exercise relieves anxiety and depression, and that your brain and body depend, in some measure, on vigorous movement to work like they are designed to. I do not doubt that the multiplying physical and psychological maladies in our day are owing in large part to not exercising enough and eating/drinking far too much sugar. For pastors in particular, Jones continues, "I'm persuaded that overeating, as the fruit of a generally indulgent lifestyle, has become a tragically acceptable sin among many Christians in North America. I'm also equally persuaded that a lot of pastors should jump on a bike, go for a run, walk, or build some modest muscle, and they'd likely get more work done. A lack of discipline in areas such as food, exercise, and drink typically reflects a lack of discipline in other areas of the Christian life." "Remember the Body: The Pastor and His Exercise," Desiring God, June 20, 2019, https://desiringgod.org.

given some the calling of singleness and with it, "having his desire under control" (1 Cor. 7:37); others "burn with passion" and find it better to marry (1 Cor. 7:9).

The question for the Christian, then, is this: If self-control is so significant—and if indeed it can be taught—how do I go about pursuing it as a Christian?

Find Your Source Outside Yourself

Professor Mischel preaches a gospel of distraction and distancing:

> The children who succeed turn their backs on the cookie, push it away, pretend it's something nonedible like a piece of wood, or invent a song. Instead of staring down the cookie, they transform it into something with less of a throbbing pull on them. . . . If you change how you think about it, its impact on what you feel and do changes.[4]

This may be a good place to start, but the Bible has far more to teach than raw renunciation. Turn your eyes and attention, but don't stop there. *Turn from*, yes, and *turn to*—not to a mere diversion, but to the source of true change and real power that is outside yourself, where you can lawfully indulge. The key to self-control is not inward but upward.

Gift and Duty

True self-control is a gift from above, produced in and through us by the Holy Spirit. Until we own that it is received from outside ourselves rather than whipped up from within, the effort we give

---

4 Druckerman, "Learning How to Exert Self-Control."

to control our own selves, if successful, will redound to our praise rather than God's.

But we also need to note that self-control is a gift we receive not passively but actively. We are not the source, but we are intimately involved. We receive the gift as we live it and strive to have self-control habituated in us. Receiving the grace of self-control means taking it all the way in and then out into the actual exercise of the grace. "As the Hebrews were promised the land, but had to take it by force, one town at a time," says Ed Welch, "so we are promised the gift of self-control, yet we also must take it by force."[5]

You may be able to trick yourself into some semblance of true self-control for a while. You may be able to drum up the willpower to *just say no* for a season. But you alone get the glory for that—which will not prove satisfying enough for the Christian.

We want Jesus to get glory. We want to live in such a way that others see our lives and give glory, not to us but to our Father in heaven (Matt. 5:16). We want to control ourselves, not in our own feeble power but in the strength he supplies (1 Pet. 4:11). We learn to say no, but we don't *just say no*. We admit the inadequacy and emptiness of doing it on our own. We pray for Christ's help, secure accountability, and craft specific strategies.[6] We trust God's promises to change our hearts, accustom us to different instinctive responses, and supply the energy for every good work (2 Cor. 9:8; Phil. 4:19), and then we act in faith that he will do it in and through us (Phil. 2:12–13). Then we thank

---

5   Edward Welch, "Self-Control: The Battle Against 'One More,'" *Journal of Biblical Counseling* 19 (Winter 2001): 30.

6   Welch counsels, "Develop a clear, publicized plan." I would clarify "publicized, in the old fashioned sense"—meaning tell a flesh-and-blood friend or family member or few, rather than post online. "Self-Control," 30.

him for every Spirit-supplied strain and success and step forward in self-control.

Christ-Control

Ultimately, our controlling ourselves is about being controlled by Christ. When "the love of Christ controls us" (2 Cor. 5:14), when we embrace the truth that he is our sovereign and God has "left nothing outside his control" (Heb. 2:8), we can bask in the freedom that we need not muster our own strength to exercise self-control, but we can find strength in the strength of another. In the person of Jesus, "the grace of God has appeared . . . training us"—not just "to renounce ungodliness and worldly passions" but "to live *self-controlled*, upright, and godly lives in the present age" (Titus 2:11–12). Christian self-control is not finally about bringing our bodily passions under our own control, but under the control of Christ by the power of his Spirit.

Because self-control is a gift, produced in and through us, Christians can and should be the people on the planet most hopeful about growing in self-control. We are, after all, brothers of the most self-controlled man in the history of the world.

All his life he was "without sin" (Heb. 4:15). "He committed no sin, neither was deceit found in his mouth" (1 Pet. 2:22). He stayed the course even when sweat came like drops of blood (Luke 22:44). He could have called twelve legions of angels (Matt. 26:53) to spare him the most horrific of deaths, yet he had the self-control to not rebut false charges (Matt. 27:14) or defend himself (Luke 23:9) but go in silence. When reviled, he did not revile in return (1 Pet. 2:23). They spit in his face and struck him; some slapped him (Matt. 26:67). They scourged him (Matt. 27:26). In every trial and temptation, "he learned obedience through what he suffered" (Heb. 5:8), and at the pinnacle of his self-control, he was "obedient to the point of death, even death on a cross" (Phil. 2:8). And he is the one who strengthens us (Phil. 4:13; 1 Tim. 1:12).

In Jesus, we have a source for true human self-control far beyond that of our feeble selves.

Self-Control in Plurality

To this point, our reflections on self-control have focused on the individual Christian and pastor-elder. But to conclude this chapter, let's expand the scope to the pastoral team—the plurality of elders—and reflect briefly on the collective self-control Christ calls his pastors to exhibit together toward the flock they're been entrusted to lead and feed.

There is a kind of power in the eldership. The elders themselves, hopefully due to their relative humility, typically feel that power least. But the congregation sees and senses it. The most respected and influential teachers in the church form a team (the council of elders) that pools these individuals' influence and authority into a whole. Indeed, the team is meant to pool its power to work on behalf—for the joy—of the congregation (as the pastors find their joy in the joy of the whole body), and to do so, the elders *as a team* need to exercise a kind of collective self-control: that in their decisions and actions together, they do not subtly gravitate toward what is easiest and most personally advantageous for the elders, but are willing and ready to put themselves through inconvenience, difficulty, and personal cost (typically in the form of time and energy) in the best interests of the congregation. The elders exist for the joy of the church, not vice versa.

This means that wise, humble, self-controlled elders will learn to take every reasonable opportunity to build trust with the people rather than presume on it. It means learning to bring the church along in major decisions and changes of course, leading with the Bible open, giving the people more time and space than seems necessary to ask questions (and answering foolish questions with patience) and challenge the elders' emerging direction in healthy, respectful ways. In other words, self-controlled elders do not presume upon the church's trust and leverage that trust to twist arms and get their way. Rather, they exercise patience as a team, seeking to not rush the congregation but introduce new ideas long before calling for a vote. They work *with their people* for their joy.

What Do Pastors Do with Power?

To conclude this chapter, let's ponder the nature of power and what it means for pastors and the church. When we talk about *power* today, we do so in a particular social climate. Even ordinary folks, unfamiliar with foreign names like Nietzsche and Foucault, have caught the drift and the negative connotations of power. This is why it might sound jarring in many ears to hear about pastoral *power*.

Power, however, rightly defined, is first a gift and blessing from God, not an evil to be avoided. Power, writes Andy Crouch, going back to creation, is "our ability to make something of the world" in fulfillment of the charge God gave our race to be fruitful and multiply and fill the earth and subdue it, and have dominion.[7] In that sense, to be human is to have power. With brains and hands, minds and muscles—and a voice—God

---

7 Andy Crouch, *Playing God: Redeeming the Gift of Power* (Downers Grove, IL: InterVarsity Press, 2013), 17.

enables us to fulfill his call and increases our power as we exercise it effectively, especially as we consolidate our human powers by working together.

So make no mistake: pastors have power—some more, some less—as it relates to their particular context in the local church. The question is not whether they have power but what kind, how much, and how they use it.

Power of Office

Both in the church and beyond, we might talk of two kinds of power. The first is *official power*, power that is tied to office.

In the New Testament, the office of *apostle* drew on the very power of Christ himself; the apostles were his official spokesmen. The apostles were a single, irreplaceable generation, the men who Christ himself discipled plus a few others like Barnabas and Paul, to whom Christ appeared on the Damascus road. In their words and writings, the apostles spoke for the risen Christ. Their living words and office died with them, but their writings endure as our living word of inspired Scripture for the church to receive, with the Old Testament, as the very word of Christ, our head. The first and greatest authority in the church, which should be unrivaled, is the authority of Christ through the writings of his apostles.

In addition to apostles, Scripture establishes the two *ongoing* offices in the life of the church, as we have seen: the lead office, called variously *pastor* (or *shepherd*, Eph. 4:11; 1 Pet. 2:25; 5:2), *elder* (Acts 20:17; James 5:14; 1 Pet. 5:1), and *overseer* (Acts 20:28; Phil. 1:1; 1 Tim. 3:1–2; Titus 1:7); along with the assisting office called *deacon* (Phil. 1:1; 1 Tim. 3:8–13). To be a pastor-elder or deacon today in the church—to hold church office—is to have, in some sense, power as a formal representative of a particular local church.

Depending on the church's polity, to be a member is to have some real, not-to-be-overlooked power as well. And whatever their polity, congregations always vote with their dollars and feet. Still, as we all intuit and expect, the officers in the church are entrusted with additional power, at least formally. As *officers*, they are *official*.

Power of Influence

Power in the church is not only *official*, drawing on the power of the institution and office, but also *unofficial* or *informal*—what we might call *influence*. And in healthy churches, teaching is especially influential. Pastors are teachers (Eph. 4:11), indeed leaders in the church are teachers (Heb. 13:7), and given the centrality of teaching in the Christian faith, it is fitting that it be so. We're setting ourselves up for trouble if the pastors and the teachers are two different groups and not essentially the same.

Jesus himself, even before his disciples recognized him in his office as Messiah, amassed great influence through his teaching. So too, throughout church history, those who have been most influential in the church, though typically officers, have been so not because they had an office but because they won trust and expanded their influence by proving themselves to be faithful and effective teachers of God's word.

After all, the gospel itself is "the power of God for salvation" (Rom. 1:16), coupled in fruitful preaching with the power of the Holy Spirit. Those who preach the gospel, and preach it well, with the Spirit's help, may gain a significant amount of "power" on Christian terms. To have that influence is not evil. The question is what pastors do with such power.

Power of Team

Still, one more dynamic to consider is the pooling (or consolidating) of power—what happens especially when men become friends and work together. This is particularly relevant to a *plurality* of pastor-elders, working as a team in a local church, which is the focus of Dave Harvey's book *The Plurality Principle*.[8] Harvey returns again and again to a central thesis: "The quality of your elder plurality determines the health of your church."

Pastor-elder teams who know and teach the Scriptures well and genuinely enjoy each other (and get along) unavoidably become a formidable center of power in a local church. Not only do they have their office and, in theory, are the church's most able teachers, but their influence is compounded by their unity and industry as a team. That consolidation can be scary for those who feel weak and insecure and carry suspicion of the team's motives.

The question though is not whether such pluralities have power, but what they will do with it. Will they use it to serve the good of the whole church or use it to serve themselves? Will they give of themselves to enrich the flock or take selfishly for their own private gain? Will they be a force for good or reinforce their own good?

Acknowledging Power

Good pastors, for good reason, do not gravitate toward talking much in public about their own power. Still, engaging the subject well, at least in private, can serve both them and their people. Harvey writes, "The wise leader acknowledges his power and leverages it wisely."[9] And here the New Testament prescription of a

8 Dave Harvey, *The Plurality Principle: How to Build and Maintain a Thriving Church Leadership Team* (Wheaton, IL: Crossway, 2021).
9 Harvey, *Plurality Principle*, 108.

plurality of pastors—a team working together—shines with one of its many bright rays of glory. Wise pastors recognize their power in the context of the team and remind each other about it. "Wise pluralities have *power dynamics* as a functional category for how their leadership affects the church."[10] In the team are more power (to use for good) and simultaneously more safety for the congregation, as individual pastors are held accountable by fellow, mature Christian brothers who are not yes-men but stand on their own two feet before God.

Doubtless you can find some conceited elders and councils, swollen with pride and selfish motives, who relish the power and influence they have in the church as their sad, little kingdom. They savor their power and guard it, and in the end they aren't as powerful as they think. But I suspect that in most healthy, faithful churches, the elders are relatively humble ("not . . . arrogant," Titus 1:7; also 1 Tim. 3:6) and often don't realize how powerful they are (as officers, teachers, and teammates) in the context of that particular local church.

Humble pastors and councils don't think often about their power, but at times they are frank with each other about it. And from time to time, it can be good for one brother to look around the circle and remind the team, "You know, guys, as the pastors and main teachers of this church, we may have a lot more power and influence than we're typically conscious of." That should not swell our pride. Rather, it should give us a holy fear and lead us regularly to our knees to ask that God make us humble and keep us faithful, that we steward the power we have on loan from him to make much of Christ and serve this church, not make much of ourselves and serve our own comforts and preferences.

---

10 Harvey, *Plurality Principle*, 110.

Leveraging Power

Leadership in the local church is not a package of conveniences but precisely the opposite. The elders, of all people, should be the most grounded and mature and most willing to forgo personal conveniences and private comforts for the sake of the good of the whole church. Good elders see leadership not as a *reward* for their past performance or present value but as a *responsibility*, taken up gladly, for the good of the flock. Good pastors know that God has given them power for serving the church, not self. For exalting Christ, not self.

Again and again, pastor-elders stand at this junction as they oversee the church: "What's easiest for us versus what's best for our people." In overseeing the church, many decisions come down to this key moment for any team of pastors: *Will we use our power—whether it's teaching or decision-making—to serve us or to serve this church?*

At such times, good pastors remember that, as John Piper writes:

> The path of suffering and sacrifice really does lead to glory. . . .
> This is [Christ's] peculiar glory—that he would condescend from such a height of deity, of power, to such a depth of naked, beaten, mocked, spit-upon, crucified humiliation—that he would do that without reviling is unspeakably glorious.[11]

Pastors like this leverage power not like the world, but like Christ—and like the apostle Paul, who says, "I will most gladly spend and

---

11 John Piper, *Living in the Light: Money, Sex, and Power* (Surrey, UK: Good Book Company, 2016), 98–99.

be spent for your souls" (2 Cor. 12:15). Such leaders "spread power around," says Harvey, and "push the power out" as they embrace the path of love, which is often the harder path.[12]

Giving without Giving In

Spreading power around and pushing it out is very different from giving in to grabs. Power, like money, can be acquired justly or unjustly. It can be earned or seized. It can be given or taken, whether outright or through emotional manipulation.

Mature pastors and congregants know this. Rather than clamor for power, healthy churches give their pastors volitional space to take proactive steps in spreading power around and pushing it out. Foolish pastors acquiesce to immature lobbying, and in doing so, they set destructive precedents and expectations. They feed an insatiable beast. The effects of rewarding those dynamics will prove devastating for the church (and for those individuals) in the long haul.

Wise pastors sniff out power grabs and are careful not to give in, but they don't leave it at that. They do more. They embrace the harder path. They take such efforts as indicators that they have work to do, far beyond holding lobbyists at bay. *We have work to do*—work that will require the powers of 2 Timothy 2:24: "The Lord's servant must not be quarrelsome but kind to everyone, able to teach, patiently enduring evil, correcting his opponents with gentleness."

"Not So among You"

Faithful, healthy pastors, and their churches, handle power differently than the world does. Not just in how we teach from the

---

12 Harvey, *Plurality Principle*, 110–11.

front but in what we say through our actions in everyday life, and especially in how we lead. We are growing into, not away from, the one who came with unrivaled power *not* to be served, but to serve:

> You know that those who are considered rulers of the Gentiles lord it over them, and their great ones exercise authority over them. But it shall not be so among you. But whoever would be great among you must be your servant, and whoever would be first among you must be slave of all. For even the Son of Man came not to be served but to serve, and to give his life as a ransom for many. (Mark 10:42–45)

We show our society that while Nietzsche and Foucault may be right about depraved aspects of humanity, our churches are led and filled with new men with new hearts who steward power with selfless grace and humility. The church, then, is a covenant community in which power, both in office and influence, can be received as the gift it is and leveraged for the joy of the church to the glory of Christ.

6

The World Needs More One-Woman Men

. . . the husband of one wife.

1 TIMOTHY 3:2; TITUS 1:6

THE "ONE-WOMAN MAN" may seem like an endangered species today in some circles. In our oversexualized and sexually confused society, it's increasingly rare to come across married men who are truly faithful to their bride—in body, heart, and mind. It may be even more rare to find unmarried men who are on the trajectory for that kind of fidelity to a future wife. Jaws will drop when a handsome, eligible bachelor discloses he's a virgin waiting for the wedding night.

Of the fifteen basic qualifications for the office of elder in the local church, *one-woman man* may be the one that runs most against the grain of our society. We're relentlessly pushed in precisely the opposite direction. Television, movies, advertising, social media, locker-room talk, and even casual conversations condition the twenty-first-century male to approach women as a consumer of many instead of as a protector of and provider for one. The cultural icons teach our men to selfishly compromise and take rather than to carefully cultivate and guard fidelity to one woman.

But what's rare in society is still easier to find, thank God, in biblically faithful churches. The true gospel is genuinely powerful and changes lives, even under such intense pressure from a world like ours. You can be pure. You can detox. You can retrain your plastic brain. You can walk a different path by the power of God's Spirit, even if that other path was once yours. In the company of others who enjoy pleasures far deeper than promiscuity, you can become the one-woman man our world needs.

For All Christians

Just because being a one-woman man is essential for church leaders does *not* mean it's irrelevant for every Christian. The elder qualifications, as we've seen, are remarkable for being un-remarkable. What's demanded of church officers is not academic decoration, world-class intellect, and talents above the common man. Rather, the elders are to be examples of normal, healthy, mature Christianity (1 Pet. 5:3). The elder qualifications are the flashpoints of the Christian maturity to which every believer should aspire and which every Christian, with God's help, can attain.

God does not mean for us to relegate one-woman manhood to formal leaders. This is the glorious, serious, joy-filled calling of every follower of Christ. It's a word for every Christian man (and every Christian woman to be a "one-man woman," see 1 Tim. 5:9). And it's relevant for married and unmarried alike.

For Husbands and Bachelors

Clearly, "one-woman man" applies to married men. In faithfulness to the marriage covenant, the married man is to be utterly committed in mind, heart, and body to his one wife. Being a one-woman man has implications for where we go, how we interact with other women, what we do with our eyes, where we let our thoughts run, what we access on our computers and smartphones, and how we watch movies and television.

It's also relevant for married men in the positive sense, not just the negative. A married Christian must not be a zero-woman man, living as though he isn't married, neglecting to care adequately for his wife and family. If you're married, faithfulness to the covenant requires your interests being divided (1 Cor. 7:35), but only with your one woman.

Do you have to be married to be a one-woman man? The challenge to be a one-woman man applies not only to married men but to the unmarried as well. Are you a flirt? Do you move flippantly from one dating relationship to another? Do you enjoy the thrill of connecting emotionally with new women without moving with intentionality toward clarity about marriage?

Long before they marry, bachelors are setting (and displaying) their trajectory of fidelity. In every season of life and every relationship, however serious, they are preparing themselves to be one-woman men, or not, by how they engage with and treat the women in their lives.

Isn't It "Husband of One Wife"?

At this point, you may be feeling the weight of this phrase "one-woman man" both for elder qualification and for Christian manhood in general. Don't our English translations read "husband of one wife" in 1 Timothy 3:2 and Titus 1:6? That seems like a clearer box to check. It's either true or it's not—none of these questions about whether your eyes and mind might be wandering unfaithfully. And nothing that might apply to the unmarried.

In a previous generation, this may have been the most debated of the elder qualifications. Some take it to require that church leaders be married; others say it bars divorcés who have remarried; others claim it was designed specifically to rule out polygamy. But one problem, among others, with each of those interpretations is that they make the qualification digital—plainly true or false—rather than analog, like every one of the other fourteen qualifications.

The traits for leadership in the local church are brilliantly designed to prompt the plurality of elders, and congregation, to make a collective decision about a man's readiness for church office. Sober-minded, self-controlled, respectable, hospitable—these are analog and unavoidably subjective categories (not easy either-ors) that require careful thought and evaluation. I believe Paul intended us to read "one-woman man" as requiring the same spirit of discernment, not as a black-and-white, no-exceptions rule. *Is this man today, so far as we know, through years of tested faithfulness, faithful to his one wife? Is he above reproach in the way he relates to women? Is he manifestly a one-woman man?*

Ask Yourself

Men, ask yourself these questions and be ruthlessly honest: Am I a one-woman man? What, if anything, in my life would call this into question? What habits, what relationships, what patterns do I need to bring into the light with trusted brothers and ask God afresh to make me truly, deeply, gloriously, *increasingly* a one-woman man?

If you're married, what is your reputation? Do people think of you—your speech, your conduct, your body language—as joyfully and ruthlessly faithful to your wife? Or might there be some question? Are you known for demonstrating self-control publicly and privately for the sake of the purity and fidelity of your marriage?

For the unmarried, what do your friendships and relationships look like with the opposite sex? Do you genuinely treat other women "as sisters, in all purity" (1 Tim. 5:2)? Are you dabbling with pornography, trying to stop, but still allowing room for it? Or have you become tragically desensitized to impurity because of the boundaries being crossed on television and in movies? In your thought life, on the Internet, in your interactions, are you a one-woman man waiting for your one woman?

In Christ, we need not be satisfied with anything less. Try as hard as you can, you will not be satisfied. But in Christ, we are called to be one-woman men in a world that expects and encourages far less. And in Christ, you have the resources you need to see that fidelity become reality. This is what God expects and makes possible in the church and requires in its leaders.

Pursuit of Purity

Before ending this chapter with a word about false teachers—and their frequent connection with sexual immorality—I thought it might be helpful to include a practical and hopeful word about the pursuit of sexual purity in our day. Expecting that many readers of this book will have come of age in the Internet Age, perhaps this word would be of some small help on your journey toward eldership or in your labors as an elder to help the many refugees of our age.[1]

It's Not Too Late

I could see the pain in his eyes. And fear.

His question was about his lack of assurance of salvation, and it was easy to tell this was not philosophical or merely theoretical. It was turmoil of soul over some besetting sin.

All it took was one clarifying question to uncover the source: guilt over his repeated return to Internet pornography. It was good he felt guilty, as I'd soon tell him. It was a sign of God's grace.

By now, such a scenario was no surprise in college ministry. Here on a Christian campus, the pastoral issue that had come up more than any other was assurance of salvation. And after some initial bewilderment and a few extended conversations, the typical culprit soon became clear: porn and masturbation.

Epidemic in This Generation

Assurance of salvation may be at an all-time low among Christians with the epidemic of porn use through ubiquitous Internet access. Sometimes it takes the form of existential angst and epistemological confusion, but often lack of assurance is the product of some deeply rooted sin. *Could I really be saved if I keep returning to the same sin I have vowed so many times to leave behind?*

In 2015 Desiring God (desiringGod.org) surveyed eight thousand of its users. The study found that ongoing pornography use was not only dreadfully common but increasingly higher among

---

1 For more on the subject, its dangers and deliverance, see Joe Rigney, *More than a Battle: How to Experience Victory, Freedom, and Healing from Lust* (Nashville, TN: B&H, 2021). I am not aware of a better book on the topic.

younger adults. More than 15 percent of Christian men over age sixty admitted to ongoing use. It was more than 20 percent for men in their fifties, 25 percent for men in their forties, and 30 percent for men in their thirties. But nearly 50 percent of self-professing Christian men ages eighteen to twenty-nine acknowledged ongoing use of porn. (The survey found a similar trend among women, but in lesser proportions: 10 percent of females, ages eighteen to twenty-nine; 5 percent in their thirties; increasingly less for forties, fifties, and sixty-plus.)

Hear His Voice Today

While the issue of online access to porn may be new in the last generation—and progressively devastating to those who were exposed to it at young ages—the invitation to repentance from besetting sin is gloriously ancient. And perhaps no biblical text is more relevant to today's struggles than Hebrews 3 and 4.

Two millennia old itself, the book of Hebrews points even further back into the past, to God's invitation to repentance in Psalm 95:7–8: "Today, if you hear his voice, do not harden your hearts" (Heb. 3:7–8, 13, 15; 4:7). While this offer of rest stretches across the centuries, the actual application to individual believers is restricted to those who have not yet fully hardened their hearts in unbelief and moved beyond repentance.

Hebrews is written to a group of persecuted Jewish Christians, tempted to abandon their worship of Jesus as Messiah (the reason for their persecution) and return to the Judaism to which they once adhered apart from Jesus. Not only is such a move theologically disastrous (in terms of how one understands God and his revelation), but it is also personally, and eternally, devastating. These early Christians were experiencing a similar hardness of heart to that which accompanies repeated sin and unfought unbelief in professing Christians today.

Into such a context, Hebrews reaches for Psalm 95 and the exhortation it holds out: "Today, if you hear his voice, do not harden your hearts." It's a word our generation desperately needs to hear.

If You Still Hear Him

The emphasis on "today" is essential. Tomorrow is not a given. What you do have is *right now*—right now as you read these words.

If you hear God's voice *today*—calling you to Christ and his holiness—and if you reject that voice, your heart will be some degree harder for it. Do not take for granted that you will have next week, next month, a year from now, or even tomorrow to find repentance.

Every time we ignore the convicting voice of grace, we inch a degree closer to judgment. Every conscious embrace of unrighteousness darkens the soul and works callouses on the heart. At some point, no warmth or softness remains. Then, like Esau, who "found no chance to repent" (Heb. 12:17), it will be too late.

But today—*today*—if you still hear his gracious voice in the promptings of his Spirit, if you still feel the guilt, if you still sense the shame, if you still know some distaste for the impurity of sin— make today your point of turning. "See that you do not refuse him who is speaking" (Heb. 12:25).

It is good that you feel bad about your ongoing sin. That's the touch of grace. You still have the chance to turn from sin's coldness to the warmth of a forgiving Christ. If your heart was already hard beyond repair, you wouldn't be bothered by sin. Your conviction is his kindness.

As Long as It's Still Today

Make today count for some new initiative in the fight. Renounce the sin while you can still muster the heart to do so. Involve a Christian friend in your struggle, with whom you can live out the priceless grace of Hebrews 3:12–13:

> Take care, brothers, lest there be in any of you an evil, unbelieving heart, leading you to fall away from the living God. But exhort one another every day, as long as it is called "today," that none of you may be hardened by the deceitfulness of sin.

Choose righteousness today. Every concrete embrace of holiness matters. Every choice against evil, every act of righteousness in heart and mind and body. Every renouncing of sin prepares you, at least in some small measures, for choosing righteousness the next time. "We are always becoming who we will be,"[2] and today really does matter. Right now counts.

Where We Have Our Hope

Most importantly, fix your eyes afresh today on your advocate and great high priest, who is able "to sympathize with our weaknesses" and "who in every respect has been tempted as we are, yet without sin" (Heb. 4:15). He is ready to dispense mercy and send grace "to help in time of need" (Heb. 4:16). We say no to sin by saying yes to joy in him.

There, at God's right hand, sits our final hope. Not in our accountability, or our resolves, or our willpower. Not in our record

---

2 Joe Rigney, *Live Like a Narnian: Christian Discipleship in Lewis's Chronicles* (Minneapolis: Eyes & Pen, 2013), 52.

in the past, nor our ability in the present, nor our potential in the future. Our great hope lies not in ourselves but outside of us, in Christ, who has overcome and in whom we too will overcome.

———

The Surprising Truth about False Teachers

Here in a book on eldership, we need at some point to address the topic of false teaching. After all, one of the central charges to pastor-elders, as we've seen, is Titus 1:9: "He must hold firm to the trustworthy word as taught, so that he may be able to give instruction in sound doctrine *and also to rebuke those who contradict it.*" So also as pastors "preach the word," we are to "reprove, rebuke, and exhort, with complete patience and teaching" (2 Tim. 4:2). We have the Scriptures, "breathed out by God and profitable," not just for teaching and training in righteousness but also "for reproof, for correction" (2 Tim. 3:16). But identifying false teachers can be far easier in theory than in practice, especially when we are awash in half-truths and deceptive words.

The question is not whether you ever hear the voice of false teachers. You do—probably every day. The question is whether you can discern which messages are false.

If you watch any television, listen to any radio or podcasts, keep up on the news, scroll social media, or interact regularly with just about anyone in modern society, you are being exposed to some form of false teaching. If you cannot identify any voices you hear as false, or misleading, it's not because you aren't being exposed but because you're falling for it in some way.

For most of church history, it took extraordinary energy and effort to influence the masses. Messages had to be copied by hand

and distributed, and teachers had to travel by foot or horseback. There were no cars or airplanes, and no printing presses, websites, or Facebook pages. But today just about every false teacher has a Twitter account.

How, then, does the church discern true teachers from false ones in a world like ours, where it's easier than ever to spread false teaching?

False Teachers Will Arise

We begin by acknowledging not just the possibility of false teaching but the certainty of it. We should not be surprised to find false teaching in the church today—even among the members of our own churches in some shade or form. Jesus and his apostles are clear that false teachers will arise. They promise it. As Jesus says:

> False christs and *false prophets will arise* and perform signs and wonders, to lead astray, if possible, the elect. But be on guard; I have told you all things beforehand. (Mark 13:22–23; see also Matt. 24:24)

Likewise, Paul warns the Ephesian elders (Acts 20:29–31) and his protégé Timothy (2 Tim. 4:3–4) that false teaching is sure to come (also 1 Tim. 4:1 and 2 Tim. 3:1–6). If we had any doubts at this point, Peter adds his voice too: "There *will be* false teachers among you" (2 Pet. 2:1).

So we should not be caught off guard by the fact that false teachers have arisen throughout church history and have multiplied in our day.

Watch Their Doctrine—and Lives

What we might find surprising—both from Jesus and his apostles— is how revealing the everyday lives of false teachers can be about their falseness. They are not just *false* in their teaching but also in their living.

Beneath their doctrinal error, however subtle and deceptive, we will find ethical compromises in tow. Not all of them come out quickly; some take time, even years. But they will become manifest. Here's how Jesus prepares us in Matthew 7:15–20:

> Beware of false prophets, who come to you in sheep's clothing but inwardly are ravenous wolves. You will recognize them by their fruits. Are grapes gathered from thornbushes, or figs from thistles? So, every healthy tree bears good fruit, but the diseased tree bears bad fruit. A healthy tree cannot bear bad fruit, nor can a diseased tree bear good fruit. Every tree that does not bear good fruit is cut down and thrown into the fire. Thus you will recognize them by their fruits. (See also Luke 6:43–44)

Jesus says it twice: *You will recognize them by their fruits.* His warning may sound clear and simple at first, but as we all know, trees don't bear fruit overnight. Eventually, however, the fruit (or lack thereof) will be indisputable. And so it is with ethical compromise. What may begin as mere whispers in a private room will soon enough be proclaimed from housetops (Luke 12:3). And so Paul instructs leaders not only to pay careful attention to their people and to their teaching, but also to their own lives (Acts 20:28; 1 Tim. 4:16).

No doubt false teachers may be difficult to recognize *in the moment*. If we don't have access to their personal lives, or their doctrinal compromises haven't yet become evident publicly in their behavior, we may find it difficult to know whether they are true. But time will tell. They will be known by their fruit—not the fruit of ministry quantity and numbers, but quality and endurance—and ultimately the quality of their own lives.

Allure of Money, Sex, and Power

In particular, 2 Peter 2 is remarkable in how it fleshes out Jesus's warning about the fruit of false teaching. Peter has little to say about compromised teaching, but he gives a litany of descriptions about compromised lives.

Verses 1 and 3 mention the generalities "destructive heresies" and "false words"—which indeed relate to teaching—but then nothing further in this chapter focuses on their teaching. Everything else is about their lives. We can boil it down to three essential categories— and all three are about character and conduct, not teaching:

- Pride, or defying authority: they deny "the Master who bought them" (v. 1); also verses 12–13 and 18.
- Sensuality, which typically means sexual sin: "many will follow their sensuality" (v. 2); also verses 10, 12–14, and 19.
- Greed, for money and material gain: "in their greed they will exploit you" (v. 3); also verses 14–15.

Again and again, Peter's descriptions relate to greed, sensuality, and pride—or *money, sex, and power*. What false teachers throughout history have shared in common is not the specific nature of their doctrinal error but the near inevitability of moral compromise in one of these three overlapping spheres.

Another way to see it is that their falseness comes out in sin against themselves, against others, and against God. In their greed, they fleece the flock for material gain. In their lust, they compromise sexually (whether fornication, adultery, or homosexuality, which 2 Peter 2 may suggest). Or in their pride, they "despise authority" (2 Pet. 2:10), and the greatest authority, who upholds all authorities, is God himself.

You Can't Study All the Counterfeits

If false teaching, then, relates not only to what teachers say and write but also to how they live, how are faithful pastors and churches to recognize and expose false teaching today? We may be able to reasonably access someone's teaching online or at a large conference, but how can we know their lives are true?

The greatest defense against false teaching is a local church community that knows, enjoys, and lives the word of God together—and holds its leaders accountable. Little, if anything, can be done to hold teachers accountable who are far away, but much is realistic and actionable in the life of the local church. Practically, then, we might be wise to proceed with extra caution toward far-away teachers who are more "at large" and not manifestly embedded in the life and leadership of a particular local church.

Our leaders need to be held accountable, and not held in such high esteem that we give them a pass on the normal Christian life. As we've seen, pastors are to be *among* the people and examples for the people. Good shepherds smell like sheep because they live and walk among the sheep and are not sequestered from the flock. We need pastors who know themselves first and foremost as sheep and only secondarily as leaders and teachers—pastors who are manifestly more excited to have their names written in heaven than they are to be used as vessels in celebrated ministry (Luke 10:20).

Jesus Will Rescue His Church

We can have our systems of accountability (and we should), and we can do our best to watch both the lives and the doctrine of our leaders (and we should),[3] but in the end there is no foolproof human system or effort. This is why 2 Peter 2:9, the apex of this chapter on false teaching, serves as such a sweet assurance—"the Lord knows how to rescue the godly from trials."

No matter how twisted the teaching, no matter how publicly shamed the church may feel over the exposé of an unethical leader, no matter how dark the days become, no matter how helpless we may feel in guarding gospel doctrine and preserving gospel-worthy lives, we have this great sustaining hope: *Jesus knows how to rescue the godly.*

Jesus is not only the greatest and truest teacher who ever lived, but he also is the great rescuer who has redeemed us from sin and will keep those who are truly his from soul-destroying error. No matter how small a minority the church may become in a place, and no matter how fragile we feel, the very one who is both the subject of true teaching and the model of true living is also our life- and soul-preserver.

As God preserved Noah (2 Pet. 2:5) and rescued Lot (2 Pet. 2:7), so the Lord Jesus will rescue his true people from the false teaching—and false living—of false teachers.

---

3 We briefly discussed disciplining elders, based on 1 Tim. 5:19–24, at the end of chap. 1.

7

Does Drinking Disqualify a Pastor?

. . . not a drunkard.

TIMOTHY 3:3; TITUS 2:7

A FEW SUMMERS AGO, surprising news rippled through some evangelical circles. The preacher of one of the largest and fastest-growing multisites in the country had been removed as a pastor from the church he planted. After a long, seemingly patient process, the other leaders in his church had deemed him unfit for ongoing ministry, citing, among other factors, 1 Timothy 3:3 ("not a drunkard") and his entrenched overuse of alcohol.

Many were taken off guard, not just because they didn't see it coming with this well-known preacher but because they never had heard of a pastor being disqualified for drinking. Sexual immorality and financial mismanagement—those tragic stories have been all too common. But the overuse of alcohol?

Teetotal Generation

Of the fifteen qualifications for pastor-elder in 1 Timothy 3:1–7, "not a drunkard" may be the one a previous generation of

43

evangelicals passed over most quickly. Not because that genera-tion was deaf to the dangers of alcohol, but because, for so many, partaking *at all* was almost unthinkable. The legacy of Prohibition in the United States (1920–1933) endured long after repeal of the Eighteenth Amendment, especially among evangelicals. In large swaths, drinking was frowned upon for all Christians and particularly pastors.

My, how the times have changed.

Of course, teetotaling wasn't assumed in every stripe of evangeli-cal association or in every region, but the vestiges of the nineteenth-century temperance movement continued to hold sway in many sectors. For my grandmother, for instance, who was both Baptist and Southern, it was almost imponderable that the same lips could touch a drink and make a credible profession of faith. I grew up in South Carolina in the 1980s and 1990s believing the same. I remember folks at our Southern Baptist church being appalled by news from around town that the new minister at First Pres would have a glass of wine with congregants.

Even as temperance and Prohibition curtailed some evils, such a sharp reaction to the perils and excesses of alcohol (especially hard liquor) doubtless created its own problems in subsequent genera-tions, but these are not typically the troubles we face today— at least not in the circles I expect most readers of this book run. The pendulum has swung. Whereas evangelicals of a bygone era may have overreached in response to the dangers of alcohol, we may find ourselves today in fresh need of church leaders who will not fall victim to the same set of new temptations our flocks are facing.

The new call is for pastors and elders stable and mature enough in the faith to not only know well their freedoms in Christ but even more: to stand ready, in love, to forgo their rights at times for the good of others.

Wine to Gladden the Heart

Paul's list of qualifications for the office of pastor-elder begins with seven desirable traits and then gives four negatives, or disqualifiers, before finishing with three final requirements. "Not a drunkard" (Greek *mē paroinon*, only here and in Titus 1:7) is the first of the four disqualifiers. Deacons, also, according to 1 Timothy 3:8, must be "not addicted to much wine." These are not requirements for teetotalism. "Not a drunkard" hardly means no alcohol whatsoever.

Psalm 104:14–15 celebrates God's good gifts in his created world, including bread and oil and "wine to gladden the heart of man." Proverbs 3:10 mentions "vats . . . bursting with wine" as a blessing, not a curse—as a promise to those who honor God. John the Baptist chose the lifestyle of the ascetic, while Jesus came eating and drinking, and both were wise and righteous (Matt. 11:18–19; Luke 7:33–35). For his first miracle, of course, Jesus made wine from water (rather than the reverse!), and Paul instructed Timothy, in what we have as holy writ, to "use a little wine for the sake of your stomach and your frequent ailments" (1 Tim. 5:23).[1]

Those who stand against the ancient attempts to teetotalize the church stand on the side of the angels, against the teaching of demons (1 Tim. 4:1–5).

Warnings We Cannot Ignore

The above affirmations, however, are by no means all that God has to say to us about wine and intoxicating drink. As John Piper

---

1 For 1 Tim. 5:23 in context, see n7 in chap. 1.

summarizes, "Even though wine was permitted and was a blessing, it was fraught with dangers."[2] In both the Old and New Testaments, the warnings far exceed the commendations (by some counts, more than three to one). That doesn't mean we ignore the clear commendations. But it does mean that we will do well, especially in our current climate, to take the warnings with all seriousness.

In every place across the canon, *drunkenness* is roundly condemned. Drunkenness often serves as a metaphor for unbelief and condemnation. Jesus and Paul connect staying awake to God to staying awake (sobriety) in this world (Luke 12:45–46; 21:34–36; 1 Thess. 5:7–8). Excess drink can be associated not just with violent anger ("not a drunkard, not violent," 1 Tim. 3:3; also Matt. 24:49; Luke 12:45) but with rebellion (Deut. 21:20), sexual immorality, and division (Rom. 13:13–14).

Proverbs links excess drink to folly (Prov. 20:1; 23:29–35; 26:9–10) and poverty (Prov. 21:17; 23:20). Here the goodness of drink in God's created world is not denied, but the itch or lust for "encore" (as C. S. Lewis called it) is exposed and challenged.[3] God's prophets pronounce woe on those who "rise early in the morning, that they may run after strong drink, who tarry late into the evening as wine inflames them! . . . Woe to those who are heroes at drinking wine, and valiant men in mixing strong drink" (Isa. 5:11, 22).

Models of Judgment

Accordingly, drunkenness becomes a recurring image of divine judgment in the prophets—in Isaiah (19:14; 24:20; 28:7–8), Jer-

---

2 John Piper, "Is Drinking Alcohol a Sin?" Desiring God, October 23, 2013, https://www.desiringgod.org/.

3 In a message titled "Christian Hedonics," Joe Rigney spoke on Lewis's use of the term *encore*. "Christian Hedonics: C. S. Lewis on the Heavenly Good of Earthly Joys," Bethlehem College & Seminary, October 8, 2016, https://www.desiringgod.org/.

emiah (13:13; 25:17; 51:7), Ezekiel (23:33), Hosea (4:11, 18), Amos (2:8; 4:1; 6:6), and Nahum (3:11). When we turn to the New Testament, drunkenness finds no place in the church but belongs to the course of this fallen world and the pattern of rebellion against God (1 Cor. 15:34; Eph. 5:18; 1 Pet. 4:3). Without exception, references to intoxication are negative (Acts 2:15; 1 Cor. 11:21; Titus 2:3)—a manifestation of the unbelief from which Christians are being saved, or otherwise will not inherit the kingdom (1 Cor. 5:11; 6:10; Gal. 5:19–21).

The dangers are real for all of God's people and yet, in some sense, even more so for leaders. Proverbs 31:4–5 warns that "it is not for kings to drink wine, or for rulers to take strong drink, lest they drink and forget what has been decreed and pervert the rights of all the afflicted." The more responsibility a leader has for the lives and care of others, the more sheep entrusted to his lot, the more tragic when the shepherd checks out and the watchman abdicates his post (Isa. 56:10–12). "Happy are you, O land, when . . . your princes feast at the proper time, for strength, and not for drunkenness!" (Eccles. 10:17).

Forgo My Freedom?

God's call on his people, and particularly on the leaders who serve as examples for the flock (1 Pet. 5:3), is not simply to acknowledge the goodness of God's creation alongside his litany of gracious warnings. God calls us to love. To look not only to our own interests but also the interests of others (Phil. 2:4). "In humility count others more significant than yourselves" (Phil. 2:3). Not just to keep our own noses clean but to learn to look past our own noses to the needs of others.

It is good to know that "nothing is unclean in itself" (Rom. 14:14), that "everything is indeed clean" (Rom. 14:20). Yes and amen. And little is distinctively Christian about such knowledge on its own. It may even be said that such "knowledge puffs up, but love builds up" (1 Cor. 8:1).

Negatively, Paul repeatedly cautions Christians not to put a "stumbling block" before others (Rom. 14:13, 15, 20–21; 1 Cor. 8:9, 13; 9:12). Or, positively said, walk in love (Rom. 14:15). Pursue what makes for peace and mutual upbuilding (Rom. 14:19). Additionally, "do not let what you regard as good be spoken of as evil" (Rom. 14:16) because of your careless, loveless words and actions in the presence of less mature brothers and sisters.

To be clear, in Paul's framing, the "weaker brothers" aren't prohibitionists who seek to press their personal convictions on the conduct of others. Rather, the genuinely weaker brothers are those who "through former association" would have their weak consciences defiled (1 Cor. 8:7). Meat sacrificed to idols in the first century is not the same as alcohol in the twenty-first. Today such a concern for the well-being of others may mean that some Christians simply choose to not partake. For others, it will mean doing so with both gratitude and appropriate caution, with awareness of context and company. And being conscientious to not contribute to a cavalier and indulgent culture, whether in the world or within the church, that will yield abuse in only a matter of time.

Even at a Feast

How might pastors today seek to practice these principles? To begin with, as husbands, fathers, and Christians, we never want to be unable to help others—whether the occasion is a feast or not. Becoming a pastor then adds to the number of lives for which we want to remain vigilant. Emergencies don't announce themselves ahead of time. And it would be wise to realize and remember that our drinks are typically larger and stronger than they were in previous generations.[4]

As fuzzy as the line between a glad heart and overuse can be, one aspect of modern life gives us a way of objectifying sobriety: operating a motor vehicle. As men ready to care for our wives and children and others, including congregants, in time of unexpected need or emergency, we never want to be unable to drive safely to a hospital. And no matter how great the feast, we never want to be unable to think clearly enough to answer serious questions about life and faith and ethics, or provide spiritual counsel to someone in need, or make the most of a teachable moment. God calls us to remain sober and available, ready to set aside our own interests to serve the needs of others in an unexpected instant. "Not a drunkard" means more than just "Knows how to toe the line and stay within the legal limits." It implies a positive vision. It calls for men who are reliable, ever vigilant, "ready in season and out" (2 Tim. 4:2)—men never checked out and incapacitated by their own lack of self-control when you call on them for help.

Qualified leaders in the church are men who have grown into the personal maturity of seeking to fill the emptiness we often feel with the fullness of Christ and his Spirit (Eph. 5:18). We lead the way in turning restless hearts Godward rather than medicating with alcohol or other substances. This is a critical test for Christ's undershepherds: where will we turn to fill an empty soul? How can we call our people to feast on Christ when we are defaulting elsewhere? Pastors are to be examples in Christian self-control (1 Tim. 3:2; Titus 1:8), to lead the way in the Pauline sentiment "I will not be enslaved to anything" (see 1 Cor. 6:12), that we might instead

---

4   Joe Carter, "Why Christians Need a Better Debate about Alcohol," The Gospel Coalition, October 27, 2018, https://www.thegospelcoalition.org/.

be gladly enslaved to our Lord and eagerly ready to act, when he calls, in love for others.

At the same time, pastors also have the opportunity to model glad-hearted moderation. Young Christians who grew up in tee-totaling contexts may only know two options: total abstinence or abuse. In certain settings, pastors can set an example, as in other areas, of wise, loving, glad-hearted celebration in the holy use of God's good gift of alcohol.

Christ Did Not Please Himself

Good leaders in the church are ready to rise to more than simply avoiding intoxication. Paul doesn't single out pastors as those called, at times, to forgo Christian freedoms for the sake of others. He would have all Christians grow into such love. Yet as with other hoped-for maturities in the faith, the church looks to the leaders to exemplify and model them (so that *all* grow into such maturity): "Let no one seek his own good, but the good of his neighbor . . . not seeking my own advantage, but that of many, that they may be saved" (1 Cor. 10:24, 33).

Relative to Christian freedoms, church leaders aren't necessarily held to a higher standard but are more rigorously held to the standard of the whole church. Leaders should be among those who best know the truth that neither partaking nor abstaining commends us to God (1 Cor. 8:8) and that we taste uniquely satisfying joys not just in the times we partake in appropriate ways *but also* in the times we abstain for the sake of love.

At bottom, what inspires such love and concern for others, in shepherds and in the flock, is our Savior himself. Paul says, "We who are strong [pastors especially?] have an obligation to bear with the failings of the weak, and not to please ourselves. Let each of us please his neighbor for his good, to build him up" (Rom. 15:1–2). Then he gives the all-important reason: "For Christ did not please himself" (Rom. 15:3).

Jesus did not simply know and exercise his divine rights. Rather, knowing his rights full well, he chose, at the proper time, to forgo them (Phil. 2:6–7) to love and rescue us. *Christ did not please himself.* That is, he found greater pleasure in the interests of others than in his own private interests. Jesus loves us like this. What a privilege and joy to receive and echo such love, as we anticipate the day we will enjoy with him, without any peril, the fruit of the vine in his Father's kingdom (Matt. 26:29).

8

Does Your Pastor Love God or Money?

. . . not a lover of money. . . . Not . . . greedy for gain.

1 TIMOTHY 3:3; TITUS 1:7

HOW CHRISTIANS HANDLE money speaks volumes about our Christ. It's one of our greatest opportunities to show ourselves distinct from the world, or just like it.

Jesus talked about money more than any other temptation. More than sex. More than power. More than heaven and hell. Some of his best-known words, in his most-remembered sermon, strike right at the heart of the polar reality deep beneath all the practical shades of gray: "You cannot serve God and money" (Matt. 6:24).

We might quickly object, *Money isn't evil in itself*—which is true. It's just paper and coins (and now digits on a screen). Money represents value, value in God's created world and humanity's God-commissioned efforts to "subdue it" into goods and services for our flourishing (Gen. 1:28). Money facilitates the movement and exchange of such God-ordained value with others. Isn't it "*love* of money" that the apostles warn us of (1 Tim. 6:10; Heb. 13:5), not money itself?

Money Talks

It is "*love* of money," but that important nuance might not create as much wiggle room for sinners as we first think. When Jesus explains the parable of the sower, he identifies the thorns choking out his gospel as "the cares of the world and the deceitfulness of riches and the desires for other things" (Mark 4:19). "Love of money" wouldn't be an unfair summary. When the apostle Paul warned of the climactic evil to come "in the last days," he said, "people will be lovers of self, *lovers of money*, proud, arrogant, abusive" (2 Tim. 3:1–2)—anticipated by the religious leaders of Jesus's day, the Pharisees, who were also "lovers of money" (Luke 16:14).

Jesus also told the parable of the rich fool, who instead of trusting in God for his future, built bigger barns to trust in his surplus, his own resources. The fool says to himself, "Soul, you have ample goods laid up for many years; relax, eat, drink, be merry." Yet in an ironic twist on the saying "Eat, drink, and be merry, *for tomorrow we die*," he doesn't even see tomorrow. God says, "Fool! This night your soul is required of you" (Luke 12:19–20).

Jesus's point for his people is plain: be "rich toward God," which means handling money in such a way that we show God, not money, to be our greatest treasure. Or to put it negatively, do not "lay up for yourselves treasures on earth" (Matt. 6:19–20; Luke 12:21) but "be on your guard against all covetousness" (Luke 12:15)—for which Jesus gives this penetrating rationale: "for one's life does not consist in the abundance of his possessions" (Luke 12:15). Do you believe that? *Your life does not consist in the abun-*

dance of your possessions. But who among us, living in the glories of God's material world, does not need a regular reminder?

Money Reveals

We Christians, of all people, have come to believe that *our life* does not consist in what we have on earth but whom we have in heaven. We look upward, with eternity in view, to "take hold of that which is truly life" (1 Tim. 6:19), not the temporal and earthly. And yet the money-loving world in which we live constantly dulls us to what is truly life.

Money is a powerful revealer of the human soul. What we do (and don't do) with money can put the depths of our inner person on display—in ways we often do not see (and show) otherwise. Money can provide a wonderful and terrifying glimpse into our deepest recesses.

The human heart is deep and complex. Who knows the heart of man besides his Maker? Well, one startling peek into a man's subjective heart is his treatment of objective dollars and cents. This is why our handling of money is such a wonderful opportunity for Christians to show the world the value of Christ—and for pastors and elders to lead the way for their people.

Not Greedy of Filthy Lucre

"Not a lover of money" is not only a qualifying virtue but an ongoing requisite for Christian leaders. The way the leadership goes, the church soon will follow. As we have seen, God appoints a plurality of pastor-elders in the church (Acts 20:28; Titus 1:5; James 5:14; 1 Pet. 5:1) not only to teach and govern together (1 Tim. 5:17), but also to serve as a collective example to the flock of the healthy Christian life (1 Tim. 4:12; 1 Pet. 5:3). What leaders do with money—both in their personal finances and together with the church's—sets the pace for the whole congregation, together and personally.

Of the fifteen qualifications for the church's lead office, "not a lover of money" (1 Tim. 3:3; memorably in the KJV, "not greedy of filthy lucre") may be the most conspicuous when compared with other lists. The synonymous attribute "not greedy for gain" appears both in Titus 1:7 and 1 Peter 5:2, as well as for deacons in 1 Timothy 3:8 (while Titus 1:11 rebukes false teachers who are "teaching for shameful gain"). The single word translated "not a lover of money" in 1 Timothy 3:3 (Greek *afilarguron*) appears again in Hebrews 13:5, for the whole church: "Keep your life free from love of money."

Why is it essential to have pastors who aren't seduced by money? Not simply so that pastoral teaching and governance aren't sold to the highest bidder (or sold at all!), but chiefly because of how pointedly our handling of money shows what we believe about God. Hebrews 13:5 makes the connection crystal clear. Why "keep your life free from love of money"? "For he has said, 'I will never leave you nor forsake you.'" Why do you need more money when you have God? Why pine for more earthly resources when you have a Father in heaven who owns everything?

The pastor who drips love of money, subtle as it may be, tells his church and the world that having God is not enough. Added to that, those who love money, Jesus says, do not truly love God. Rather, we need leaders who show the church and the world that God, not money, is our refuge and hope and safety and comfort and peace.

Root of All Evils

At the heart of Christianity is the claim that *God himself is our true life* (Luke 12:15). It is tragic beyond words for a professing

Christian to pursue life in more and more earthly possessions—and an even greater tragedy for leaders in the church. Modern society constantly inundates us with messaging that implies true life consists in more stuff (or just the right amount of uncluttered luxuries) and greater spending power. And if the pastors of the church aren't cutting unambiguously against the grain, in their teaching and in their lives, who will rescue the flock from this deadly trap? If the pastors aren't themselves aware and vigilant about the danger, who will awake the congregation? Pastors who are not enamored with riches are able to preach the way Jesus and the apostles did about earthly possessions and lead their congregations through one of the greatest snares in the Christian life.

Besides the all-important message it sends, the love of money is not a small danger in the human soul, only to be magnified in our leaders. Paul says, literally, it is "the root of all evils"—meaning, according to John Piper, that love of money

> corresponds to the root longing for the things money can buy minus God. That is why all these *many desires* "plunge people into ruin and destruction" (1 Timothy 6:9). . . . All evils come from that root desire—the desire for anything minus God. No exceptions. . . . All sin, "all evils," come from this desire, this love—represented in 1 Timothy 6:10 by love for the currency of satisfaction minus God.[1]

In other words, the kind of heart that loves money (desiring more and more human resources) in place of God is the kind of heart that produces *all manner of evil*, and is the very essence of evil in

1 John Piper, "Is the Love of Money Really the Root of All Evils?" Desiring God, February 7, 2017, https://www.desiringgod.org/.

us: preferring other things to God. Love of money, then, is not an isolated flaw or foible. It provides a penetrating peek into the recesses of a soul's rebellion against God. In due course, the truth will come out. And the repercussions will be all the more disastrous when the love of money becomes manifest among leaders.

Cheerful Givers

Thankfully we have more to look for, and pray for—in ourselves and in our leaders—than simply "not a lover of money." Hebrews and 1 Timothy both are explicit about the positive virtues as well: "be content with what you have" (Heb. 13:5; also 1 Tim. 6:8) and "be generous and ready to share" (1 Tim. 6:18). Why line our lives of vapor with gold when copper will do? When God does the miracle of unseating love for money in a human heart, he plants in its place an increasing eagerness to give, and to do so with joy. "Each one must give as he has decided in his heart, not reluctantly or under compulsion, for God loves a cheerful giver" (2 Cor. 9:7).

Christ intends for his church to be led by men who are not only free from the tyranny of money, but who know and regularly recall his words, "It is more blessed to give than to receive" (Acts 20:35). Christ wants leaders who are not reluctant givers, but cheerful ones—and not just individually but together as a team of leaders in order that our churches too become cheerful givers as a body. Pastors model how Christians handle money not only in what they say in sermons and write in church newsletters, but perhaps especially at congregational meetings, as they explain the annual budget and cast vision for congregational giving and how we as a church view our finances. Pastors, don't miss these precious teachable moments when it's time for the budget proposal or update. For some of our people, this is the most direct, intentional instruction they receive about how Christians think about finances.

God's Money, Wise Managers

As Christians and as churches, our call is not to pinch every penny and show reticence to spend God's money, but to spend it well. Jesus wants his people to be spiritually savvy with their cheerful generosity, righteous managers of his resources, using them with eternity in view, serving God, not sin (Luke 16:9). Pastors who love money cannot fulfill their calling to be righteous managers of God's money. "No servant can serve two masters, for either he will hate the one and love the other, or he will be devoted to the one and despise the other. You cannot serve God and money" (Luke 16:13).

Could the stakes be any higher for our pastors and elders not to love and serve money? As gray as it can seem in practice, Jesus assures us that at bottom it is black or white. One or the other. God or money. Test your heart, not just once but regularly. In Christ, we want to be free from the love of money, and we want leaders who love and serve God. This means we look for leaders content with what they have and cheerfully generous with others. We cannot afford leaders who love and serve money.

Worthy of Double Honor: On Pastors' Pay

Let the elders who rule well be considered worthy of double honor, especially those who labor in preaching and teaching. For the Scripture says, "You shall not muzzle an ox when it treads out the grain," and, "The laborer deserves his wages." (1 Tim. 5:17–18)

Elders who lead well, writes Paul, are to be "considered worthy of double honor." What is double honor?

"Double honor" means both (1) the honor of deserved respect as leaders and (2) the honor of deserved remuneration, or payment (*honoraria*). Good pastors are *worthy* not only of the church's respect but also of financial support in some form. Being "considered worthy" means the elders may receive pay from the church, or may not. Paul doesn't require that all pastors be paid or that all be volunteers, but he establishes a principle that is applicable to churches and pastors everywhere. He establishes the justice of pastors being compensated for their work of teaching and leading in service of the church but does not force all pastors to make use of that right. At Cities Church, as at many others, we have both vocational and nonvocational pastor-elders—both paid and unpaid pastors.

To establish this principle of justice, Paul gives explanation in 5:18. Note the word "For" (or "Because") at the beginning of verse 18. Then he provides two quotations. The first is from the Old Testament, Deuteronomy 25:4: "You shall not muzzle an ox when it is treading out the grain." It would be cruel to put a muzzle on an ox so that he is unable to eat any of the grain as he works to separate it from the chaff. And God does not want his people to be cruel. He wants them to be generous, not exacting. And if this for an ox, how much more for fellow humans, including pastors?

The second quotation is from Jesus, in Luke 10:7: "The laborer deserves his wages." Not only did the Old Testament establish the principle implicitly, but Jesus himself applies it to Christian ministry. It's a brief but powerful case for the fundamental justice of pastors receiving some kind of financial remuneration for the investments of their work—and also it's a remarkable testimony to how early and how authoritative were the Gospels. Paul wrote this letter in the mid-60s, and already at this point, the sayings of Jesus in the Gospels were available and functioning alongside the Old Testament as Christian Scripture.

First Timothy 5:18 argues ("For") that it is justice, not kindness or mercy, for a church to doubly honor its pastors with respect and remuneration. Some will receive that right and bless the church through their willingness to give their vocational life to the church's needs. And others, like Paul himself, will forgo that right and bless the church by supporting themselves through labors other than pastoral ministry.[2]

As we saw in chapter 3, the word *labor* is key in verse 17, and the "especially" clause does not introduce us to two different categories of elders based on teaching and ruling: "Let the elders who rule well be considered worthy of double honor, *especially those who labor in preaching and teaching.*" Rather, all elders, according to 1 Timothy 3:2, must be skillful in teaching. As we've seen, in

---

2 My sense is that pastoral teams function best in the long haul when composed of some mix of both vocational and nonvocational elders. In the good times, the more vocational pastors, the better. They are a great gift to the church in giving their full-time work life and best energies to the church and its mission. In the difficult times, perhaps especially when there is tension within the church, or even within the staff, the more nonvocational pastors, the better. Because these men do not draw their livelihood from the church, they can be a stabilizing influence in lean seasons and, depending on the structure, less beholden to the lead pastor. Depending on how the paid staff is structured, elder teams that are heavy on vocational against nonvocational, or vice versa, will present drawbacks over time. Some church bylaws require particular ratios. From my observations over the last twenty years, I see wisdom in elder teams aiming to have as many (or more) nonvocational elders as vocational, whether this is a simple majority, or even a 2:1 ratio.

the New Testament, teachers are leaders, and leaders are teachers. Ephesians 4:11 even puts "pastors and teachers" together as one category (literally, "the pastors-and-teachers," *tous poimenas kai didaskalous*). The distinction introduced in 1 Timothy 5:17 is more along the lines of vocational versus nonvocational.[3]

---

3 For more on pastors' pay, see Collin Hansen, "Piper on Pastors' Pay," The Gospel Coalition, November 6, 2013, https://www.thegospelcoalition.org/, as well as appendix 3, "What's the Best Way for a Pastor to Negotiate His Salary?," in Dave Harvey, *The Plurality Principle: How to Build and Maintain a Thriving Church Leadership Team* (Wheaton, IL: Crossway, 2021), 161–66. In particular, Harvey counsels vocational pastors to "look at the whole package," not just salary figures; warns men moving from the private sector to a church staff that they likely have "a substantial salary reduction coming [their] way—possibly 40–60 percent," and reminds them, "the final reward for your role is not delivered in your monthly paycheck." Harvey also cautions pluralities to not allow "the instincts of thrifty elders to determine the culture of salary setting." Indeed, the opposite of not loving money is not miserliness but generosity.

9

The Tragedy of Distracted Dads

He must manage his own household well, with
all dignity keeping his children submissive, for if
someone does not know how to manage his own
household, how will he care for God's church?

I TIMOTHY 3:4–5

THE GRATUITOUSLY DISTRACTED and often unexamined lives of modern unmarried men might be concerning enough. Then the seriousness of the problem rises higher when we say, "I do." And even more when we bring children into the world.

One of the greatest needs wives and children have—and all the more in our relentlessly distracting age—is dad's countercultural attentiveness. Perhaps human attention never has been more valuable. Today the largest corporations in the world no longer compete for oil but for human attention. And when attention is short and scarce, one of the greatest emerging tragedies of this new era is *distracted dads*. And in the church, their digital-age analog: distracted pastors.

Qualification for Christian Men

"He must manage his own household well" (1 Tim. 3:4). The risen Christ, through his apostle, requires as much of any officer in the church, whether pastor-elder or deacon (1 Tim. 3:4–5, 12). As is plain from the rest of the leadership qualifications, however, these traits aren't meant to set leaders apart from the congregation but to make them "examples to the flock" (1 Pet. 5:3) of every Christian's calling. Christ means for these attributes to be true of us all, and so it is essential that they be modeled, at minimum, in the leadership. By extension, Christ means for every dad to manage his household well.

This qualification to "manage his own household well" forges a special relationship, among the other requirements, between church leadership and domestic husbanding and fathering. Why must a pastor be one who manages his household well? "For if someone does not know how to manage his own household," Paul reasons, "how will he care for God's church?" (1 Tim. 3:5). Such caring *attentiveness* is at the heart of pastoring—keeping watch (1 Tim. 4:16; Heb. 13:17) and paying careful attention (Acts 20:28)—and at the heart of fathering.

Learning to be a Christian man goes in both directions: pastors first learn to lead at home, and fathers learn from the pastors to "shepherd the flock" (1 Pet. 5:2) of their own household. On-duty lifeguards must not be hypnotized by a smartphone. Nor shepherds watching over their flocks. And if such is the case for *sheep*, how much more should a father keep watch and fight distraction for the sake of his wife and children?

His Own Household

Twice in 1 Timothy 3:4–5 Paul says "his *own* household," not just "household." In doing so, he implies a distinction between the man's household and the church, which is God's household (1 Tim. 3:15; see also Eph. 2:19; 1 Pet. 4:17). Pastors are *household managers* in God's household, and being called to such, they first manage their *own* households ably as a prerequisite.

Our families, then, are our first pastorates. If our families are being led poorly—exposing deep faults in our leadership, whether inattentiveness or simple inability—it doesn't make sense to make us leaders in the church and multiply the effects of those same faults in God's family. Glaring gaps in domestic leadership need not extend to the church (though they are checked in plurality). But mainly, if our family already needs more of us, better not to take even more of dad's attention away from the home.

Even on the other side of ordination, as Thabiti Anyabwile comments, "Paul warns against men who could be too preoccupied with the affairs of the church and too little occupied with what's going on under their own roof."[1] One's *own* household, then, is a testing ground, and an ongoing test, for leading in the church.

How Does He Manage?

What, then, does it mean for a man to *manage* his household well? Elsewhere in the New Testament *manage* (*proistēmi*) can be translated "lead" (Rom. 12:8) or "rule over" (1 Thess. 5:12; 1 Tim. 5:17). Such *leading*, for one, requires attentiveness and rules out negligence. God calls fathers and pastors alike to be, at minimum, *responsive* to the needs of those in their charge.

But *leading* also implies more than mere responsiveness. Leadership requires initiative and proactivity. Good initiative progresses over time, rather than regresses, on the spectrum from mere

1 Thabiti Anyabwile, *Finding Faithful Elders and Deacons* (Wheaton, IL: Crossway, 2012), 96.

responsiveness toward proactivity. Leadership entails "being out ahead" mentally and emotionally: thinking ahead, planning ahead, taking initiative to draw others into shared life together.

Christian leadership, then, is formed and shaped by the example of Christ, who did not "lord it over" his people but gave his own life for their eternal good (Mark 10:42–45). So also we fathers and pastors must not be domineering with our God-given authority but gentle (more on that in chapter 13). We use it for building up, not tearing down (2 Cor. 13:10). Not for selfish, private ends but self-sacrificially, for the good of the whole household.

Good fathers, and good pastors, habitually choose to inconvenience themselves for the sake of their flocks rather than presuming on what feels most personally convenient. They bear the cost themselves for the gain of the household, rather than angle for personal gain whatever it costs the family.

Take Care of Your Home

We do have another verb in 1 Timothy 3:5 that helps explain what Paul has in mind by "manage" in this context: "care" (*epimedeomai*). "If someone does not know how to manage his own household, how will he *care* for God's church?" God calls fathers and pastors to *care for* their flocks, which confirms the Christ-shaped vision of Mark 10:42–45.

The only other place in the New Testament where this verb for *care* appears is (twice) in the parable of the good Samaritan:

He went to him and bound up his wounds, pouring on oil and wine. Then he set him on his own animal and brought him to an inn and *took care* of him. And the next day he took out two denarii and gave them to the innkeeper, saying, "*Take care* of him, and whatever more you spend, I will repay you when I come back." (Luke 10:34–35)

This kind of *taking care* of others—with energy and gentleness, strength and compassion, diligence and love—is at the heart of what it means for dads and pastors to *manage their households*. Not just as the good Samaritan did, but as the one to whom the parable points (Jesus) did in his life and leadership. We are his innkeepers, instructed to be his eyes and hands in caring for his church until he returns.

What Does "Well" Mean?

What, then, does it mean for a man to manage his household "well"? Oh, the apostolic brilliance of that qualifier. To some, it may sound like a low bar. *Just "well"?* To them, *well* may seem like welcomed leniency. To others, however, this is a glimpse of grace and a reason for hope.

While the qualifier *well* does provide a gracious subjective element, the objective facet must not be lost on us: overall fruitfulness, not failure, in leading at home. *Well* does not mean perfection, but it does mean something. *Well* does not mean "poorly." The man's leading should be fruitful and improving. Of course, overall healthy and productive households have their moments, even days on end, of chaos and floundering and failure rather than perceived fruitfulness. Those who lead *well*, though, recognize the strain, renew their attentiveness, make a plan, turn a corner, and respond by giving more of themselves to relieve burdens and patiently restore peace.

However low of a bar *well* may sound to some ears, the wise and godly man (as with the other elder attributes) will not take a minimalist approach to his own household but regularly evaluate what can be better. Leading at home or in the church is not something any man gets on top of for good. Busy households, without upkeep, tend quickly toward disorder. Active households, like living sheep, incline toward chaos and need the regular attention and investment of the shepherd, not semiregular checkups.

And with the addition of children—and growth of children into more activities and levels of awareness and responsibility—the kind of energy and attention that was adequate in previous seasons no longer proves sufficient. Over time, especially in young adulthood, the demands of fathering increase, not decrease. Managing a household well is not static but ever changing, and changing in such a way that it demands more, not less, from dad.

Managing Different Relationships

Typical households include wife and children (and sometimes others) as well as material possessions. Taking care of the inanimate stuff is the easiest aspect of managing. Caring well for *people* is the most challenging. However, managing the material is not to be neglected. Certain men gravitate toward or away from dealing adequately with the stuff or from caring well for the people. We each have personal penchants to identify and necessary adjustments to make.

But leading a household is first and foremost about taking care of people.

For (and with) His Wife

The first and most important person in a man's household is his wife—and he feels a unique tension (and privilege) in caring well for her. On the one hand, she is a member of the household and deserving of his greatest attention and care and emotional provision and investment. On the other hand, she is his comanager. Accord-

168

ing to Paul, a Christian man is not the lone master of his domain. Married women also "manage their households" (1 Tim. 5:14).

Dad has an associate, "a helper fit for him" (Gen. 2:18), for whom he thinks and cares in fundamentally different ways than he does for the children. A good manager treats his comanager differently from the other workers under his leadership. God did not design Christian households to be mini-monarchies where the husband rules as king with his wife as a childlike subject. Rather, she is the queen, and together they manage the household, even as he carries a unique burden of leadership and owes his comanager a special kind of care.[2]

For the husband, being head in his home doesn't center on his enjoying the greatest privileges, but on gladly shouldering the greatest burdens. Being head means going *ahead* and apologizing first when both are at fault. It means taking the small, humble initiatives in conflict and turmoil that his wife does not want to take. It means treating his comanager with unrelenting kindness, even when she's less than kind. It means exercising true strength by inconveniencing himself to secure her good, rather than serving himself by presuming on her. And, of course, it includes vigilance in being a one-woman man (chapter 6) utterly committed in mind, heart, and body to his one wife.

For His Children

After his wife, and with her, a Christian man *takes care* of his children. In 1 Timothy 3:4 the phrase "with all dignity" modifies "keeping his children submissive." There are dignified and undignified ways to raise submissive children.

---

2 For more on this important aspect of the complementary callings of men and women, see John Piper, "Do Men Owe Women a Special Kind of Care?" Desiring God, November 6, 2017, https://www.desiringgod.org/.

Domineering and heavy-handedness are undignified and ruled out by the nature of Christian *management* and *caretaking*. Even if abusive fathering remains hidden from the public eye for years, it will catch up with a man as his children become adults and realize what he was doing. God means for a father to teach and train his children *with dignity*—in a respectable way, appropriately engendering respect from his children, and his wife, in how he treats them, even at their worst moments. Their sinful conduct is not justification for his. Paul captures the heart of it in one stunning sentence: "Fathers, do not provoke your children to anger, but bring them up in the discipline and instruction of the Lord" (Eph. 6:4).

Not only are children different from a wife, but also children have their various stages of growth. In partnership with their mother, dignified fathering takes that into account and adapts accordingly.

Does an Unbelieving Child Disqualify an Elder?

A father's management and care for his children raises a perennial question: How submissive must a pastor's children be to not disqualify him from office? Or, more to the point, must a pastor's children be *professing believers*, in good standing with the church, for the pastor to be qualified for office?

Clearly, 1 Timothy 3:4–5 makes no such requirement, but some (understandably) stumble over the language of Titus 1:6: "His children are *believers*." That way of translating the Greek (*pista*) sounds like a pastor-elder's children must be (at least) professing Christians. However, we should note the same word is often translated "faithful" elsewhere, depending on context.[3] And when we step back to take in the full context in Titus, the meaning becomes clear enough. Not only

---

3 To give a sense of the balance, in forty-five of the sixty-seven instances in the New Testament, the ESV translates *pista* as "faithful." Granted, other New Testament uses do not determine

does the companion list of qualifications in 1 Timothy 3 highlight *submission* in a pastor's children (rather than, say, regeneration), but what immediately follows in Titus 1:6 also clarifies: "His children are believers and *not open to the charge of debauchery or insubordination.*"

Paul also adds further explanation in the next verse: "For an overseer, as God's steward, must be *above reproach*" (Titus 1:7). So, the issue at hand is not the eternal state of the child's soul, but the nature of the elder's fathering. Is he above reproach as a father? Does the child's behavior betray faults in the father's leadership? Quite apart from whether the child is unbelieving or not (something a father cannot control), is the child faithful *to his father* in a way that good fathering can, in fact, secure?[4]

Childrearing done well requires attending to countless and seemingly ceaseless needs. Often a father has his wife at his side, and together, as they share the burdens, the work becomes lighter and feels freshly doable, even enjoyable. But where does a man turn when his wife already carries as much as God means for her to bear? She is his comanager, but he is the head. And God designed men to bear the final burden and carry the greatest weights, even and especially when they are too great for his wife to shoulder with him.

Who Cares for Dad?

God means for dads to frequently come to the end of themselves and learn what it means to lean on him and, in faith, keep moving. In the moments when fathers most soberingly feel the weight of being the buck-stopper at home or as pastors in the church, God

---

this one, but it is helpful to know that translating *pista* as "faithful" is not unusual but even typical.

4 For more on this question, Justin Taylor gives five reasons for this view in response to the question, "You Asked: Does an Unbelieving Child Disqualify an Elder?," The Gospel Coalition, November 2, 2011, https://www.thegospelcoalition.org/.

wants them to know that they themselves have a Father and that he does not call them to pretend to be the hero in their own strength, but to ask for his help, lean on him, and roll their burdens onto his shoulders. Both pastor-elders and husband-fathers need the solace and blessing of 1 Peter 5:6–7:

> Humble yourselves, therefore, under the mighty hand of God so that at the proper time he may exalt you, casting all your anxieties on him, *because he cares for you.*

Before and beneath God's call that fathers *care for* their households and for God's church is his care for them. Before he says to fathers and pastors, "You go, and do likewise" (Luke 10:37), he first is the good Samaritan to them. He comes to them in those moments when they're feeling half dead on the side of the road. He binds their wounds, pours out his own precious oil and wine, picks them up off the ground, brings them to the inn, and *takes care of them* (Luke 10:34) at great cost to himself and with a promise to return (Luke 10:35).

Rightly was it said about Jesus, "He has done all things well" (Mark 7:37). Surely such is the case with his household and bride, the church. He has and does manage his household well, and that is a dad's great comfort not just *if* but *when* he feels inadequate, even in his best efforts, to manage his own household well.

───

Inconvenient Headship

My grandfather died in August 2017 at the age of ninety-three. For almost a century, he gave himself in service to the needs of others. He was one of the most manifestly unselfish people I have ever known.

He gave himself for his country, serving in World World II. He was wounded in combat and received two Bronze Stars for heroic valor. When he came home from the war, he taught ROTC, studied poultry husbandry at Clemson, and then completed forty years in the South Carolina poultry industry. He served as a deacon in his church, and often invested even more as chairman. And when he retired from work in the late 1980s, he did not retire from serving others. In fact, his serving became all the more demanding and selfless.

In his golden years, he gave himself for his children and grand-children. He and Grandmommy didn't move to Boca Raton but leveraged their retirement years to serve family and church in new and fresh ways. They tirelessly sacrificed for the good of others. As the oldest child, I had a front-row seat for how Granddaddy in particular made life workable for our family of six in those unusu-ally demanding little years (with four kids age nine and under).

Then, not long after I graduated from college and moved across the country, Grandmommy developed severe dementia and was no longer able to function as normal. It all happened so fast. Without much warning, everything fell to him. A lifetime of private instincts and habits came quickly into full view. Would he care for her when it cost him most? When it meant surrendering the idyllic retirement he'd anticipated for decades? Would he trade golf for going to a litany of doctors, old friendships for pressing needs, and vacations for daily vigilance?

Soon they were together in assisted living, and eventually she needed professional care and attention, but all along, Granddaddy was there with remarkable faithfulness, concern, and service. For ten years he cared for her daily until she died in late 2014.

He was a true husband who *gave himself* for the good of his wife.

He Gave Himself

Six times the apostle Paul says that Jesus "gave himself" for his people. He "gave himself for our sins to deliver us from the present evil age" (Gal. 1:4). He "gave himself as a ransom" (1 Tim. 2:6). He "gave himself for us to redeem us" (Titus 2:14). "Christ loved us and gave himself up for us" (Eph. 5:2). And for Paul (and us), Jesus's self-giving love is not only corporate but personal: he "loved *me* and gave himself *for me*" (Gal. 2:20). In Jesus's giving of his own self for us, God demonstrates his love (Rom. 5:8). Ephesians 5:25 makes the connection to earthly husbands:

> Husbands, love your wives, as Christ loved the church and *gave himself up for her.*

In modern times, the word "submit" in Ephesians 5:22–23 turns heads, but that's not the heart of the matter for Paul. Rather, what he lingers over and gives more space and attention to explaining (in more than three times as many words) is his radical charge to husbands to *give yourself up for her*—as Jesus did for his church.

But in the ups and downs and endless shades and ambiguities of everyday domestic life, what does it mean for a Christian husband to *give himself up for her*, and for pastors to give themselves up for their churches?

Giving In vs. Giving Yourself

It's an important question for Christian husbands (and pastors) to ask themselves because weak and selfish *giving in* to a wife's fleeting preferences may appear on the surface to be strong and selfless *giving himself*. And there is all the difference in the world between a husband giving in and giving himself for her.

God doesn't *call* husbands to *be* the head. He simply says the husband *is* the head (Eph. 5:23). The question is not whether the man will be head, but what kind of head will he be? An absent one? A lazy one? An evil, abusive one? A bullied one? Or will he be a true husband, the kind Jesus is to his church? The husband's calling is to be a head *like Christ*—which is the sort of headship provided by one who is also Savior. "The husband is the head of the wife even as Christ is the head of the church, his body, *and is himself its Savior*" (Eph. 5:23).

Jesus made it plain what headship means *in Christian terms*: not lording it over but serving:

> You know that those who are considered rulers of the Gentiles lord it over them, and their great ones exercise authority over them. But it shall not be so among you. But whoever would be great among you must be your servant, and whoever would be first among you must be slave of all. For even the Son of Man came not to be served but to serve, and to give his life as a ransom for many. (Mark 10:42–45)

But every husband needs help with that kind of serving. Is any old semblance of service adequate? How do we know when we're serving as one who *selflessly gives himself* rather than as one who *selfishly gives in*? Consider four questions we husbands (and pastors) can ask of our patterns and individual acts of service to discern whether we're simply giving in or giving of ourselves like Christ.

Four Questions for Christian Husbands

1. Loving Self or Her?

First, am I loving myself or loving her? Or maybe a better way to put it: Am I being (sinfully) selfish, or serving my wife with (holy) self-interest?

Three times Ephesians 5:28–33 says husbands are to love their wives *as they love themselves*—an understated application of Jesus's affirmation of Leviticus 19:18: "Love your neighbor as yourself" (Mark 12:31). If such with every neighbor, how much more with my wife?

In the course of our marriages, we make hundreds of small, intuitive decisions on a daily basis that affect our wives. We don't stop to ponder and reflect on all these. But when we do, perhaps even multiple times a day, we come to moments of decision, emotional forks in the road. What is the loving choice and action here? Before taking action, I find it helpful to ask myself, Am I loving me or her? Is this selfish or self-interested?

Selfishness seeks my own private good at her expense. Self-interest finds my joy in hers. *Giving in* is a lazy, selfish kind of sacrifice. *Giving of myself* is typically demanding and depleting, but it is gloriously rewarding to find my good in hers.

2. Dutifully or Joyfully?

Second, am I serving my wife dutifully or joyfully?

Begrudging service, perhaps surprisingly, is often a form of giving in. Something is not right when we grit our teeth and just get it done. We may indeed be doing what we sense is required externally in that moment, but if we're not doing it *gladly*, we may be just giving in instead of truly giving of ourselves.

True masculinity is "the *glad* assumption of sacrificial responsibility."[5] Jesus gives himself up for his bride, not dutifully but "for the joy that was set before him" (Heb. 12:2). God calls heads to serve "with joy and not with groaning" (Heb. 13:17), "not under compulsion, but willingly, as God would have you" (1 Pet. 5:2). He expects no less of husbands. And his Spirit stands ready to help those who ask.

3. Her Sin or Her Sanctity?

Third, am I catering to sin or pursuing holiness? First, it's a question for me. In undertaking a particular "sacrifice," am I giving in to my own sinful proclivities, or am I pursuing real holiness (which is typically the harder avenue, not the easier)? Then, turning to consider my wife, will this sacrifice cater to her sin or contribute to her holiness?

Ephesians 5:25–27 addresses the motivation that drives true husbandly sacrifice: her sanctity. "Christ loved the church and gave himself up for her, *that he might sanctify her*, having cleansed her by the washing of water with the word, so that he might present the church to himself in splendor, without spot or wrinkle or any such thing, *that she might be holy and without blemish*." Our sacrifices and service will not prove neutral. They will contribute in the end to sin or sanctity, which leads to a final question—and the one I often find most helpful.

4. Convenient or Costly?

Lastly, is my supposed sacrifice for my wife convenient for me or costly? Is it the easy action to take or the tough one? Is it a form of

---

5   Douglas Wilson, "'Father Hunger' in Leading the Home," Desiring God 2012 Conference for Pastors, January 30, 2012, https://www.desiringgod.org/.

laziness in disguise, or does it require physical or emotional energy? Will this be personally convenient or have some real, personal cost?

Jesus's giving himself for his church was not convenient. It was not accomplished by his choosing the path of least resistance. And not just at the cross, but throughout his life. So also today as he works by his Spirit in the church. And in marriage, this is a vital way in which our union points to his gospel. Not just by our being Christians, but by the husband in particular caring for his wife in such a surprising way that the world sees the surprising care of Christ for his church. The world expects husbands to act when it's convenient, or they've been bullied into it. What catches eyes and reveals genuine love is costly initiative.

When to Make Momma Happy

It may indeed be true that when momma ain't happy, ain't nobody happy. But true husbandly sacrifice doesn't just seek to make momma happy *now*, but for endless ages to come.

Such a husband knows that simply *giving in* is not just easy, convenient, and weak but will destroy both her joy and his in the long run. And such a husband knows that gladly *giving himself for her*, as I so memorably saw my grandfather model, is not only costly and the heart of real sacrificial service, but what builds her joy, and his, forever. Good pastors have learned this at home and bring to the church their collective willingness to *give themselves* for her.

PART 3

HONORABLE

Men before a Watching World

*An overseer must be above reproach. . . . He must
be well thought of by outsiders, so that he may not
fall into disgrace, into a snare of the devil.*

1 TIMOTHY 3:2, 7

This third and final part begins and ends, like the elder qualifications in 1 Timothy 3:1–7, with "above reproach" and its complement "well thought of by outsiders." In part 3 the public nature of office will be particularly in view. In fact, the tenor of the whole list from beginning to end is strikingly public. Such is the nature of *office*—of being an official leader in the church. Even as we've noted that the qualifications are largely unremarkable but, in essence, the virtues of everyday healthy Christianity, there is an irreducibly public nature to *office* that is not the same expectation and assumption of every member in the church.

After "above reproach," which I take as the overall umbrella or summary term for the requirements, we'll look at what may be the least understood of the list: "respectable." Then comes the often forgotten "hospitable" (and its evangelistic impulses), followed by two disqualifications, one with its opposite explicit, the other implied: "not violent but gentle" and "not quarrelsome" (but peaceable).

Throughout this study we have taken our bearings from 1 Timothy 3 primarily, then Titus 1 secondarily. The list in Titus includes three virtues that do not appear in Timothy's list: a lover of good, upright, and holy.[1]

Holy and Righteous and Good

Interestingly, these three—holy, righteous, and good—appear together in Romans 7:12, as Paul writes about God's law-covenant arrangement with the people of Israel prior to the coming of Christ: "The law is holy, and the commandment is holy and righteous and good." That is to say that these adjectives are not insignificant or marginal in the Bible. Perhaps Paul thought them so basic that they went without saying in 1 Timothy 3 as he wrote to the more established church in Ephesus, but maybe the more touch-and-go nature of the newly planted church in Crete meant he not only left out "not a new convert" in Titus but also felt the need to express such obvious biblical values. One way we might think together of

---

1   In fact, all three appear in Titus 1:8. The Titus list includes essentially two words for *self-controlled* (*sōphrona* and *egkratē*). The first appears in the 1 Tim. 3 list; the second does not. Since the second (which the ESV translates as "disciplined") has a very similar semantic range as the first, I have chosen not to treat it as a fourth distinct term in the Titus list.

these three is "lover of good" as *toward* the world, "upright" as *in* the world, and "holy" as *apart from* the world.

Lover of good (*philagathon*). Philippians 4:8 well summarizes the kind of man the elder is to be *in relation to his world*: "Whatever is true, whatever is honorable, whatever is just, whatever is pure, whatever is lovely, whatever is commendable, if there is any excellence, if there is anything worthy of praise, think about these things." Far from being a call to remove ourselves from the world and just think happy, Christian thoughts, Paul's charge here is to a form of cultural engagement, as commentators Moisés Silva and Gordon Fee have argued.[2] Paul's call is to look for the good, the true, the honorable, and the excellent in the surrounding society, by God's common grace, and consider these things. So elders too should be men like this, who see the world with realistic yet hopeful eyes and can spot and point out the good.[3]

Upright (*dikaion*). "Upright" or "righteous" is one of the more common load-bearing words in the New Testament, and especially for Paul. The adjective (*dikaios*) appears seventy-nine times, and the verb (*dikaioō*), "to justify" or "declare righteous," appears thirty-nine times, mainly in Romans 3–5 and Galatians 2–3 (though also in Luke–Acts, as well as notably in James 2:21–25 and Matthew 11–12).[4] Unlike Paul's special project in Romans and Galatians, where

---

2 Moisés Silva, *Philippians*, Baker Exegetical Commentary on the New Testament (Grand Rapids, MI: Baker, 2005), 196–98. Gordon Fee, *Paul's Letter to the Philippians*, New International Commentary on the New Testament (Grand Rapids, MI: Eerdmans, 1995), 413–21.

3 I've written on this reading of Phil. 4:8 as the foreword to *Make Mature Multiply: Becoming Fully-Formed Disciples of Jesus*, ed. Brandon Smith (Austin, TX: GCD Books, 2014), 12–17.

4 For my modest effort to address in a single article the *dikai-* word group and the doctrine of justification by faith alone (and that the real surprise is not James's teaching but Paul's), see "The Most Scandalous Verdict: How James Prepares Us for Justification by Faith," Desiring God, July 26, 2018, https://www.desiringgod.org/.

he uses *righteous* in a surprising way—by faith in Christ, we are declared righteous, though we ourselves are not righteous but ungodly—here *righteous* or *upright* means real, lived-out righteousness (as in Matt. 11–12 and James 2). Elders are not just justified by faith; they have learned to live righteously in the world. They are seen as upright.

Holy (*hosion*). *Holy* is not mere separateness or otherness. The seraphim in Isaiah cry, "Holy, holy, holy" and mean far more than "Other, other, other" or "Separate, separate, separate." When they cry, "Holy," they ascribe to God infinite value and worth. God is not just *other*. He is both other *and better*. He's not just set apart but an infinite cut above, incomparable in his value and worth. For the pastor-elders (and all Christians who follow their example), being holy not only means distinctness, otherness, and separation from the world. It is an otherness that is better. There is a value or worth or attractiveness to the otherness. This winsome and attractive holiness will be unmistakable in the best of elders.

10

The First Requirement for Christian Leaders

An overseer must be above reproach.

1 TIMOTHY 3:2; TITUS 1:7

IF YOU TRIED to capture in a summary term a single qualification for the office of pastor-elder in the church, what would it be?

Some of us may have the reflex to say immediately with great confidence, "He must be a Christian." Indeed, he must—but that should be required of all church members so far as we can discern. The apostle Paul, at least, was willing to assume new birth when it came to listing qualifications for overseers and deacons.

What about "a gifted teacher"? Surely that's vital for leaders of the church, as people of the Book, as we lingered over in chapter 3. It is essential in the pastor-elders (though not in its deacons), but it's not what Paul lists first and as overarching. Others might point to ability in oversight and administration. Some may say, "He must aspire to the work," which is needful, as we saw in chapter 1, but in Paul's way of reckoning, that's a prerequisite, not the summary qualification. Others may venture, "a model Christian," which would be the flip side of the coin of the answer we're looking for, though not the precise way Paul says it here.

What a Pastor Must Be

When we first open to both lists of elder qualifications in 1 Timothy 3:1–7 and Titus 1:6–9, we might be surprised to find a summary trait that seems like such a low bar, in a sense: "above reproach."

> An overseer must be *above reproach*. (1 Tim. 3:2)

> . . . if anyone is *above reproach*. . . . For an overseer, as God's steward, must be *above reproach*. (Titus 1:6–7)

In both lists, "above reproach" comes first. Then another dozen-plus follow. In coming first, "above reproach," says Thabiti Anyabwile, is "an umbrella term for all the other requirements that follow."[1] Philip Towner agrees: "This is the essential requirement for the candidate."[2] As does Bill Mounce: "What it entails is spelled out in the following eleven attributes and three specific concerns."[3] So while "above reproach" may seem pretty minimal at first pass—and in some ways it is—upon further reflection we may see why Paul begins here, as the trait is fleshed out in the specific aspects that follow.

1   Thabiti Anyabwile, *Finding Faithful Elders and Deacons* (Wheaton, IL: Crossway, 2012), 57.
2   Philip Towner, *The Letters to Timothy and Titus*, New International Commentary on the New Testament (Grand Rapids, MI: Eerdmans, 2006), 250.
3   Towner, *Letters to Timothy and Titus*, 169.

Oh, to Be above Reproach!

As low-bar as "above reproach" may sound to some ears, with just a little reflection we can discover some of the wisdom in it. For one, consider the unavoidably public nature of formal office in the church. In appointing particular individuals to be pastor-elders or deacons, the church marks them, both internally to the church and externally to the world, as models and representatives, in some reasonable measure, of what the church is and stands for. "Above reproach" at the head of the list shows that "right from the outset, the public nature of the office is in view with its peculiar demands."[4]

Paul's list in 1 Timothy 3:1–7, in admirable literary fashion, ends on a note similar to how it begins: "He must be *well thought of* by outsiders." *Above reproach*, as the summary term, may be seen to include both a man's internal reputation (in the church) and external (in the world). However, at the outset of the list, the accent is naturally on the internal (in v. 2), before the eyes of the church, with the particular application to the external ("outsiders") in the final qualification (in v. 7).[5]

Bigger than You Think

To begin, let's not overlook the actual meaning of "above re-proach." This banner qualification is not just "innocent" or "ac-quitted," but "above reproach." We are looking for men not just technically righteous but *above* being reasonably charged with wrong in the first place. The term, according to George Knight, means "not open to attack or criticism . . . not objectively

---

4 John Piper, "Biblical Eldership, Session 1: Shepherd the Flock of God among You," Desiring God, May 1, 1999, https://www.desiringgod.org/.

5 In chap. 15 we will draw out the distinctive emphasis ("outsiders") of the final qualification.

chargeable."[6] He's not one who makes a practice of tiptoeing close to the line of righteous reproach. Whether a man is technically innocent (or not) is not the entirety of the concern for church leadership. He might be unnecessarily controversial in a way that betrays immaturity or lack of sober-mindedness. We want a pastor to be not only forensically righteous but also "the kind of man whom no one *suspects* of wrongdoing or immorality" due to his own indiscretion, immaturities, or imbalances.[7]

But how much suspicion? How much controversy is counterproductive? That is what particular local-church pluralities will have to wrestle with in their specific contexts. They are best positioned to discern of a potential officer:

- Is he regularly the subject of charges, whether justly so or not, due to his own lack of prudence? It's one thing to speak the truth and stand your ground. It's another to use the truth to satisfy your own lust for attention.

- Will having him as a pastor-elder prove a regular distraction and hindrance to the council and to the church? If his discretion or qualifications are frequently called into question, not strictly because of the truth but due to his way of presenting it, perhaps he needs more time to live faithfully, develop fresh habits, and build a new reputation before encumbering the church with his lapses. Again, a man may be technically righteous and yet of such a reputation that it would be counterproductive to invite him into church office.

---

6 George Knight, *The Pastoral Epistles*, New International Commentary on the New Testament (Grand Rapids, MI: Eerdmans, 1999), 155–56.
7 Anyabwile, *Finding Faithful Elders*, 57.

Note also, it's one thing to consider a man who is already controversial as a candidate. It's another when a man becomes controversial in the course of his calling. In the former, wise pluralities may be slow to bring him into office, while in the latter, being ready to stand by him. And to help him discern how much the truth itself is ruffling feathers and how much is his way of going about it.

As pluralities, we will do well to lean more toward the maximalist bar for "above reproach," rather than the minimalist. False charges, let's be clear, are not grounds for disqualification; however, the nature and reasonability of accusations should be carefully considered—and repeated public accusations or suspicions against a man may well mean it is unwise to appoint him to office.

Examples to the Flock

As mentioned above, "a model Christian" is essentially the other side of the coin from "above reproach." This seemingly low bar for eldership does have some important truth to convey about our pastor-elders. First, as Don Carson has memorably observed, the lists of qualifications, summarized with "above reproach," are "remarkable for being unremarkable." There is no requirement for particular achievements in formal education, world-class intellect or oratory, or manifest giftedness above the common man. Rather, these qualifications are the sort of traits we want in every Christian in time. What we're looking for in our pastor-elders, in essence, is normal, healthy, model Christianity. There are a couple caveats, as we saw in chapters 2 and 3. He must not be a recent convert, and he must be equipped, eager, and effective in teaching, relative to the particular congregation (not the church at large), to be a fitting leader of the people of the Book. However, this list, beginning with "above reproach," is the stuff of everyday Christianity. Christ means for all his church to aim at and progress in being "above reproach." It's the goal of all (as we've observed over and again), and because of that, requisite in the elders.

But note also that in pagan contexts, the moral distance between new converts and mature Christians may be all the greater than we're used to in historically Christian contexts. As low-bar as these requirements may seem to some today in gospel-developed locales, such men may have been more difficult to find in the first century. And perhaps we ourselves increasingly will find the same to be true if society becomes significantly more post-Christian.

Fundamental, then, to leadership in the local church is an exemplary function. Pastors are to not only be *able teachers* of God's word and *competent governors* of his people, but also examples of the kind of increasingly Christlike life toward which the whole congregation is progressing. The pastors unavoidably are "examples to the flock" (1 Pet. 5:3; also 1 Tim. 4:12). The pastors are to be those we hold up to the church and say, in essence, "Be like him," without feeling the need to make immediate qualifications.

"Above reproach," as we see in Titus 1:7, also communicates a kind of modesty and humility in the very nature of the calling: "An overseer, *as God's steward*, must be above reproach." Leaders in the church are not rulers in their own right. They are *stewards*, not kings, not stars, not performers. Pastors are God's stewards of his word and his people, and church office is not a personal possession but an assignment to steward. And part of stewarding, among other things, is not drawing inordinate attention to the steward himself while eclipsing the one to whom you're called to point.

Why Reputation Matters

The entirety of the list of qualifications, with "above reproach" as the summary, focuses on public reputation in a way that could make some of us uneasy. As John Piper observes, "Coming at the head of the list [above reproach] puts a tremendous emphasis on what a person's reputation is. The focus here is not a person's relationship to the Lord, but how others see him."[8]

We are in Christ, and right with God, based not on our reputation and life but on Christ's. Let it be heard in all the church, and beyond. However, our focus in this book is not every Christian but *formal leaders*. Christian leadership is not the same as Christian salvation, and we do well to keep the distinction clear in our minds, as Jesus did for his disciples: "Do not rejoice in this, that the spirits are subject to you [in ministry], but rejoice that your names are written in heaven [in Christ]" (Luke 10:20).

When it comes to formal leadership, one reason reputation matters is that the reputation of the church and its Lord matters. Paul demonstrates this with special clarity and focus in Titus 2 where he commends holiness and obedience "that the word of God may not be reviled. . . . So that an opponent may be put to shame, having nothing evil to say about us. . . . So that in everything they may adorn the doctrine of God our Savior" (Titus 2:5, 8, 10).

When the early church chose the seven, the first qualification (of only two!) was "of good repute" (Acts 6:3; the other was "full of the Spirit and of wisdom").

Called to Be Blameless

One after another, as "above reproach" is fleshed out in a dozen-plus specific aspects in 1 Timothy 3 and Titus 1, we see a pattern

8 Piper, "Biblical Eldership."

that Christian leaders are not called to a fundamentally different Christian life from the church. Rather, the leaders are to
be exemplary, "above reproach," in the very lifestyle to which
Christ, through them, calls the whole flock. Paul speaks to all
Christians when he says that Christ "has now reconciled [you] in
his body of flesh by his death, in order to present you holy and
blameless and above reproach before him" (Col. 1:22). "Blameless" (as is required of deacons, 1 Tim. 3:10) is another way of
saying "above reproach."

Throughout history, God's people have been called to be and
celebrated as "blameless." Noah was commended as such (Gen.
6:9). Abraham was called to be blameless (Gen. 17:1), as were God's
people as a whole (Deut. 18:13). Job was said to be blameless (Job
1:1, 8; 2:3); so also Daniel (Dan. 6:22).

When we open to the New Testament, we hear of the blame-
lessness of Zechariah and Elizabeth (Luke 1:6). And Paul's regular
call and attribution to the church is to be blameless: he chose us
in Christ before the foundation of the world to make us blameless before him (Eph. 1:4), that is, blameless one day soon at the
day of Christ (1 Cor. 1:8; Phil. 1:10; 1 Thess. 3:13; 5:23) and
blameless in our generation (Phil. 2:15; 1 Thess. 2:10). So also
Jude, in his beloved benediction, declares the glory of "the only
God" who "is able to keep you from stumbling and to present
you blameless before the presence of his glory with great joy"
(Jude 24).

"Blameless" may sound to our ears like a higher bar than "above
reproach"—especially if we think it to mean "sinless." But that is
not what *blameless* means. We sinners cannot yet be perfect, but
we can be blameless. Perhaps no passage captures the dynamic of
sinful yet blameless like 1 John 1:7–10:

If we walk in the light, as he is in the light, we have fellowship with one another, and the blood of Jesus his Son cleanses us from all sin. If we say we have no sin, we deceive ourselves, and the truth is not in us. If we confess our sins, he is faithful and just to forgive us our sins and to cleanse us from all unrighteousness. If we say we have not sinned, we make him a liar, and his word is not in us.

If you would be blameless, don't pretend to be sinless, but do with your sins what God, in Christ, would have you do: own and confess them, lay hold on God's forgiveness in Christ, and walk in the light. And when you are at fault and justly to blame, walk toward it rather than run away from it. Admit your wrong and seek peace with God and men. And though not sinless, you will be blameless before God. You yourself are not without blemish, but you have a Savior who is (Heb. 9:14; 1 Pet. 1:19).

This much, and more, Christ requires of formal leaders in his church. It is inevitably a public calling, in the church and beyond. And so for the good of the flock and the good of the gospel in the world, Christ through his apostle bids us to appoint pastors and deacons whose lives are exemplary. They are to be above reproach. No reasonable or founded blame or reproach can be leveled against them as they happily and undistractingly lock arms with a team of pastors to care well for the whole of the flock.

11

How Pastors Win (and Lose) Respect

... respectable.

1 TIMOTHY 3:2

OF THE FIFTEEN distinct elder qualifications in 1 Timothy 3:1–7, one in particular may be the least understood: "An overseer must be . . . *respectable*" (1 Tim. 3:2). What does it mean for a pastor to be respectable?

We should acknowledge that there may be less to go on with "respectable" than any other qualification. The Greek *kosmios* appears only twice in the New Testament: here and just verses earlier, in 2:9. However, *kosmios* is largely synonymous with *semnos*, which the ESV translates as *dignified* in 1 Timothy 2:2; 3:8, 11; and Titus 2:2 (the related noun *dignity* appears in 1 Tim. 3:4 and Titus 2:7). This is not a lot to go on (eight texts for starters) compared to other qualifications, but the picture begins to take shape, as we'll see.

Orderly Life, Worthy of Respect

What does it mean, then, to be respectable?

In the adjective *kosmios*, you can hear the noun *kosmos*, which means not only the "world" or "universe" but its orderly arrangement. There is a fixed structure and order to the world as God made it. The sky is above. The ground is beneath our feet. The ground slopes up into mountains, and down to the oceans. The planets and stars have their orbits. In the *kosmos*, God's ordered world, everything has its place; it is arranged by its designer. It is *put together*.

Perhaps what gets at "respectable" as well as anything else is the concept of an "orderly life" that puts others at ease and engenders trust.[1] Philip Towner says *kosmios* "conveys the ideas of 'seriousness' and 'appropriateness.'"[2] Similarly John Piper says, "The idea seems to be one of not offending against propriety—a person who comports himself in situations so as not to step on toes unnecessarily."[3] Respectability loves others by not being rude (1 Cor. 13:5).

Positively, one source captures it as "having characteristics or qualities that evoke admiration or delight."[4] Again, this is very similar to *semnos*, that is, *dignified*, meaning "to evoke special respect." *Evoke* may be the key verb: to evoke reverence, evoke respect. In other words, it's to help others take you seriously for Jesus's sake. To present yourself as "worthy of respect," carrying with it a sense

1   Donald Guthrie, *Pastoral Epistles: An Introduction and Commentary*, Tyndale New Testament Commentaries (Grand Rapids, MI: Eerdmans, 1991), 92.

2   Philip Towner, *The Letters to Timothy and Titus*, New International Commentary on the New Testament (Grand Rapids, MI: Eerdmans, 2006), 170.

3   John Piper, "Rethinking the Governance Structure at Bethlehem Baptist Church: A Biblical Examination of Key Terms," Desiring God, revised April 27, 2000, https://www.desiringgod .org/.

4   Walter Bauer, *A Greek-English Lexicon of the New Testament and Other Early Christian Literature*, ed. Frederick W. Danker, 3rd ed. (Chicago: University of Chicago Press, 2000), 561.

of seriousness or holy dignity. Noble, esteemed, admirable. Not being frivolous or crass or indecent.

Respectable, then, is irreducibly external. It "refers to a person's outward deportment or outward appearance."[5] It's "an observable quality of behavior with an inward source."[6] Also, respectable appearing after self-control "is almost predictable. It occurs frequently alongside 'self-control' in the literature, the two together completing a picture of honorable and dignified bearing."[7] Inward self-control, outward respectability.

To be sure, the kind of dignity or respectability to which God calls his people and his pastors is not simply outward appearance, words, and behavior but a manifestation of inward virtue. It's a subtle quality that demonstrates internal stability and is not an outward show. It elicits respect and demonstrates worthiness of trust. It is a genuine external expression of inner maturity—not hollow or faked.

And it is fitting that those who would be considered *the elders* of the church would be respectable, as respect is the kind of posture that is fitting toward maturity—respect for the old (Deut. 28:50) or respect shown to elders (Lam. 5:12)—a holy deference in view of age or status. To be respectable means "to be held in high regard," and again, on the proper terms: God's, not necessarily the world's.

Why Is It Necessary?

Why would it be necessary for the elders, the pastors, in the church to be respectable?

5 Bill Mounce, *Pastoral Epistles*, Word Biblical Commentary (Nashville, TN: Thomas Nelson, 2000), 173.
6 Towner, *Letters to Timothy and Titus*, 262.
7 Towner, *Letters to Timothy and Titus*, 252.

First, Christ not only calls for pastors to be "respectable" (1 Tim. 3:2) but for all Christians to live "godly and *dignified* in every way" (1 Tim. 2:2). And one way Christ shows he's serious about his followers as a whole being respectable is by requiring this virtue of his undershepherds. Christ means for his church's pastor-elders to live, teach, and serve as examples for the flock (1 Pet. 5:3). Pastors model the kind of holy dignity the church is to demonstrate to the world, to win the world, and image Christ, and not build up unnecessary barriers.

Also, pastors being *respectable* corresponds to the church's call to *respect* its leaders:

> We ask you, brothers, to respect those who labor among you and are over you in the Lord and admonish you, and to esteem them very highly in love because of their work. (1 Thess. 5:12–13)

Good pastors help the flock in its call to respect its leaders. Christ calls his church to respect its leaders, and he calls its leaders to do their part to be respectable—make respect easier, not more difficult. Church, respect your leaders. Leaders, be respectable. We acknowledge the difference between being *respect-ed* and *respect-able*. We are not charged to be respected; that lies beyond our control. But we can be respectable.

So good pastors and growing Christians will want to ask not only about elder candidates but about themselves:

- Am I reliable? Do I engender trust?
- Do I live and speak and present myself in such a way, as a representative of Christ and his church, to help people take Jesus seriously, for one, and me seriously for Jesus's sake?

- Does the way I carry myself in the church and in the world help others experience serious joy in Jesus because of me? Or do I needlessly undermine God's worth by talking, dressing, or behaving foolishly?

Good leaders, out of love for their people, seek to cultivate and maintain a kind of humble, godly dignity that encourages, rather than discourages, respect from others. They make it easier, not harder, for the flock to take them seriously as they take Jesus seriously.

As workers for the joy of their people, they want to help, not hinder, the church as it fulfills its part of the dance: to obey and submit to the shepherds in such a way as to "let them do [their work] with joy and not with groaning"—for the advantage of the church (Heb. 13:17).

Conduct, Comments, and Clothing

Practically, then, what forms might such respectability and holy dignity take? Without pretending to be exhaustive, let's look at three that the texts on dignity would lead us toward.

1. How We Live (Conduct and Lifestyle)

The KJV renders *kosmios* in 1 Timothy 3:2 as "of good behavior," which is an important aspect of being respectable, even though, as we'll see, more is included.

How we carry ourselves in life cultivates respect and trust, or not. How we treat our brothers and sisters in Christ—Jesus called it "love"—either shows the world we are his, or not. "By this all people will know that you are my disciples, if you have love for one another" (John 13:35). And how we treat the members of our family, with whom we may be quickest to let our guard down, demonstrates dignity or lack thereof (1 Tim. 3:4). Also how we deal with "outsiders" demonstrates to others whether we are worthy of respect, or not (Col. 4:5–6; 1 Thess. 4:12).

By our conduct, our behavior, we signal inward rest and security and stability—or neediness. We evidence whether our hearts are satisfied in God and ready to overflow to meet others' needs, or not. We show ourselves to be starved for undue attention or eager to generously give our own attention to others. Humility demonstrates concern for others, while outward ostentation or carelessness broadcasts an inward emptiness aching to be filled.

Regarding lifestyle, how we steward our bodies is not irrelevant.[8] But maybe the most important word to add here in this section on conduct is the other mention of dignity in the elder qualifications in 1 Timothy 3:4: "He must manage his own household well, with all dignity keeping his children submissive."

Dignified dads. We covered godly fathering in chapter 9, so we'll just briefly touch on it here. What does it mean for a father to keep his children submissive "with all dignity"? It might be a reference to the children submitting with dignity. However, it seems far more likely, since the qualifications are mainly about the man, not his children, that the father "with all dignity" keeps his children submissive. In other words, it speaks to "the manner in which authority is exercised over the children" and shows "a measure of suitability to exercise authority over church members."[9] The question is not just, "Can he keep his kids (and the church) in line?" But, "How does he do it?" Is he harsh, threatening, overbearing, domineering? Or does he do it with dignity—through forethought, words, and persuasion?

---

8 For more on body stewardship, see n3 in chap. 5.
9 Towner, *Letters to Timothy and Titus*, 256.

As we all know, there are undignified ways to keep children submissive. This is not how the family or the church should be led. Homes need dads, and churches need pastors, who are not passive but who actually lead, through humble initiative, and do so in a certain way—as 1 Peter 5:3 says, "not domineering over those in your charge, but being examples to the flock."

Ephesians 6:4 speaks to such respectable fathering: "Fathers, do not provoke your children to anger [undignified], but bring them up in the discipline and instruction of the Lord." Bob Yarbrough, in his excellent commentary on the Pastoral Epistles, says we need "big men, not little autocrats"—men who demonstrate "forgiveness, care for others, prayer and regard for God's word, self-sacrifice, loving service, respect for others, listening to others, finding joy in what pleases others rather than oneself, making personal changes and forsaking sin for the sake of improved relations with other family members, in many cases seemingly endless delayed gratification, and much more. . . . This task requires big men, not little autocrats."[10]

2. What We Say (Communication and Teaching)

Respectability also encompasses our speech in the assembly, in conversation, and in the words we publish for the world online. When Paul requires dignity (*semnos*) of deacons and their wives, he pairs it twice with their speech: they "must be dignified, not double-tongued . . . dignified, not slanderers" (1 Tim. 3:8, 11).

In a special way, pastors show themselves respectable, or not, through their teaching, their words: "In your teaching show integrity, *dignity*, and sound speech that cannot be condemned" (Titus 2:7–8). Being skillful at teaching or "teachers at heart" is what sets

---

10 Robert W. Yarbrough, *The Letters to Timothy and Titus*, Pillar New Testament Commentary (Grand Rapids, MI: Eerdmans, 2018), 200.

the elders apart from the deacons. Leaders in the church are those, says Hebrews 13:7, who speak the word of God through their teaching, which makes the respectability of our words so critical.

We pastors would do well to pray earnestly for the sanctification of our speech, that our words would not be crass or crude or too clever or too sophisticated but substantive and accessible. We want our words to be faithful to God's word and clear to our congregation. In a world of communication drowning in frivolity, we pray that our words would have a seriousness to them (serious joy!) and prove reliable and worthy of respect.

Faithfully and compellingly preaching and teaching God's word is the heart of a pastor winning (or losing) the trust and respect of his people. The well of genuine authority in the church is the trustworthy word of Christ. So the elder "must hold firm to the trustworthy word as taught, so that he may be able to give instruction in sound doctrine and also rebuke those who contradict it" (Titus 1:9). Respectability extends beyond our words and teaching, but for pastor-teachers "rightly handling the word of truth" (2 Tim. 2:15) comes first. The sheep hear their Savior's voice (John 10:3, 4, 16, 27) in his word, and as they hear his voice faithfully and compellingly proclaimed—in a manner worthy of respect—they grow in their trust of and respect for the preacher.

Comments online. A new phenomenon in our day is that some pastors regularly publish casual and often uncareful words on social media for their people and others to see. We do well as pastors to think about our words being respectable, not only in the pulpit and in the context of corporate worship but everywhere we put our words—and especially when we put them online to be read by anyone at any time. Yarbrough includes these comments on 1 Timothy 4:7 ("Have nothing to do with irreverent, silly myths"):

Some ideas or proposals are so far beyond the pale of plausible that a pastor has no time or business giving them the dignity of extensive attention. This does not mean writing people off crudely (cf. Titus 3:2 ["show perfect courtesy toward all people"]). But overall, Paul's view (and example) is to focus on and promulgate the truths of Christ and the faith, not to be distracted with undue attention to aberrant beliefs. There are contemporary analogies, for example, in conspiracy theories, so-called urban legends, and endless issue-oriented (and often polemical) blogs and websites from which most pastors find it wise to recuse themselves.[11]

Amen. Brother pastors, let's "focus on and promulgate the truths of Christ and the faith"—in our preaching and teaching and conversations and letters and text messages and online, if we feel any sense of call and interest investing minimally there. And after all we've seen in recent years, with conspiracy theories and urban legends and endless issue-oriented polemics, I can't help but resonate with Yarbrough's word, and encouragement, that "most pastors find it wise to recuse themselves."

Positively, when Yarbrough mentions Paul's "example" in parentheses in the quote above, he adds this footnote:

It is an ongoing source of scholarly frustration that Paul is not more specific about the names and views of his opponents. He tends to focus on what he holds to be true and redemptive rather than allow gospel detractors to set the agenda for his remarks or exhaust his energies in venting so as to profile them.

11 Yarbrough, *Letters to Timothy and Titus*, 238.

That's an important word for pastors today: Paul "tends to focus on what he holds to be true and redemptive" and does not "allow gospel detractors to set the agenda." He doesn't say that gospel detractors don't *inform* Paul's ministry. Indeed they do! We have thirteen letters from Paul that give evidence to his being informed by or aware of error. But being aware of and responding to error through a "focus on what we hold to be true and redemptive" is a far cry from *letting error set the agenda.*

So may God give pastor-elders today the grace, if online, to be *respectable* in their online presence, no matter how base the world's standards become. Pastor-elders owe it to their people and to the name of Christ—and to model it for their people—not to lose their witness with the triviality and frivolity of online behavior that is unworthy of their church's respect.

3. How Pastor-Elders Dress (Clothing)

Finally, then, and perhaps least important, though not unimportant, respectability relates, unavoidably, to how pastor-elders dress. God made this visible, material world and made humanity *in his image*, to visually represent and display him in the world. An image is irreducibly visual.

As we mentioned, the only other occurrence of *kosmios* in the New Testament comes just sentences earlier in 1 Timothy 2:9: "Women should adorn themselves in *respectable* apparel, with modesty and self-control." How we dress, relative to mature societal expectations and norms (not immodest trends), engenders respect or undermines it. And God means for his people, beginning with the leaders, to be the kind of people who, in both primary and secondary matters, seek to make respect easier for others, not more difficult.

It is at least juvenile, if not self-absorbed, to attempt to draw special attention, whether positively or negatively, by the way we dress. For pastor-elders this cuts both ways: preaching in an old hoodie and ratty jeans, or in designer kicks and a $5000 leather jacket. Love and maturity lead good pastors to consider others from a full heart and to try within reason to put them at ease rather than shock, offend, distract, or entice.

We are unavoidably saying something to others with how we dress and comport ourselves. Here, we as Christians will want to be especially diligent not to take our cues from the unbelieving world. As society continues to devalue marriage and cultivate a hook-up culture in which dress subtly (if not overtly) signals sexual availability, we will want to think carefully and fundamentally differently about how we dress. We cannot simply take our bearings from the world.

The image of an ambassador might be helpful for pastors. They are not kings. They are ambassadors. A good ambassador doesn't dress to look like a king or eclipse the king. Nor does he dishonor the king by wearing conspicuous rags. Rather, the ambassador seeks to honor the king whom he represents, not draw attention to himself. This is true for all Christians but especially so for pastors. They do not want their clothing to be conspicuous, either because of how fashionable they are or how surprisingly casual and informal.

As ambassadors for Christ, pastor-elders can dress to honor the King and not distract from him or draw attention to themselves. They can dress to put others at ease and engender trust as Christ's spokesmen as they open his word through their teaching.

God at Work

Again, true dignity is not staged or put on. True respectability is an outward echo of inward peace. It gives the world a glimpse into the internal maturity God sees and is himself working in Christ's undershepherds.

We all know there is a kind of pretend dignity that's not natural to a person's maturity but put on for show, typically to compensate for some insecurity or sense of inadequacy. Such "dignity" is not produced by a heart satisfied in God, seeking to put others at peace, but by a restless, growling stomach seeking to fill itself with others' attention and approval. Faux dignity is selfish rather than selfless. It dresses, acts, and speaks "up" to protect and posture itself above others.

But selfless dignity serves. It comes down from its heights to associate with others, bring up the lowly, and foreground the needs of others.

Soon enough all the façades will fall. The curtains will swing back, the makeup will wear off, and every tree will be known by its fruit (Luke 6:44). The true dignity and genuine respectability that remain will be the kind that didn't begin with us and isn't decisively owing to us.

Being respectable does not mean that pastor-elders won't be mistreated, that they won't be falsely accused, or slandered, maligned, or insulted. In fact, being genuinely respectable, on God's terms, might make them a target of the evil one. But there is a respectable, dignified way to handle mistreatment. Indeed, when unfairly and poorly treated, true dignity shines its brightest. There's a time to simply remain silent, like Jesus, before accusers. Other times pastors need to own and apologize for any part that's theirs. And other times, they may say calmly, "Bring forward the evidence."

They crucified the most respectable man who ever lived. And we respect him all the more because of how he handled it.

And he is the one now at work in and through us to free us from self and miraculously make us look not only to our own interests but also to the interests of others. In humility we count others more significant than ourselves, and we do what we can, within reason, for others and for Christ, to be worthy of respect.

12

Love for Strangers and
the Great Commission

. . . hospitable.

1 TIMOTHY 3:2

THE TWELVE OF US sat in silence on the edge of our seats. You could have heard a pin drop.

Three of us had pilgrimaged from Minnesota to muggy Orlando and its stifling August humidity for a weeklong intensive course on evangelism with Steve Childers. Fortunately, Reformed Theological Seminary is as air-conditioned as it is Reformed.

With only a dozen students on board for five 9-hour days with one of the country's top church-planting strategists, it was a rich week, to say the least. During these precious hours, the Beijing Olympics were playing second fiddle to learning about the advance of the gospel around the world and in personal conversation.

Time and again Childers had thrown us curveballs. He knew how to keep us on our toes. But now he had us nothing short of captivated.

"You know what the key to evangelism in the twenty-first century will be, don't you?"

Childers wasn't talking about the Global South but about the Western Hemisphere—and America in particular. I'm sure he could see on our faces how eager we were for his answer. *Wow, the key*, we were thinking. *This is huge.*

He paused and smiled his memorable world-evangelism grin. He waited. Still waiting. Still paused. Still nothing. Hold it—hold it. I was almost ready to burst with, "Just c'mon already!"

Finally he lifted the curtain.

"Hospitality."

Then another long pause to let it sink it.

Hospitality and Post-Christendom

In an increasingly post-Christian society, the importance of hospitality as an evangelistic asset has been growing in recent years. Increasingly, the most strategic turf on which to engage the unbelieving with the good news of Jesus may be the turf of our own yards and homes.

When people don't gather in droves for stadium crusades, or tarry long enough on the sidewalk to hear a gospel presentation, or look up from their phones, or take out their earbuds, what will you do? Where will you interact with the unbelieving about the realities that matter most?

Invite them to dinner.

For several of us in Childers's class, the lights went on after his semidramatic revelation. Biblical texts on hospitality came springing to mind. He wasn't making this up; he was reading the Scriptures. This wasn't an innovative strategy but ancient, even if it was beginning to feel newly relevant. A biblical theme we'd previously assumed to be marginal, perhaps even antiquated, was emerging again as a significant avenue for evangelism in secular times.

Love for Outsiders

The New Testament word for *hospitality* (Greek *philozenia*) is a compound of *love* and *stranger*. Hospitality has its origin, literally, in love for outsiders, for the unfamiliar and uncomfortable.

One of the more memorable charges is Hebrews 13:1–2: "Let brotherly love continue. Do not neglect to show hospitality to strangers, for thereby some have entertained angels unawares." Yes, love the brothers, says Hebrews, but make sure you don't forget this. And don't neglect to love strangers as well.

Love for fellow Christians is essential—some call it "the final apologetic," based on John 13:35: "By this all people will know that you are my disciples, if you have love for one another." There is an *especially* to our love for Christian brothers and sisters, as Paul writes in Galatians 6:10: "As we have opportunity, let us do good to everyone, and especially to those who are of the household of faith." Yet vital as it is, there's a way in which loving those who love you may not be all that impressive. "Do not even unbelievers do the same?" asks Jesus (see Matt. 5:47). But showing love to outsiders, to strangers, that's surprising. Indeed, that's countercultural. Especially in times in which we're becoming increasingly suspicious of strangers. Showing love and concern *for strangers* has the fingerprints of a heavenly Father on it.

Seeking to Show Hospitality

In Romans 12, as the apostle Paul points us to important flashpoints for how our lives will increasingly look when claimed by the gospel, he says, "Rejoice in hope, be patient in tribulation, be constant in prayer. Contribute to the needs of the saints *and seek to show hospitality*" (Rom. 12:12–13).

It could be that this charge to hospitality is another way of saying "contribute to the needs of the saints," but it seems more likely that this "and" (like Heb. 13:1–2) adds love for strangers to love for brothers and sisters. Both-and: let brotherly love (*philadelphia*) continue, and don't overlook stranger love (*philozenia*) as well. It's another summons to demonstrate kindness to outsiders—like the kind a wealthy man on the island of Malta showed Paul in Acts 28:7: "Now in the neighborhood of that place were lands belonging to the chief man of the island, named Publius, who received us and entertained us hospitably for three days." Paul and those who survived the shipwreck were utter strangers to Publius. Yet he, the chief man of the island, and clearly a man of means, welcomed these strangers and hospitably received them as guests. And *for three days*, which is no brief stay.

Outsiders from around Town

Keep thinking through the New Testament mentions of hospitality and see that it's no peripheral theme, which brings us to this chapter in a book on local-church leadership. Hospitality even finds its way into such a prominent place as both lists of elder qualifications:

An elder "must be . . . hospitable." (1 Tim. 3:2)

An elder, "as God's steward, must be . . . hospitable." (Titus 1:7–8)

How many of us pastor-elders stay mindful of this requirement? Not just about prospective elders: *Is he genuinely hospitable? Does he give evidence of a Christlike love for strangers—not fear of, not indifference toward?* But also, in an ongoing sense, about current pastor-elders: *Do we still love strangers? Do we still ache for those who seem far off to come near and be found in Christ? And are we willing to take uncomfortable steps that the proximity of hospitality entails?* I suspect hospitality may have fallen out of consciousness in many places today. Yet here it is in both 1 Timothy and Titus, to govern the selection of elders—and as a virtue that must continue in their lives and leadership. And not just individually, but collectively.

It matters tremendously how the elders orient toward "outsiders" and those who are "strangers." The elders set the tone and ethos for how the church will engage with the world and with unbelievers. As we'll consider in chapter 15, some Christians and churches may be taken aback to read that an elder "must be well thought of by outsiders" (1 Tim. 3:7), but in a society becoming more secular, with the church increasingly at the margins, we might begin to see this value in new light. If the elders who are to be "examples to the flock" (1 Pet. 5:3) don't themselves engage on the front lines with the city's unbelieving, it's unlikely the flock will take up a mission the shepherds are avoiding.

Inviting in the Believing as Well

Lest we swing the pendulum and think the charge to hospitality no longer enjoins us to care for fellow believers, 1 Peter 4:9 and 3 John 5–8 stand ready to bring the balance. Fellow believers can be "strangers" to us as well. Consider 1 Peter 4:9 in context, with verses 8–10:

> Above all, keep loving one another earnestly, since love covers a multitude of sins. *Show hospitality to one another* without

grumbling. As each has received a gift, use it to serve one another, as good stewards of God's varied grace.

So full Christian hospitality includes inviting in other believers as well, caring for each other at inconvenient times and in uncomfortable ways, "washing the feet of the saints," contributing to the needs of the saints, and so on. Hospitality is not just for making converts but for the Great Commission task of making disciples as well (more on that below). And there's more.

Strategic Hospitality

Christian hospitality also serves Jesus's global mission by inviting in traveling missionaries. This might be really outside the box for some readers. If so, perhaps it's a call for prayer for your church to be more globally engaged. John's third epistle commends this kind of care for gospel workers on furlough:

> Beloved, it is a faithful thing you do in all your efforts *for these brothers, strangers as they are*, who testified to your love before the church. You will do well to send them on their journey in a manner worthy of God. For they have gone out for the sake of the name, accepting nothing from the Gentiles. Therefore we ought to support people like these, that we may be fellow workers for the truth. (3 John 5–8)

Brothers and strangers both. Brothers in Christ, yet strangers till now. But "they have gone out for the sake of the name" of Christ. John says that "we ought to support people like these." So let your hospitality include not only unbelieving neighbors and coworkers, but also traveling missionaries sent out for global gospel propaga-tion. John Piper calls it "strategic hospitality":

> Strategic hospitality . . . asks: How can I draw the most people into a deep experience of God's hospitality by the use of my home . . . ? Who are the people who could be brought together in my home most strategically for the sake of the kingdom? . . . Strategic hospitality is not content to just have the old clan over for dinner again and again. It strategizes how to make the hospi-tality of God known and felt all over the world, from the lonely church member right here, to the Gola farmers in Tahn, Liberia. Don't ever underestimate the power of your living room as a launching pad for new life and hope and ministry and mission![1]

What a vision for the use of our homes for Christ's global cause—and good pastor-elders and their wives and families long to lead the way with a heart like this.

Why We Love Strangers

Full-orbed Christian hospitality makes room for fellow believers and global gospel carriers; however, let's not quiet the main note we're striking here, the evangelistic one—inviting in the outsider, welcoming unbelievers onto our turf and into our space in hopes of bringing Jesus into theirs. This is the note struck in the elder qualifications and will lead our churches into the kinds of hospitable hearts that will birth evangelism and disciple-making and church planting and world missions.

---

1 John Piper, "Strategic Hospitality," Desiring God, August 25, 1985, https://www.desiringgod .org/.

The reason this is no minor biblical theme is that the streams of hospitality flow from the well of God himself. Christians love the stranger because we have been loved by the Father when we ourselves were strangers. Hospitality rises in its purest form when we heed Paul's counsel, "Remember that you were at that time separated from Christ, alienated from the commonwealth of Israel and strangers to the covenants of promise, having no hope and without God in the world" (Eph. 2:12).

In Jesus, we find ourselves to be the former enemy who now has been welcomed, the sinner who is saved, the stranger who is loved. "God shows his love for us in that while we were still sinners, Christ died for us" (Rom. 5:8). And welcomed strangers, who remember it, want to be the kind of people who are quick to welcome other strangers.

Church Planting

If we were to identify where in the elder qualifications is the main evangelistic impulse—for gospel expansion and growth, for drawing in "other sheep" (John 10:16), rather than being content with the same old flock—I would put it in *hospitality*. Those willing and eager to open their homes to strangers are typically those willing and eager to open their lives to make disciples and open their hearts (and prayers and finances) for church planting and global missions.

At Cities Church we have found that our shared mission as a plurality of elders to plant new churches has had powerful effects in drawing us together and bringing health and balance to the work of shepherding our own flock. Healthy churches grow. And healthy elders want to grow healthily. And strong, energetic, holy, ambitious churches produce more than enough mature, effective leaders than that producing church needs. This is normal, Great Commission–fulfilling church life. Christ builds his kingdom through healthy churches raising up more equipped, eager, effective leaders than needed so that they can share them with the world through church planting and missions—like the church in Antioch, which was willing not just to send out a few leaders but to *send out its very best*: two men named Paul and Barnabas (Acts 13:2).

Tim Keller writes in his short article "Why Plant Churches":

The vigorous, continual planting of new congregations is the single most crucial strategy for (1) the numerical growth of the body of Christ in a city and (2) the continual corporate renewal and revival of the existing churches in a city. Nothing else—not crusades, outreach programs, parachurch ministries, growing megachurches, congregational consulting, nor church renewal processes—will have the consistent impact of dynamic, extensive church planting.[2]

Note well that remarkable claim about planting new congregations: it is, Keller says, "the single most crucial strategy" for both growth and renewal in a city. Hospitable pastor-elders are the kind of men who want to "reach our city," and will want to take Keller seriously when he says that "the only widescale way to bring in lots of new Christians to the Body of Christ in a permanent way is to plant new churches." And for pastor-elders teams in particular, "our attitude to new church development is a test of whether our mindset is geared to our own institutional turf or to the overall

---

2   Tim Keller, "Why Plant Churches," Redeemer City to City, January 1, 2002, https://redeemercitytocity.com/.

health and prosperity of the kingdom of God in the city."[3] Good pastors have hearts like that: not fixed on their own turf but pining for the overall health and thriving of the church through the city.

Elders Making Elders

One more topic to address here under the heading of hospitality is *disciple-making*. And not simply disciple-making in the big Great Commission picture but in its specific application to the pastor-elders in 2 Timothy 2:2: "What you have heard from me in the presence of many witnesses entrust to faithful men, who will be able to teach others also." *Disciple-making*, in my use of the term, is the process in which a maturing believer invests himself, for a particular period of time, in one or just a few younger believers, in order to help their growth in the faith—including helping them also to invest in others who will invest in others.

It's especially vital for new and young believers. A discipler is like a personal trainer to help "new plants" get established and moving forward in the faith. The goal isn't to always have the personal trainer watching over you but to learn spiritual health and fitness for yourself and eventually be able to help others also. I'm not a stickler for the mentality that says, "Always have your Paul and always have your Timothy." I love the instinct behind it but find it overstates the enduring need for a Paul, even if it rightly challenges us to remain deliberate to invest, as we're able, in Timothys. New believers don't need a Timothy (a disciple) right away; they just need a Paul (a discipler). And more mature believers don't necessarily need a Paul, but I sure want to encourage them to find some Timothy to invest in.

3   Keller, "Why Plant Churches."

Such disciple-making requires both some minimal structure and margin to let life happen. It's both engineered and organic, trellis and vine, truth-speaking and life-sharing. Quantity time is the soil in which real quality time grows. The vast majority of Jesus's time with his men wasn't formal. Mark 3:14 says that "he appointed twelve (whom he also named apostles) *so that they might be with him.*" We too need to "be with them" to have the kind of effect Jesus had on his men, which eventually the authorities saw in Acts 4:13: "Now when they saw the boldness of Peter and John, and perceived that they were uneducated, common men, they were astonished. And they recognized that they had been with Jesus." Tom Nelson highlights the importance of what Michael Polanyi calls "tacit knowledge,"[4] that is, "the kind of knowing that is difficult to capture in propositional terms or categories, but that emerges in the context of a close relationship and in the imitation of another."[5] "By watching the master and emulating his efforts in the presence of his example, the apprentice unconsciously picks up the rules of the art, including those which are not explicitly known to the master himself."[6]

Calling All Pastors

While I was in college, I was discipled and learned to do the same. As a college junior, I chose to live on a freshman hall, invested in a few particular men, and sought to be for them what my discipler had been for me the previous two years. Then in 2003 I moved to Minneapolis with a Campus Outreach team and for four years lived

4 Michael Polanyi, *Personal Knowledge* (Chicago: University of Chicago Press, 2015), 53.
5 Tom Nelson, *The Flourishing Pastor: Recovering the Lost Art of Shepherd Leadership* (Downers Grove, IL: InterVarsity Press, 2021), 94.
6 Polanyi, *Personal Knowledge*, 53.

at the University of Minnesota, seeking to evangelize and disciple men in that vision Paul gave Timothy about raising up "faithful men, who will be able to teach others also."

Now, as a pastor, I'm blessed to labor with a team of eight others who take 2 Timothy 2:2 seriously as a charge to pastors. We believe that the principles of 2 Timothy 2:2, lived out in a church over time, will produce disciple makers beyond just the pastors, but we take that text as a mandate first and foremost to us as pastors. *Pastors, amid all the other demands and pressures of your work (and it is unavoidably broader than simply personal disciple-making), don't miss this vital endeavor: make sure to entrust the gospel to faithful men who will be able to teach others also.*

Robert Coleman's 1963 classic *The Master Plan of Evangelism* laid out a vision for such disciple-making in an era when so much energy and attention was going to crusades and revival meetings. Coleman was not opposed to big evangelistic gatherings; he participated in them. But he was adamant that they weren't enough—or the main strategy for gospel advance. Instead Coleman commended the "lifestyle of the Great Commission" and pointed readers to observe in the life of Christ that his ministry revolved around his investment, his discipling, of his twelve men.[7]

Jesus did indeed *bless the masses* with his public teaching, but he gave the lion's share of his time to *invest in the few*, his men (the twelve), whom we call his "disciples." He called them to a particular season of learning under him. "Follow me, and I will make you fishers of men" (Matt. 4:19). For three and a half years, they learned under his personal tutelage and care. And having been discipled by him, there would have been little doubt in their minds what

---

7   Robert E. Coleman, *The Master Plan of Evangelism* (Grand Rapids, MI: Revel, 1963).

their Master was calling them to when he said, "Make disciples of all nations" (Matt. 28:19).

So also the apostle Paul, having been discipled by rabbis in his youth, followed suit in his manifest personal investments in younger associates, Timothy and Titus among them, and he encouraged Timothy to disciple the church's next generation of leaders and teach them to do the same.

13

The Strongest Men Are Gentle

. . . not violent but gentle.

1 TIMOTHY 3:3

LENNIE IS FAMOUS for his lack of gentleness.

One of the lead characters in John Steinbeck's *Of Mice and Men*, Lennie is a giant of a man, strong as an ox, with a mild mental disability. He has big muscles and a big heart. He loves petting soft things but doesn't know his own strength. First, he unintentionally kills a mouse he is stroking. Later it's a puppy. Finally, he accidentally and fatally breaks a woman's neck.

Lennie's problem isn't his strength. Strength is a gift. Others benefit from Lennie's strength, especially his friend George. What Lennie needs is not to jettison his strength but to gain the ability to *control* his strength and channel it into good purposes, to use his power to help others, not harm them.

No Meekness without Might

Revelation 6 gives us a stunning glimpse of divine judgment. A sixth seal is opened. The earth quakes, the sun goes dark, the moon turns to blood. Stars fall, and the sky is rolled back like a scroll. The earth's kings and "the great ones and the generals and the rich and the powerful . . . [hide] themselves in the caves and among the rocks of the mountains" (Rev. 6:15). So terrified are they at "the wrath of the Lamb" that they call to the mountains and rocks to fall on them:

> Fall on us and hide us from the face of him who is seated on the throne, and from *the wrath of the Lamb,* for the great day of their wrath has come, and who can stand? (Rev. 6:16–17)

They would rather be crushed to death than face omnipotent wrath. Did you do the double take? Excuse me, "the wrath of *the Lamb*"—the Lamb being Jesus Christ? How's that? We know Christ to be gentle, meek and mild. Who would cower before *him* like this? Before God the Father, of course, we expect that. But the Lamb, gentle Jesus?

Those of us who love that Christ is gentle and lowly need not be afraid to rehearse that his wrath is horrific. To know the sovereign power and unmatched strength of Christ—and the sheer terror of those who realize they have opposed him—will both keep us from misunderstanding his gentleness and make his remarkable gentleness all the more impressive.

Gentle and Lowly

We dare not minimize the portrait of Christ in Matthew 11:28–30 simply because many are at home with this emphasis today. This is a penetrating self-revelation from Christ himself—and all the more if he is sovereign and strong and his wrath is terrifying:

Come to me, all who labor and are heavy laden, and I will give you rest. Take my yoke upon you, and learn from me, for I am gentle and lowly in heart, and you will find rest for your souls. For my yoke is easy, and my burden is light. (Matt. 11:28–30)

It is no accident that these words have been greatly celebrated. Such an invitation from such a person is precious beyond words. We owe our very life, and the joy that is to come for us, to his gentleness and lowliness.

And his gentleness toward his people is all the sweeter as we learn what sovereign strength lies beneath it. His gentleness is not a replacement for his sovereign strength that soon will horrify those who have rejected him. Rather, his gentleness cushions the application of his great power as he marshals it in service of his weak people. Our Jesus is indeed gentle—and he is not only gentle. As Dane Ortlund writes, "'Gentle and lowly' does not mean 'mushy and frothy.'"[1] Mistake not his gentleness for weakness. *Gentle* is not code for *weak*. Gentleness is not the absence of strength but the addition of virtue to strength.

And in our day, when we seem to be increasingly uncomfortable with the danger of *other people's* power and strength, it's vital that we see this in Jesus and throughout the Scriptures. Power in its various forms is a good gift from God to be used by his people for the ends

---

1 Dane C. Ortlund, *Gentle and Lowly: The Heart of Christ for Sinners and Sufferers* (Wheaton, IL: Crossway, 2020), 21. Ortlund highlights Jesus's "restraint" (53) as he "deals gently" (Heb. 5:2) with his own. "What elicits tenderness from Jesus is not the severity of sin but whether the sinner comes to him. Whatever our offense, he deals gently with us. If we never come to him, we will experience a judgment so fierce it will be like a double-edged sword coming out of his mouth (Rev. 1:16; 2:12; 19:15, 21). If we do come to him, as fierce as his lion-like judgment would have been against us, so deep will be his lamb-like tenderness for us (cf. Rev. 5:5–6; Isa. 40:10–11). We will be enveloped in one or the other. To no one will Jesus be neutral" (54).

of his kingdom. And like other good gifts, power is perilous when wielded improperly. The better the gift, the more perilous in the hands of sinners. The answer to the dangers of strength is not its loss, but the godly exercise of power in the gaining of a Christian virtue called *gentleness*.

Bring Gentle Back

Gentleness today may be the single most misunderstood Spirit-produced virtue of the nine listed in Galatians 5:22–23: "The fruit of the Spirit is love, joy, peace, patience, kindness, goodness, faithfulness, *gentleness*, self-control." Two millennia later, *gentleness* is often used as positive spin for *weakness*. But gentleness in the Bible is emphatically not a lack of strength; it's the godly exercise of power. Gentleness does not signal a *lack of ability* but the *added ability* to steward one's strength so that it serves good, life-giving ends rather than harmful ends.

Take rain, for instance. Hard rain can destroy life, while "gentle rain" gives life (Deut. 32:2). Violent rain can do more harm than good. The farmer prays not for weak rain, or no rain, but for *gentle rain*. The means of delivery is important. We need water (as power for life) delivered gently, not destructively. *Gentle* doesn't mean *feebly* but *appropriately*; it means giving, not taking, life.

So also, "a gentle tongue is a tree of life" (Prov. 15:4). Gentle doesn't mean weak, but fittingly strong with life-giving restraint—giving something good not in a flood but in due measure. Or consider sailing. A gently blowing wind (Acts 27:13) answers a sailor's prayer, while a violent wind spells trouble (Acts 27:18).

The virtue of gentleness is seen best in God himself, who "comes with might" (Isa. 40:10). How does he wield his strength toward his people? "He will tend his flock like a shepherd; he will gather the lambs in his arms; he will carry them in his bosom, and *gently* lead those that are with young" (Isa. 40:11). Violence is the destructive use of strength (Isa. 22:17). Gentleness is its life-giving exercise.

What Our Daughters Want

When the apostle Peter contrasts good power with bad, just rulers with the unjust, he describes good leaders as "good *and gentle*" (1 Pet. 2:18). The opposite of a crooked master isn't a weak one—who wants the protection of a weak lord?—but "good and gentle." We want *gentle* leaders, not *weak* ones. We want leaders with strength and power, not to use against us to our harm, but to wield on our behalf for our good to help us. This is what makes the image of a shepherd so fitting in both the Old and New Testaments. Sheep are manifestly weak and vulnerable. They need strong shepherds, not weak ones. They need shepherds who are "good and gentle" and will use their power to help the sheep, not use and abuse them.

My three-year-old daughter doesn't want a weak daddy. She wants me to be strong—and to use that strength to help her, not hurt her. And what she needs most is not for me to flex my muscles to threaten her. It's clear enough that daddy is bigger and stronger. She needs to see that I'm gentle. That her daddy is not only strong enough to protect her, but that she can trust me to use my strength to serve and bless her, not harm her.

Weak men are often preoccupied with showing and talking about their strength. Truly strong men give their energy and attention not to showing off their strength but to demonstrating their gentleness. They are able to rightly exercise their manifest power for others' good. Insecure men flex and threaten. Men who are secure in their strength and the strength of their Lord are not ashamed, but eager, to let their gentleness be known to all (Phil. 4:5).

Gentle Men for the Church

It should be no surprise, then, that Christ requires such of the leaders in his church: "not violent but gentle" (1 Tim. 3:3). As we've seen, among the fifteen qualifications in 1 Timothy 3, four are negatives: "not a drunkard, not violent . . . , not quarrelsome, not a lover of money." Only one of these negatives is paired with an explicit positive: "not violent *but gentle*." Perhaps the reason Paul doesn't provide the positive virtue for the other three negatives is that none of them are easy to capture in a single word. Yes, pastors are to *stay sober*, *make peace*, and *be generous*, but none of those simple contrasts captures the full range of the desired positive trait like *gentle*.

Among other implications, what it does say for "not violent"— with its simple positive "gentle"—is that Paul assumes that the elders will be strong. They will have power. These are mature Christian men who teach God's word to the church. And they are not alone, acting as isolated individuals in the church, but they *consolidate male power* in the plurality of the council. The question will not be whether such elders have strength, but whether they can be trusted with it. Have they shown, individually and as a team, that they know how to use this strength to help others, not harm them, and that their hearts are set on helping the flock, not taking advantage of it? We want such men as pastors who know and have demonstrated how to channel God's good gift of strength with appropriate restraint and self-control. As individuals and as a team, they must be gentle.

It's clear from elsewhere in the Pastoral Epistles that Paul sees *gentleness* as critical, not optional, in Christian leadership. "As for you, O man of God, . . . pursue . . . gentleness" (1 Tim. 6:11).

True gentleness in the pastors not only gives life to the flock but also models for the flock how it can give life to the world: "Remind them to be submissive to rulers and authorities, . . . *to be gentle*, and to show perfect courtesy toward all people" (Titus 3:1–2). And perhaps most significant of all for leaders: "The Lord's servant must not be quarrelsome but kind to everyone, able to teach, patiently enduring evil, *correcting his opponents with gentleness*" (2 Tim. 2:24–25).[2] Even the correcting of opponents, which we might assume, if anything, could be undertaken fiercely—perhaps even violently—is to be done with gentleness.

Gentleness Himself

In the end, whether as congregants or pastors, whether as men or as women, husbands or wives, fathers or mothers, bosses or employees, genuine biblical gentleness is formed and filled by God himself in Christ. When we admire his gentleness—and he is its paragon—we do not celebrate that he is weak. Rather, as his feeble sheep, we enjoy that not only is our Shepherd infinitely strong, but he is *all the more admirable* because he knows how to wield his power in ways that give life to, rather than suffocate, his beloved.

Our Lord is not like Lennie. Mighty and meek, Christ came not as a domineering and abusive king but as a *good and gentle* Lord. He descended gently into our world in Bethlehem, almost without notice, grew in wisdom and stature in Nazareth, taught with toughness and tenderness in Galilee, and rode into Jerusalem "humble, and mounted on a donkey" (Matt. 21:5) to lay down his own life for us. "When he was reviled, he did not revile in return; when he suffered, he did not threaten, but continued entrusting

---

2 More on this vital text to come in the next chapter (14) on pastors not being quarrelsome.

himself to him who judges justly" (1 Pet. 2:23). Not because he was weak or powerless—he could have come down from the cross or called twelve legions of angels—but because he was powerful enough to be Gentleness himself.

And he invites us still today with the beloved disclosure that takes nothing from his power but adds to it and what makes him so remarkable: "I am gentle and lowly in heart." So, we, like the apostle Paul, both receive and seek to imitate "the meekness and gentleness of Christ" (2 Cor. 10:1), which doesn't take anything away from being strong, but requires it.

In his strength, Christ has freed us from the need to flex, and he commissions us to let our gentleness be known to all (Phil. 4:5). He gives his undershepherds power and strength for serving the flock, not subjugating it. He gives his people influence and authority to steward without being protective of it or becoming jealous when he gives more power to others.

Whatever influence we have, in the church and in the world, is not ours by right but on divine loan to use for his great purposes—with gentleness.

Admire His Mercy—and Might

The day is coming when the wicked would far rather quietly pass out of existence than stand before the omnipotent Christ whom they have scorned and rejected. His sheer power and sovereign strength will terrify them. But not so for his people. We will delight in his strength. We will admire his power.

We will glory that he has made us his own and wields all authority in heaven and on earth for our deep and enduring joy and will lavish it on us forever in the life-giving proportions of true gentleness.

14

How Do Pastors Pick Their Fights?

. . . not quarrelsome.

1 TIMOTHY 3:3; 2 TIMOTHY 2:24

NOT A BRAWLER. The four-hundred-year-old King James Version (KJV) translates 1 Timothy 3:3 with surprising timelessness. Of the full list of fifteen, this qualification for pastor-elder is one of just four negative traits. Modern translations say "not quarrelsome" (ESV and NIV) or "not pugnacious" (NASB), but the language of the KJV has endured. We still know what a brawler is, and it doesn't take much foresight to recognize what a problem it would be to have one as a pastor. Or, God forbid, a whole team of brawlers.

However, a nuance that "not a brawler" may lack is distinguishing between the physical and verbal dimensions of combat. This is the upside of "not quarrelsome." In 1 Timothy 3, the physical, if there were any question, has been covered already: "not violent but gentle" ("no striker," KJV). What's left is the temperamental, and especially verbal.

We all know by the war within us how the flesh of man finds itself at odds with the Spirit of God. By nature we are prone to quarrel when we should make peace, and not ruffle feathers when we should speak up. And in a day in which so many are prone to sharpness online and cowardice face to face, we need leaders who are "not quarrelsome" and at the same time have the courage to "reprove, rebuke, and exhort, with complete patience and teaching" (2 Tim. 4:2). We need men who "contend for the faith" (Jude 3) without being contentious. We need pastors who are *not brawlers*—and yet know when (and how) to say the needful hard word.

We need men who know how to disagree without creating unnecessary division. We need pastors and elders with sober minds and enough self-control to avoid needless controversies, and with enough conviction and courage to move gently and steadily toward conflicts that await wise, patient leadership.

Men Who Make Peace

The flip side of the negative "not quarrelsome" would be the positive *peaceable*. Titus 3:2 is the only other New Testament use of the word we translate "not quarrelsome" (*amachon*): "Remind [Christians] . . . to speak evil of no one, *to avoid quarreling*, to be gentle, and to show perfect courtesy toward all people" (Titus 3:1–2). James 3, which warns, "Not many of you should become teachers, my brothers, for you know that we who teach will be judged with greater strictness" (James 3:1), also directs us to "the wisdom from above," which is bookended by peace:

> The wisdom from above is first pure, then *peaceable*, gentle, open to reason, full of mercy and good fruits, impartial and sincere.

And a harvest of righteousness is *sown in peace by those who make peace.* (James 3:17–18)[1]

Healthy pastors are peacemakers at heart, not pugilists. They don't fight for sport; they fight to secure and defend true peace. They are not wolf hunters but competent defenders of the flock. They know first and foremost—as Christ's representatives to their people—that our God is "the God of peace" (Rom. 15:33); our message, "the gospel of peace" (Eph. 6:15); our Lord Jesus himself made peace (Eph. 2:15; Col. 1:20) and "is our peace" (Eph. 2:14), preaching "peace to you who were far off and peace to those who were near" (Eph. 2:17). Christian leaders want real peace—enough to not avoid the necessary conflict that may be required to secure it.

Making peace is not unique to Christian leaders. Rather, we insist on it in our leaders so that they model and encourage peace-making for the whole church. "Blessed are the peacemakers," said our Lord, "for they shall be called sons of God" (Matt. 5:9). "Let us pursue what makes for peace" (Rom. 14:19). "Strive for peace with everyone" (Heb. 12:14). "If possible, so far as it depends on you"—*all of you* who are members of the body of Christ—"live peaceably with all" (Rom. 12:18).

This kind of peacemaking means not only leading our flocks in preserving and enjoying peace but also in making the peace that requires confrontation. Some controversies cannot be avoided—and we engage not because we simply want to fight and win, but because we want to win those being deceived and protect the flock

---

[1] If you are looking for a passage of Scripture to guide your regular prayers for your pastors, these would be wonderful virtues to pray for. I have tried to capture James 3:17 as a guide for "Seven Ways to Pray for Your Leaders," Desiring God, January 27, 2016, https://www.desiringgod.org/.

from their deception. God means for leaders in his church to have the kind of spiritual magnanimity to rise above the allure of petty disputes and to press valiantly for peace and Christ-exalting harmony in places angels might fear to tread.

What Brawlers Fail to Do

Paul's letters to Timothy and Titus are particularly helpful in this regard, as the veteran apostle gives his counsel to younger leaders in the thick of church conflict. Perhaps no single passage is more perceptive for leaders in times of conflict than 2 Timothy 2:24–26. More than any other, this charge expands what it means for pastors to be peaceable and "not quarrelsome." Alongside 1 Peter 5:1–5, 1 Timothy 3:1–7, and Titus 1:5–9, I would put this text as one of the most important words in all the Bible for church leaders:

> The Lord's servant must not be quarrelsome but kind to everyone, able to teach, patiently enduring evil, correcting his opponents with gentleness. God may perhaps grant them repentance leading to a knowledge of the truth, and they may come to their senses and escape from the snare of the devil, after being captured by him to do his will.

Paul fleshes out the negative "not quarrelsome" with four great, positive charges.[2] First is "kind to everyone." The presence of conflict does not excuse a lack of kindness. How pastors carry themselves in conflict is as important as engaging the right battles. And the Lord calls his servants not to be kind just to the sheep while treating potential wolves like trash, but to be "kind to ev-

2   Bill Mounce, *Pastoral Epistles*, Word Biblical Commentary (Nashville, TN: Thomas Nelson, 2000), 535.

eryone"—both to the faithful and to those who at present seem to be opponents.

Then comes "able to teach," which, as we've seen, includes both ability and inclination (1 Tim. 3:2), and is the main trait that distinguishes pastor-elders (1 Tim. 3:1–7) from deacons (1 Tim. 3:8–13). In the previous verse (2 Tim. 2:23), Paul refers to "foolish, *ignorant* [*apaideutos*] controversies"—literally, "untaught" or "uneducated." How many conflicts in the church begin in, or are fueled by, honest ignorance, and need pastors to come in, with kindness (not with guns blazing), to provide sober-minded clarity and instruction from God's word? The people need patient teaching on the topic. In the New Testament, pastors are fundamentally teachers, and Christ, the great teacher, doesn't mean for his undershepherds to put aside their primary calling when conflict arises. Conflict is the time when humble, careful, Bible-saturated teaching can be needed most.

Next is "patiently enduring evil." Rarely do serious conflicts resolve as quickly as we would like. And whether some genuine evil is afoot or just an honest difference of opinions, good pastors lead the way in patience. That doesn't mean resigning themselves to inaction, or letting conflict carry on needlessly without attention and modest next steps, but patiently walking the path of a process—not standing still and not bull-rushing the issue, but faithfully and patiently approaching the conflict one step at a time. The pastors should be the most patient and least passive men in the church—and therefore the most able to deal with conflict and make genuine peace.

Our Great Hope in Conflict

The fourth and final charge from 2 Timothy 2 is "correcting his opponents with gentleness" (v. 25). In commending kindness, teaching, and patience, Paul doesn't leave aside correction. God calls pastors to rightly handle his word (2 Tim. 2:15), which is profitable not only for teaching but for correction (2 Tim. 3:16). The goal is, first, protection of the flock from error and then restoration of those in error "in a spirit of gentleness" (Gal. 6:1).

The pastor's heart for peace, not mere polemics, comes out in the kind of soul that endures in needful conflict: we pray that "God may perhaps grant them repentance" (2 Tim. 2:25). We long for restoration, not revenge (Rom. 12:19). We pray first for repentance, not retribution.

And we remember that the real war is not against flesh and blood—especially within the household of faith. Our final enemy is Satan, not our human "opponents." We want them to come to repentance—to "come to their senses and escape from the snare of the devil" (2 Tim. 2:26)—through kindness, humble teaching, patience, and gentle correction—remembering that "we do not wrestle against flesh and blood, but against the rulers, against the authorities, against the cosmic powers over this present darkness, against the spiritual forces of evil in the heavenly places" (Eph. 6:12). We do not first want to be rid of our opponents but to win them back from Satan's sway.

Hardest on Themselves

How, then, do pastors pick their battles? What foolish controversies do they wisely avoid, and what conflicts require their courage to address kindly, patiently, and gently with humble teaching?

First, as we have noted again and again in this book, pastors do not work solo in the New Testament. Christ not only put teachers in charge of his churches, but a plurality of teachers. And he intends for countless prudential issues in pastoral work to be worked out in the context of a team of sober-minded, self-controlled, self-sacrificial leaders who check one another's blind spots and shore up each other's weaknesses. Together, such men learn over time to be hardest on themselves, not their flock.

The heart of Christian leadership is not taking up privileges, but laying them down; not gravitating toward the easy work, but gladly crucifying personal comfort and ease to do the hard work to serve others; not domineering over those in their charge, but being examples of Christlike self-sacrifice for them (1 Pet. 5:3). A pastor learns to contend well, without being contentious, "by seriously applying the word of God to himself before he applies it to others."[3] When trying to discern between *silly controversies to avoid* and *conflicts to engage with courage*, pastors might ask:

- Is this conflict about me—my ego, my preferences, my threatened illusion of control—or about my Lord, his gospel, and his church? In other words, is this for my glory or Christ's? Am I remembering that my greatest enemy is not others, or even Satan, but my own indwelling sin?

- What is the overall tenor of my ministry, and our shared ministry as a team? Is it one fight after another? Are there seasons of peace? Do I appreciate peace, or does it strangely make me nervous and send me looking for the next fight? Do I need conflict because I crave attention and drama? Is securing and then preserving Christian peace clearly my goal?

- Am I going with or against my flesh, which inclines me to fight when I shouldn't and back down when I should kindly,

3   Tom Ascol, "Elders Are Not Quarrelsome," *Tabletalk* magazine, November 2018, https://tabletalkmagazine.com/.

patiently, gently engage? As the servant of the Lord, not self, am I avoiding petty causes that an unholy part of me wants to pursue, while taking on the difficult, painful, righteous, and costly causes that an unholy part of me wants to flee?

- Am I simply angry at my opponents, desiring to show them up or expose them, or am I compassionate for them, genuinely praying that God would free them from deception and grant them repentance? Am I inclined to anger against them? Are tears for them even a possibility?

God means for his ministers, together, by his Spirit, to strike the balance, dynamic as it can be. They can learn to avoid foolish controversies and move wisely toward genuine conflicts. They can be unafraid of disagreements while not creating divisions. In a world of haters, trolls, and brawlers, pastors are to be men, set apart by Christ to lead his church, who fight well, in love, for peace.

———

Conflict: Opportunity for Grace

Of course, not all who aspire to be pastor-elders are bent toward pugnacity. Far and away more, it seems to me, both pastors and Christians are not drawn to conflict but would much rather avoid it. Likely you know the feeling. The sour taste in your mouth. The heavy feeling in your heart. That unpleasant aura of conflict that everything in you wants to avoid.

It's so much easier to talk about niceties and comment on the weather and the playoffs than to embrace the awkward moment and actually address the elephant in the room.

We can be painfully quick to believe the lie that if we just avoid the conflict, or at least minimize it, then it will diminish over time and eventually go away. But wisdom speaks a different word. Sure, we can forebear some offenses and get over some personal frustrations, but rooted interpersonal conflict doesn't go away with inattention. It festers. It deepens. And it comes back with a vengeance.

Conflict Is Inevitable

Relational conflict among us should not surprise us as Christians. We need not be ashamed that it exists and that we're involved. We should expect it. The world is complicated and fallen, and we are complex creatures and fallen. Conflicts will come. They are unavoidable. In fact, the lack of any conflict over extended periods of time may speak more to unhealthy avoidance in us than admirable peaceability.

Yes, conflict is inevitable in the church as well. Christians often have conflict with each other—true, genuine, faithful Christians. The question is not whether conflicts will come but how we will handle them.

In healthy churches, the leadership doesn't announce, "There are no conflicts here; nor will there be." Rather, the refrain will be that conflicts arise, and when they do, we won't run from them. We won't neglect to address them head on, with proper patience and gentleness. We can't afford to leave them alone. We have a God and gospel big enough even for this.

Occasion for Grace

One reason that avoiding conflict is such a problem is precisely that it worsens with negligence. It doesn't just go away. But another reason is that it cuts us off from the most significant opportunities for grace. This is the way God often does his deepest work in a world like ours. It's not when things are peachy keen, fine and dandy, when all seems right with the world. Rather, it's in the toughest times, the hardest conversations, the most painful relational tensions that the light of his grace shines brightest and transforms us most profoundly into his Son's likeness.

The high points of the history of God's people are accounts not of fleeing conflict but moving toward it in hope, believing God will be at work in the tension, pain, and mess. Such is the story of the prophets—Moses with the stubborn people he refused to abandon; Elijah at Carmel squaring off against the prophets of Baal; the embattled Isaiah, Jeremiah, and Ezekiel brought into increasing conflict, seemingly at every oracle, with a hard-hearted people they had been commissioned to serve.

So it was with the apostles. When tensions emerged in the fledgling church between Hebrews and Greeks, they dealt with disunity quickly and did not let it fester. God had a gift to give these young believers in Acts 6—seven newly appointed formal leaders to serve the people's needs—and it came not through shying away from conflict but through straightforwardly tackling their troubles. And when conflict arose again along the same fault lines, this time over circumcision, the apostle Paul didn't avoid or neglect it but wrote letters and traveled to Jerusalem to address it in person (Acts 15:2).

For Gospel Advance

When Peter's lapse in judgment at Antioch led him to choose separation from Gentile believers, "fearing the circumcision party" in Jerusalem (Gal. 2:12), again Paul moved toward the conflict, not away. "I opposed him to his face," he writes (Gal. 2:11), and with it, Peter and the gospel witness in Antioch were restored.

The life of Paul, we might say, could have seemed to be a series of one unchosen conflict after another—each one a catalyst for the ongoing progress of grace. He wrote to the Philippians about "the same conflict that you saw I had and now hear that I still have" (Phil. 1:30)—a conflict, which he says, "really served to advance the gospel" (Phil. 1:12).

He recounted to the Thessalonians how not cowering from conflict was essential to the gospel coming to them. "Though we had already suffered and been shamefully treated at Philippi, as you know, we had boldness in our God to declare to you the gospel of God in the midst of much conflict" (1 Thess. 2:2). His thirteen letters stand as a tribute to the fact that he wasn't afraid to address emerging conflict and to do so with grace, and see what good God had in store for his people precisely because of it.

Pattern of Christ

Of course, our most compelling emblem of not shying away from conflict but turning to take it head on is the founder and perfecter of our faith, who for the joy that was set before him endured the cross (Heb. 12:2).

The trajectory of Jesus's life was toward need and inevitably toward conflict, not flight. He set his face like flint to go to Jerusalem, to the great conflict at Calvary, to rescue us from our greatest conflict, eternal separation from God because of the rebellion of our sin against him.

Being saved by him, we Christians—which means, literally, "little christs"—learn increasingly to follow in his steps, empowered by his Spirit, to move toward conflict, toward need, toward pain, toward tension, looking past the imposing awkwardness and difficulty that lies before us to the promise of joy on the other side.

Lord's Servant in Conflict

The examples of Paul and Jesus turning deliberately to address conflict rather than run from it don't lead pastors, as we've seen, to become bull-headed and pugnacious and to develop a penchant for a good fight. Rather, their gospel-thickened skin frees them to lean in—with kindness, patience, gentleness, and a teacher's heart—to the cauldrons of conflict that would otherwise send them fleeing.

As we consider that difficult and threatening conversation that needs to happen—to gently remove the speck from our brother's eye, to address the elephant in the room—we acknowledge our weakness. In our own strength and ability, we will be unable to address conflict with both intentionality and kindness. But we couple this admission with a prayer for the strength of Christ himself, made available to us by his Spirit. And we move forward in faith, knowing that if tribulation, distress, persecution, famine, nakedness, peril, and sword cannot separate us from the love of Christ (Rom. 8:35), then neither can our relational clashes. No matter how tense. No matter how intimidating.

For the Christian, and church leaders all the more, conflict is not something to avoid or ignore. It is an opportunity for the triumph of grace.

15

Why Christians Care
What Outsiders Think

He must be well thought of by outsiders, so that he
may not fall into disgrace, into a snare of the devil.

I TIMOTHY 3:7

IT MAY BE the most unexpected of the qualifications for teaching office in the church. Yes, pastor-elders must be able to teach. Not a drunkard? Of course. But well thought of by outsiders? Hold on. Do outsiders have a say about who leads in the church?

Of the fifteen qualifications for pastoral office in 1 Timothy 3:1–7, Paul may have saved the most surprising for last. As we've seen, the first twelve focus mainly on character and multifaceted Christian maturity, with almost no explanation (and no real surprises). He slows down, however, and gives more context for the final three. "Manage his own household well" in verse 4 gets an explanation ("for") in verse 5. Verse 6 explains "not a recent convert" in terms of not becoming "puffed up with conceit." And the last qualification comes with its "so that" in verse 7: "He must be well thought of by outsiders, so that he may not fall into disgrace, into a snare of the devil."

Well thought of by outsiders—how many of us would have seen this coming? Some might have even assumed the opposite, that *the collective disdain of outsiders* would be a badge of Christian honor and show what a great weapon a man must be for Christ's kingdom.

They Crucified Christ

Doubtless there is a place for a holy disregard for what unbelievers think. After all, we shouldn't be caught off guard when they "suppress the truth" of God as Creator and sustainer (Rom. 1:18), as speaker (in the Scriptures), and as Redeemer (in the gospel). We need not be bewildered when the world acts and responds like the world.

Is it not the words of Christ himself that best prepare us to not be "well thought of" by outsiders? "Blessed are you when others revile you and persecute you and utter all kinds of evil against you falsely on my account" (Matt. 5:11). "No prophet is acceptable in his hometown" (Luke 4:24). "If they have called the master of the house Beelzebul, how much more will they malign those of his household" (Matt. 10:25). "Woe to you, when all people speak well of you" (Luke 6:26). The world crucified Jesus. Outsiders martyred the apostles, one after another. Surely we should take very little stock in what outsiders think, especially in what they think of those who declare the truth of Christ as central to their calling.

Yet here, as the final qualification for the church's lead office, we hear that pastor-elders must be well thought of by outsiders.

Try to Please Everyone?

In Christ we have good reason not to be shaken by every opinion of outsiders. But we also must beware of letting one biblical truth masquerade as the whole.

For some temperaments, it may be easy to settle into an unholy, careless lack of concern about what outsiders think, but the Scriptures say more than simply turn a deaf ear to outside opposition or hostility. Those of us who are surprised by the final qualification also may stumble over just how much the New Testament has to say about having a genuine (though not ultimate) concern for what unbelievers think.

We may champion Paul for his courageous, in-your-face declarations like Galatians 1:10: "Am I now seeking the approval of man, or of God? Or am I trying to please man? If I were still trying to please man, I would not be a servant of Christ." And 1 Thessalonians 2:4: "We speak, not to please man, but to please God who tests our hearts." Yet this same apostle also writes, in 1 Corinthians 10:33, "I try to please everyone in everything I do." That is a sweeping statement. I try to please *everyone* in *everything*. If a pastor today made such a statement, how quickly might self-appointed guardians of biblical fidelity be all over him?

So, which is it? Do pastor-elders seek to please men or not? Do they care about human approval or not? And, more specifically, how are pastor-elders to relate to those outside the church?

Associate with Outsiders

Of the apostolic voices, Paul has the most to say about outsiders. His first mention of outsiders, in 1 Corinthians 5:9, clarifies that his previous instructions "not to associate with sexually immoral people" did not mean the immoral of the world but the immoral in the church (1 Cor. 5:10). His point was not to separate from outsiders but from the one "who bears the name of brother" while remaining in unrepentant sin (1 Cor. 5:11).

> What have I to do with judging outsiders? Is it not those inside the church whom you are to judge? God judges those outside. "Purge the evil person from among you." (1 Cor. 5:12–13)

To be true to the church and the world, we judge within the church on clear sin issues (all the while not judging each other on issues of preference, Rom. 14:3–4, 10, 13). But as the apostle lays that burden on us, he lifts another: "God judges those outside." We are liberated from the need to judge "the sexually immoral of this world, or the greedy and swindlers, or idolaters" (1 Cor. 5:10). Rather, we happily associate with outsiders and seek to be means of their redemption by exposing them to the gospel of Christ and its counterintuitive fruit in our lives.

Be Aware of Outsiders

Paul prominently reckons with outsiders again in 1 Corinthians 14. This time the context is corporate worship, and far from ignoring outsiders or planning in such a way as to turn them off, Paul wants to engage them. To win them. To be clear, he does not instruct the church to orient its worship *to* outsiders but to keep them in mind, albeit secondarily, when considering the intelligibility of the corporate gathering.

Rather than the indecipherable terms of tongue speaking, Paul would have the church speak prophetically in its public gatherings in words understandable and clear to all: "How can anyone in the position of an outsider say 'Amen' to your thanksgiving when he does not know what you are saying?" (1 Cor. 14:16). His hope is evangelistic:

> If . . . the whole church comes together and all speak in tongues, and outsiders or unbelievers enter, will they not say that you are out of your minds? But if all prophesy, and an unbeliever or outsider enters, he is convicted by all, he is called to account by all, the secrets of his heart are disclosed, and so, falling on his face, he will worship God and declare that God is really among you. (1 Cor. 14:23–25)

Be Alert to Outsiders

Beyond 1 Corinthians, we find Paul's healthy concern for the gospel's reputation in the Pastoral Epistles. Whether it's the conduct of widows (1 Tim. 5:14), slaves (1 Tim. 6:1; Titus 2:10), or young women (Titus 2:5), Paul would have us seek "in everything [to] adorn the doctrine of God our Savior" (Titus 2:10) and not bring any warranted reviling on the name, teaching, and word of God (1 Tim. 6:1; Titus 2:5). He would have us be concerned "to show perfect courtesy toward all people" (Titus 3:2) and care that our good works "are excellent and profitable for people" (Titus 3:8).

It matters to the apostle and to Christ that we "walk properly before outsiders" (1 Thess. 4:12), and it should matter to us. Christ expects his church, in the power of his Spirit, to "walk in wisdom toward outsiders, making the best use of the time. Let your speech always be gracious, seasoned with salt, so that you may know how you ought to answer each person" (Col. 4:5–6).

As we give an answer and provide a defense to anyone who asks the reason for the hope that is in us, Peter adds his voice to the concern with outsiders: "Do it with gentleness and respect, having a good conscience, so that, when you are slandered, those who revile your good behavior in Christ may be put to shame" (1 Pet. 3:15–16). Our apologetic is not only carefully chosen words with a kind demeanor but a life that benefits others, even outsiders. "This is the will of God, that by doing good you should put to silence the ignorance of foolish people" (1 Pet. 2:15).

Ask about Outsiders

Now we need to come back to Paul's own explanation of the qualification. Surprising as it may seem, this concern for outsiders actually makes for a fitting final requirement for elders, as it echoes (and extends) the first and overarching qualification: "above reproach." At the outset of the list, the accent was on the eyes of the church, but now we see a man's reputation matters beyond the church as well.

Paul's own explanation for including "well thought of by outsiders" is this: "so that he may not fall into disgrace, into a snare of the devil" (1 Tim. 3:7). The concern is with "disgrace" (or "reproach," Greek *oneidismos*). Surely, not all disgrace. But unnecessary disgrace. Unrighteous reproach. Disgrace from outsiders that is deserved because of sinful attitudes or actions present in the church's leaders. In one sense, of course, every Christian represents Christ, and yet the stakes rise when the church formally recognizes some as officers. They are "official," with a title, and accordingly their public failures do even greater harm to the name of Christ and his church.

Such disgrace, then, is "a snare of the devil"—a trap he loves to lay to sink the faith of some in the church and solidify the world in its unbelief. The church is right where Satan wants it when its leaders are disgraced among outsiders. Why? Because the devil wants to keep outsiders from the gospel. He wants outsiders to remain just that, outside the church, and in his clutches. He loves when Christian leaders, of all people, give outsiders just cause for disgust. And he loves to use modern media to magnify it.

It's one thing to be a fool for Jesus but quite another to be foolish just as much on heaven's terms as the world's. So we ask about outsiders when we consider candidates for office: What do outsiders think, and why?

Audience of More?

While we ought to care and investigate what outsiders think about our church and its pastors, Jesus is clear that we do not serve two masters. We have one Lord. First and foremost, we please Christ, not man. Our first and final allegiance is to him, our God. And yet, as we have seen, Christ is not our only audience. He is ultimate but not only. We also seek to please others when doing so is not at odds with pleasing our Lord. We pray our lives can do both. We aim to please God and also men besides.

Life in a fallen world, of course, is not always so easy. At times, and maybe increasingly in the days ahead (as in the times of the early church), pleasing God and pleasing man will be at odds. And when we come to such junctures, Christians say, with Peter and the apostles, "We must obey God rather than men" (Acts 5:29). As for our first and final allegiance, we say with Paul, "We speak, not to please man, but to please God" (1 Thess. 2:4).

Why Care about Outsiders

To be clear, the world does not choose the church's leaders. The thoughts and opinions of outsiders are not ultimate. But they do matter. We shouldn't ignore them, or presume disgrace to be a mark of faithfulness. To the question, "Should we care what outsiders think?" the biblical answer is just as much yes (if not more so) as it is no. But most significant is why: that they may be saved. We want both to keep believing sheep in and to win more from the outside, as Paul did:

> To those outside the law I became as one outside the law (not being outside the law of God but under the law of Christ) that I might win those outside the law. . . . I have become all things to all people, that by all means I might save some. (1 Cor. 9:21–22)

> Give no offense to Jews or to Greeks or to the church of God, just as I try to please everyone in everything I do, not seeking my own advantage, but that of many, that they may be saved. (1 Cor. 10:32–33)

In the end, outsiders matter to us because they matter to Christ. He has other sheep, he says, to bring in (John 10:16). He delights to make outsiders into friends and brothers as he has done with us. And we hope and pray that he has many more in our cities who are his (Acts 18:10).

Outsiders matter to us because such were all of us. But we have been brought in. And good pastors know, firsthand, that Christ loves to make us frail, former outsiders his means for bringing in more, and for leading his church with such hearts and dreams and prayers.

Commission

Christian Leadership versus Modern Celebrity

Now I commend you to God and to the word of his grace, which is able to build you up and to give you the inheritance among all those who are sanctified.

ACTS 20:32

WE ARE LIVING in a society increasingly more fit to create celebrities than develop real leaders. And it is, of course, much easier to do the former than the latter.

Another way to say it is that we are prone to create faux leaders rather than true leaders. *Celebrities*, at least the way I'm using the term here, are people who garner mass attention as objects of our interest and entertainment but do not serve in significant measure to lead, guide, or help our lives for the better. To put it in stark terms, we might say that:

- Celebrities make headlines. Leaders make sacrifices and hard decisions.
- Celebrities get rich. Leaders enrich the lives of others.

- Celebrities receive inordinate attention from those who follow them. Leaders are eager to give their attention to those whom they lead.
- Celebrities are in it for their own benefit. Leaders are in it for the benefit of others.
- Celebrities angle for the spotlight. Leaders spotlight the good in others and in some great, worthy cause.

Just because someone has many followers—whether it's album or book sales, concert attendance, downloads, social media metrics—does not mean he is truly a leader.

And as we have seen in these pages, when we come to the Bible, we find a world of difference between the substance of true leadership and the emptiness of twenty-first-century celebrity. Yet even in the church, it's easy for us to be confused about the differences.

Emotional Farewell

As we say farewell here at the end of this book, let's do so with the apostle Paul and the way he said farewell in Acts 20 to the elders of the Ephesian church. This passage pulls back the curtain on the nature of true leadership. Here we see one of the greatest leaders in the history of the world in one of the most solemn and emotional moments in the story of the early church.

Paul gathers the leaders from the young church in one of the world's leading cities. He had spent three years with them; now, like Jesus, he is headed to Jerusalem and anticipating that trouble awaits him there—like his Lord, he may be walking into the very jaws of the lion in coming to the ancient city that killed its prophets.

En route, Paul summons the leaders from the Ephesian church to meet him on the beach at Miletus. Ephesus is inland, about thirty miles from the port city of Miletus. There Paul meets them and gives what is essentially his last will and testament for them. It is the only major speech in Acts addressed to Christians, which makes it more like his letters than his other speeches in Acts.

Five Differences between *Celebrity* and *Leader*

As we come to this scene now, some two millennia later, it is remarkable to see the leadership on display in the instruction and life of the apostle Paul and how such a vision contrasts with the prevailing notions in our world today.

Our faux leaders today—our mere celebrities—are typically the rich and famous who are mainly receivers, not givers. Typically they are not really one of us, but a cut above the masses in looks, smarts, skills, and access. They are not commoners but pursued by their own paparazzi of whatever sort. They are often at great pains not to offend—at least not to offend a certain group of people, the social elites and the scrupulously politically correct. They have learned to tell their followers what they want to hear. They typically are in it for personal benefit and advantage, not ready to endure for a great cause whatever the cost. And some are even ready to have as much control of our lives as we'll give them—ready to tell us exactly what to do and how to live—because they are so manifestly successful that we should do what they've done.

But the biblical portrait and the life and teaching of the apostle Paul provide a very different paradigm for leadership. In God's common grace, we find some points of overlap but also many stark contrasts. And Acts 20 helps illumine for us at least five that we should take note of and make sure are part of our framework for true leadership in the church and in our families and other spheres. We want our understanding and practice of leadership to be Christian, from the Scriptures, not imbibed from the world around us.

Let's look, then, as we conclude, at five ways that true Christian leaders are different from today's mere celebrities.

1. Christian Leaders Live among the People

> You yourselves know how I lived among you the whole time from the first day that I set foot in Asia, serving the Lord with all humility and with tears and with trials that happened to me through the plots of the Jews. (Acts 20:18–19)

"Living among the people" is not only about accessibility and not being removed from the commoners but about identity. Christian leaders identify with their people—not *above* them but *with* them. They know deep down that they are first and foremost sheep and secondarily shepherds. Jesus is the great shepherd; they serve him ("serving the Lord," verse 19) as undershepherds, but there is no fundamental difference between church leaders and the congregation.

As such an influential teacher and apostle, Paul could have lived a cut above the people. He could have claimed special privilege, kept largely to his generous accommodations, and descended on occasion to deliver his words of wisdom to the rank and file. Yet Paul "lived among" them from the first day, and his whole time in Ephesus. He was one of them. He never removed himself from the people but identified with them—"with all humility and with tears."

So it is with true leaders today. While celebrities distinguish themselves from the masses with privileges and amenities, fences and security, Christian leaders live among the people. They know they are first and foremost sheep. Their basic identity is being sheep of the good shepherd, not in being his undershepherds. Their greater joy is not in being leaders, but in being saved. They are more excited about Jesus's ministry than their own, which relates to what we see in Acts 20.

Paul is speaking to the leaders of the Ephesian church, and yet it is here in the Bible for all Christians to read and know. Christian leadership is not a moose lodge with clandestine initiation rights and top-secret information. All the essential information is public and out in the open. Here in Acts 20, for all to see, is the emotional final message Paul gave the Ephesians elders. And the Pastoral Epistles were addressed to Paul's protégés Timothy and Titus, but crafted for the whole church at Ephesus and Crete and beyond to hear. That's because there is no fundamental difference between the official leader and the rest of the congregation.

In some sense, all Christians are called to become teachers, as Hebrews grieves: "By this time you ought to be teachers" (Heb. 5:12). That's why Acts 20 is relevant for the whole church, not just formal officers. Yes, we do make a place for remembering our leaders (Heb. 13:7) and respecting and esteeming them (1 Thess. 5:12) and doing what we can, within reason, to let them lead with joy (Heb. 13:17). But we don't give them a pass on normal, human, Christian accountability. We hold them to the fire as one of us, as sheep, and no less.

This relates to one thing we should note briefly here in Acts 20:28, which says: "Pay careful attention to yourselves and to all the flock, in which the Holy Spirit has made you overseers, to care for the church of God, which he obtained with his own blood." Leaders must pay careful attention *to themselves*. They themselves are sinners and must first and foremost pay attention to their own indwelling sin and proneness to wander.

So Christian leaders are not removed from the flock or treated as a cut above the rest or given fundamentally different treatment, but rather they live among the people as, first and foremost, members of the flock.

2. Christian Leaders Tell the Whole Truth

Not only are real-life relationships essential (living among the flock), but also intentional in declaring to the flock "anything that [is] profitable," that is, "the whole counsel of God." Paul says:

> I did not shrink from declaring to you anything that was profitable, and teaching you in public and from house to house, testifying both to Jews and to Greeks of repentance toward God and of faith in our Lord Jesus Christ. (Acts 20:20–21)

> I testify to you this day that I am innocent of the blood of all, for I did not shrink from declaring to you the whole counsel of God. (Acts 20:26–27)

Unlike our mere celebrities who calibrate their words to tell their followers what they want to hear, Paul says twice that he "did not shrink from declaring." The first time, he says he did not shrink from declaring "anything that was profitable"; the second, "the whole counsel of God." In other words, Paul unfolded for the people all of God's words, all of God's revelation, his whole counsel, all God has to say to humanity. As Paul says in 2 Timothy 3:16, "All Scripture is breathed out by God and *profitable* for teaching, for reproof, for correction, and for training in righteousness." The "whole counsel" in verse 27 is what is "profitable" in verse 20.

Paul "did not shrink from declaring," because every generation has its pressures to silence some aspects (if not many) of what God has revealed. Every generation tempts us to declare only part of God's counsel:

Yes, yes, tell us all about the love of God, but do not tell us that he has righteous wrath toward those who have rebelled against him, that he has laws we have broken, and that those who don't embrace Jesus as the one shield from his wrath will experience eternal, conscious justice in hell.

Don't talk to us about our sin. Don't talk to us about God being the designer and creator of human sexuality, that he is one who truly knows and reveals the purpose and context for sex, and that he does not affirm all to which we consent and prefer.

Don't tell us he is absolutely sovereign and that his rule and reign and prerogative are deeper and extend further than my seemingly free choices.

Say what you will to build my self-esteem and prop up my sense of autonomy and entitlement, but don't preach to us the whole counsel of what God has revealed about himself and humanity and his world.

Mere celebrities will buckle under this pressure. In fact, they likely buckled long before they became celebrated. They could tell how ears were itching in their age and knew how to tickle them. But true Christian leaders will not buckle. They tell the whole truth, like Paul, and don't shrink from declaring "the whole counsel of

God"—which will not harm people, however much it hurts, but prove eternally profitable.

3. Christian Leaders Are Not Scared Off by Hardship

And now, behold, I am going to Jerusalem, constrained by the Spirit, not knowing what will happen to me there, except that the Holy Spirit testifies to me in every city that imprisonment and afflictions await me. But I do not account my life of any value nor as precious to myself, if only I may finish my course and the ministry that I received from the Lord Jesus, to testify to the gospel of the grace of God. And now, behold, I know that none of you among whom I have gone about proclaiming the kingdom will see my face again. (Acts 20:22–25)

I know that after my departure fierce wolves will come in among you, not sparing the flock; and from among your own selves will arise men speaking twisted things, to draw away the disciples after them. Therefore be alert, remembering that for three years I did not cease night or day to admonish every one with tears. (Acts 20:29–31)

Hear at least two types of hardship in these verses—and they are representative of the many types of hardships leaders will face and must endure:

- hardship for Paul: "Imprisonment and afflictions await me" (v. 23)
- hardship for the Ephesian elders: "Fierce wolves will come in" (v. 29)

Celebrities are in as long as it's personally advantageous. True leaders endure through hardship, whether the affliction of circumstances or the conflict of difficult relationships.

Here again is another place we see the shared fundamental identity of Christian leaders with every believer, as Paul taught every Christian, not just the leaders, in Acts 14:22: "Through many tribulations we must enter the kingdom of God." Christian leaders must not be scared away by affliction and conflict, because these are the precise times when the flock most needs leadership and care. Leaders aren't mainly there for the good days and the easy times. The time the church most needs calm, firm, gracious, sober-minded, courageous, unflinching leadership (like admonishing with tears, Acts 20:31) is when hardship comes. If the shepherds run, who will protect the sheep from wolves—and from themselves?

4. Christian Leaders Trust God and His Gospel

Because God is who he is and the message of the gospel is what it is, Christian leaders are free to be influencers, not controllers. They don't commend themselves and their wisdom to their people, but God and his gospel. They are happy to influence the flock and point them toward God, entrust them to the Holy Spirit, and not have the final control. Like Paul, in Acts 20:32:

> Now I commend you to God and to the word of his grace, which is able to build you up and to give you the inheritance among all those who are sanctified.

What is this "word of his grace"? Paul mentions God's grace in Acts 20:24: "I do not account my life of any value nor as precious to myself, if only I may finish my course and the ministry that I received from the Lord Jesus, to testify to *the gospel of the grace of God.*"

So verse 24 speaks of "the gospel of the grace of God," and now verse 32, "the word of his grace." These are two ways of getting at the same reality. The very message that Paul gives his life to spread is the same message to which he entrusts these Ephesian elders whom he dearly loves and anticipates never seeing again.

At first glance, this might seem like a leadership fail. "C'mon, Paul, can't you do better than this? These are leaders in the church. Don't you have some special word just for leaders? Don't you have some surprising insight or creative charge you can give them?"

But Paul knows that the gospel to which he gives his life is the same gospel that not only brings us into the kingdom but is the very message on which we live every day of our lives and will for all eternity. It is not some new, creative instruction or fresh leadership insight, but it is the gospel that "is able to build you up and to give you the inheritance among all those who are sanctified." Again we see the leader's fundamental identify with the people.

So Paul says farewell to these dearly loved Ephesian elders with whom he invested three years of his life. He will not seek to control them from afar, apostle though he is, but leaves them to the wise hand and Spirit of God. And the message he commends to them is not some new leadership insight or counsel but the very heart of Christianity, that *Jesus saves sinners.* This message gives new life to the lost—and it's what builds up and sustains the found. Paul is no motivational speaker to rally the strong; he is a preacher of good news to the weak. When a church and its leaders are constantly gospel-minded and relentlessly gospel-occupied, that church is not shallow but truly Christian.

5. Christian Leaders Know the Joy of Giving

The leaders' holy pursuit of joy is no mere icing on the cake; this is an essential ingredient in the mixture of what true leadership is. As we have seen and said again and again, Christian leaders are to be workers *with you* for your joy. This is at the very heart of what it means to lead and what it means to be Christian. The best leadership training in the world is Christianity. No other vision of reality and everyday life so transcendently prepares so many diverse people for and sustains them in the true labor of leadership. The ultimate curriculum in leadership is the gospel. Paul says:

> I coveted no one's silver or gold or apparel. You yourselves know that these hands ministered to my necessities and to those who were with me. In all things I have shown you that by working hard in this way we must help the weak and remember the words of the Lord Jesus, how he himself said, "It is more blessed to give than to receive." (Acts 20:33–35)

Christian leadership on the horizontal plane is fundamentally giving, not receiving. Unlike the modern notion of celebrity, it is not about receiving attention and status and money and private benefits; rather, it is fundamentally about giving yourself, your time, your energy—sacrificing your private interests—to find your (greater) interest and joy in the good of others. It's not fleecing the flock for its attention, but paying attention to the flock for its good and protection and health. True Christian leadership is fundamentally self-sacrificial in the pursuit of greater, deeper, longer-lasting joy.

Paul's emotional farewell address on the beach connects to the first half of Acts 20 (vv. 1–16). He is headed to Jerusalem, working hard to bring financial help from the Gentile churches to the weak and needy Jerusalem church. He left Ephesus (v. 1) to swing back to Macedonia and Greece to get the collection. Now he's coming back through and is hurrying to get to Jerusalem by Pentecost, when worshipers en masse will have arrived from out of town.

So Paul's life backs up his words. He is living this reality when he says these essential words for leaders: "Remember the words of the Lord Jesus, how he himself said, 'It is more blessed to give than to receive'" (v. 35).

Knowing this and feeling this deep down—that it truly is better, happier, to give than receive—is essential for leadership in the church. Pastors are workers with you for your joy, who labor best for the true joy of their people when they themselves are joyful in Christ (Heb. 13:17).

Thanks

I did not choose eldership. Fifteen years ago, in my mid-twenties, I could have quickly rattled off a dozen other topics I'd rather teach and write on someday. But such surprises and unexpected turns are typical of Christ's *calling*, are they not? How boring if our lives played out like we planned as naïve collegiates or seminarians! More to the point, Christ's wise plan and call lead us to meet real-life needs, not foist our preferences on the world. Okay, enough for the reprise of chapter 1.

I might then say that eldership chose me—or better, Christ made the appointment, and did it through means. Specifically, this book began with a tangible need at Bethlehem College & Seminary (the eldership class) and an invitation from Tom Steller. I remember well the meeting with Tom in late 2011 or early 2012. Thank you, Tom, for the opportunity and for your trust. It has been a great privilege and joy, since the fall of 2012, to talk eldership—and the countless related topics—with the cohorts of seminarians at Bethlehem. These chapters took shape slowly over the course of a decade with the golden input of one class after another. Thank you, dear brothers, who shared insights, asked hard questions, pushed back on my quirks, and exposed gaps in my thinking and experience.

Doubtless many errors and oversights remain in this text, but I
believe there are far fewer because of your feedback—and I'm sure
even some remain despite your input to the contrary. And thank
you to dean Brian Tabb for keeping me in this spot as long as you
have and to former president Tim Tomlinson and new president
Joe Rigney for letting this happen on your watch.

The book took shape through one eldership class after another,
but the first seeds were sown long before that—first in the instincts
of spiritual leadership I learned from my own father and in my
teen years through Seth Buckley. While a student at Furman University I was personally discipled through the ministry of Campus
Outreach, first by Faamata Fonoimoana and then by Matt Lorish.
Thank you, dear brothers. How can I ever trace the effect of those
deeply formative collegiate years?

Next, thank you, Ken Currie. I came to Minneapolis with
Campus Outreach in the fall of 2003. From then until we planted
Cities Church in the winter of 2015, Ken shaped my vision and
instincts for on-the-ground eldership and pastoral ministry more
than anyone. The frequent references to and prominence of *plurality* in this book are owing to Ken. I saw in him an awareness
and enjoyment of pastoral ministry as teamwork that I found
compelling, consistent with Scripture, and remarkably effective
in the real world. Along with Ken, thank you, Paul Poteat and
Matt Reagan. We labored together in the ministry of Campus
Outreach and then as Bethlehem elders. We watched Ken and
learned it together.

Twelve years at Bethlehem led to the planting of Cities Church,
and that now has been my context for almost eight years. Thank
you to the founding fathers, willing to take a risk with your
own lives and families, to leave one great church with dreams of

multiplication: Michael Thiel, Jonathan Parnell, and Joe Rigney. God has been so kind to us. Now he has added Kevin Kleiman, David Easterwood, Josh Foster, Mike Polley, Ryan Griffith, Kenny Ortiz, and Max Kozak. Brothers, what a team. Thank you for your friendship and for putting up with a brother who was working on a book about what we do. And thank you, people of Cities Church, to whom this book is dedicated. I thank God for your faithfulness and graciousness going on eight years, especially through the pandemic. Your pastors are indeed able to work with you *from joy* for your joy. You have done your part to keep us from groaning and have put wind in our sails.

Simultaneously with Bethlehem and then Cities Church has been the immeasurable influence and encouragement of John Piper, who has been to me pastor, father, teacher, and friend. I quote John a lot in this book. His influence, like Ken's, is hidden, if not conspicuous, on just about every page. And thank you to the teaching and leadership teams at Desiring God. We're not a local church but a parachurch, yet I love how we've found fresh ways to work as a team and benefit from some of the best principles of plurality in leadership.

Thank you, friends and partners for the gospel at Crossway. Each project with you is an increasing honor and joy. And thanks especially to Lydia Brownback, whose editorial skill, expertise, and attention to detail impress not only authors but fellow editors.

Thank you to my dear wife, Megan, and our four kids. I'm writing these thanks on a Saturday morning. You have been so supportive in the book-writing process. You don't begrudge these few evenings and weekends—even as we all prefer when it dovetails nicely into weekdays. You are my joy and the best of daily manifestations of God's mercy and grace.

Finally and most importantly to the Chief Shepherd—thank you, Jesus, Shepherd and Overseer of my soul. Thank you for your smile and broad shoulders, ready to take every burden your undershepherds roll your way in prayer. You indeed are great, as God-man, and greatly to be praised. What unspeakable grace to find our names written in heaven, love your salvation, and say evermore that *you* are great.

Appendix 1

Who Are the Deacons?

THIS BOOK FOCUSES on the lead or teaching office of the church, that of pastor-elder-overseer. With such a focus we can't help but at times refer to the other office instituted in the New Testament, the assisting office, that of deacon. The seven chosen jointly by the apostles and the church in Acts 6 are not called "deacons," but for two millennia Christians have treated these "proto-deacons," as we might call them, as an analog, in relation to the apostles, of what was to come later in relation to elders in local churches.

Even though this book does not focus on deacons, it may prove helpful to give at least a basic sketch in this short appendix of the diaconate. For a longer treatment, I would highly recommend Matt Smethurst's *Deacons*.[1] So who are deacons, and what do they

---

1 Matt Smethurst, *Deacons: How They Serve and Strengthen the Church* (Wheaton, IL: Crossway, 2021). On the question of whether 1 Tim. 3:11 refers to deacon wives or deaconesses, I would recommend Smethurst's fair and helpful summaries of the arguments for and against. It's a difficult question in context. Few admit to much certainty either way. My own view, which is the minority view today (though not in church history)— and not just among evangelicals but on the elder team with which I serve—is that Paul had deacon *wives* in mind in v. 11, not women deacons. Among other reasons, the fact

do? Here's how we've summarized deacons in three statements at Cities Church.

1. Deacons Meet Specific Needs

Deacons are commissioned by the elders (and congregation), and serve under the elders, to meet specific needs in the life of the local church. As the needs and demands of church life increase and change, deacons are commissioned to serve the congregation and work with the elders and make it possible for the elders not to neglect the work of teaching, prayer, and oversight. Deacons are, as Mark Dever says, "fundamentally encouragers and supporters of the ministry of the elders."[2]

The role of deacon is a flexible one in terms of the kind of work to which deacons attend. In church history, deacons have been lead ministers of mercy (as in Acts 6) or financial and property administrators. Yet the functions of deacons are not plainly defined in the New Testament, like the main tasks of the elders (to lead and feed or teach and govern), and we think the reason is that this is meant to be a flexible role that can be designed to meet the needs of the local congregation in its particular context and season of church life.

At Cities Church deacons help the elders with leadership of our midweek community groups (one of our main priorities) and

---

that "deacon" is an office implies some measure of ecclesial authority, which the early church would have restricted to men. However, the most important issue in my view is that we get the complementarian dynamics right. If we appoint deaconesses as leaders of ministries that do not require them to exercise church authority over men, it is a very different discussion than if *deacons* serve as de facto elders, as in some churches. I suspect that New Testament deacons, as official title-carrying assistants to the elders, exercised a measure of authority that made it fitting for them to be men yet engaged in the kind of practical ministry work where their wives were often at their sides, thus prompting Paul to provide four brief qualifications here for deacon wives.

2   Mark Dever, "A Display of God's Glory," Nine Marks, accessed March 30, 2022, https://9marks.org.

preparation and execution of various aspects related to corporate worship and children's ministries, and they contribute to the overall unity and flourishing of the flock by meeting various needs in the life of the church (like attending to finances).

2. Deacons Represent the Church

It is no small thing to be assigned a title in the church. By being formally recognized and commissioned by the elders and the congregation, deacons represent the church both to the church family and to outsiders. This is one reason why, in many churches, the elders don't simply appoint deacons on their own but come to the congregation for formal affirmation. Our hope is that conferring an official title on the deacon is not mainly for the sake of personal honor and encouragement but to help him in executing his role.

At Cities Church each deacon is assigned to a particular pastor-elder who oversees and guides the diaconal work and is the point of affirmation and accountability. One of the ways in which deacons are held accountable for their work is by holding title and office, which can be removed for discipline.

3. Deacons Are Spiritual

Deacons are to be spiritual. In other words, they must genuinely meet the qualifications of 1 Timothy 3:8–13, which focus not on practical effectiveness, efficiency, and skill but on character and Christian spirituality. The simple qualifications for "the seven" in Acts 6:3—"of good repute, full of the Spirit and of wisdom"—are a good summary of the longer list in 1 Timothy 3:8–13.

One particular qualification to note here: deacons are to "hold the mystery of the faith with a clear conscience." They must deeply believe and be able to represent the gospel in word. Deacon is not an office where "less spiritual" people can be official so the church can capitalize on some specialty or skill they have. Deacons are not just skilled at the specific work to which they're called but are *examples to the whole flock of the kind of service and sacrifice for others that should be true of all of us in the church.* As officeholders, deacons, like the elders, model what mature Christianity is for the church and the wider world.

In particular, we want to see in the deacons the kind of attitude and readiness that every Christian, and the whole church, might have in initiating and carrying through on meeting others' needs.

Appendix 2

A Word for Leaders

On Plurality and Team Dynamics

CHRISTIAN LEADERSHIP is not for the lone wolf. The labor is too important when souls are in the balance, and all of us are simply too frail and shortsighted with too much indwelling sin and too many blind spots to go at it on our own.

Whatever the role, whether on the college campus, in the inner city, among an unreached people group, or in the local church, we desperately need each other in all of life and especially in leadership. Christian leadership is a team sport, and in a post-Enlightenment society still deeply affected by modernist individualism, the biblical model of plurality in leadership is a desperately needed corrective and a powerfully redemptive grace.

Team leadership does not mean there is no "chief among equals." That's both inevitable and good among any group, that one person eventually functions as the senior or the final buck-stopper (though not boss)—we might as well name that and make it plain. But the clear model in the New Testament is team leadership in the local church—"plurality," we call it. "Without exception," writes Gregg Allison, "every time the New Testament mentions the government of a particular church, the leadership structure is a plurality of elders."[1]

Wiser Together

Before providing a dozen additional benefits of plurality in leadership, here is a headlining principle: *We are wiser together.* "Without counsel plans fail, but with many advisers they succeed" (Prov. 15:22). "By wise guidance you can wage your war, and in abundance of counselors there is victory" (Prov. 24:6).

The vast majority of decisions we face in life each day are not clearly laid out in biblical dos and don'ts. The way we learn to do "what is good and acceptable and perfect" is by being "transformed by the renewal of [our] mind, that by testing [we] may discern what is the will of God" (Rom. 12:2). We don't live following a list. Rather, God remakes us from the inside into increasingly new people, and as we're "renewed in the spirit of [our] minds" (Eph. 4:23), we exercise wisdom as we "try to discern what is pleasing to the Lord" (Eph. 5:10). As we are "filled with the knowledge of his will in all spiritual wisdom and understanding" (Col. 1:9), we learn to "approve what is excellent" (Phil. 1:10).

Plurality in leadership, then, is the corporate manifestation of such sober-mindedness, sanctified levelheadedness. The toughest decisions we face in leadership are not clear dos and don'ts. And in leadership, the messes multiply and the decisions become more difficult. What we desperately need is to exercise a collective wisdom stemming from God's remaking of us, not just individually but together. We need to supplement each other's judgment and

---

1 Gregg Allison, *Sojourners and Strangers: The Doctrine of the Church*, Foundations of Evangelical Theology (Wheaton, IL: Crossway, 2012), 293.

seek to discern together God's path for the ministry we lead. This is why one of the first characteristics required of elders in the church is "sober-mindedness" (1 Tim. 3:2).

A Dozen More Gifts

When we have carefully guarded the door to leadership on the way in, and we know each other well enough to confirm that we're walking together in the light, then we can exercise great trust in the team's sense of direction. We are significantly wiser together than alone.

Of course, there are drawbacks to plurality in leadership. Even though it's more likely that an individual will be led astray, whole groups have been deceived and corrupted. And as Alexander Strauch concedes, "Team leadership in a church family can be painfully slow and terribly aggravating."[2] That's true. But on the whole, the benefits of leading together far outweigh going at it alone.

Here, then, are a dozen more benefits, among others, to supplement the truth that we indeed are wiser together. (These are not meant to heap discouragement on those who are in singular leadership situations and would love to be surrounded by fellows but have none. Rather, I hope they will give you incentive to keep praying for and investing in the lives of future teammates in ministry.)

1. More Strengths, Fewer Weaknesses

Plurality in leadership means filling out our limited giftings with the talents of others and pooling our complementary gifts to do the work more effectively. God gives "gifts that differ according to the grace given to us" (Rom. 12:6). Even among leaders, there are varieties of gifts, service, and activities (1 Cor. 12:4–6).

---

2   Alexander Strauch, *Biblical Eldership: An Urgent Call to Restore Biblical Church Leadership* (Colorado Springs, CO: Lewis & Roth, 1995), 44.

Leadership is better when together we are "good stewards of God's varied grace" (1 Pet. 4:10).

And as we pool our strengths, we make up for our deficiencies. Leading together covers many of our weaknesses. In a team setting, our individual lapses in judgment cause less damage, if any; other voices can speak up and point in another direction. It's okay to be imperfect; others can see our blind spots and bring correction. And leading together can guard against domineering tendencies in individual leaders as peers stand alongside to sharpen and challenge them.

2. Healthier Teaching

It's good for individual teachers to make their provocative points, have their well-placed hyperboles, and exhibit their own winsome quirks and idiosyncrasies. But when they're alone over the long haul, they can introduce wobbles and imbalances into local church life. Any group with only one teacher will become painfully like that leader if you give it enough time.

At the heart of Christian leadership is speaking God's words (Heb. 13:7). So pastors and elders must be skillful in teaching (1 Tim. 3:2; Titus 1:9). And it's just as important to have a plurality of elders in public teaching as it is in private meetings and decisions. Also, when there is a team of qualified teacher-leaders, they can teach in various settings. In this way, there are multiple significant influences on the people. No one teacher has all the gifts and all the balance that a healthy, vibrant church needs.

3. Lightening the Workload

Pastoral leadership can be demanding. Not only are there the proactive labors of preparation and delivery of public teaching and the long meetings to make mind-bending decisions; there is also the intensity of responsive ministry to needs in the flock. When we lead together, we share the heavy load that shepherding can be at times. When we divide the labor and distribute the weight of ministry, we make everyday life more livable for leaders and protect them from exhaustion and burnout.

4. Being Pastored and Accountable

Plurality in leadership also provides essential care and accountability. When the church's most public leader has peers who can speak into his life, and hold him to the fire, there is less room for subtly taking advantage of privilege and making self-serving decisions. And for every Christian shepherd, our more fundamental identity is being one of the sheep (Luke 10:20). Pastors need to be pastored. We all need to be held accountable and have some structure for being called out if we get off track as well as led proactively into greener pastures.

5. More Safety Together

We Christian leaders often encounter situations that seem far beyond us as individuals. We simply don't know what to do or what counsel to give. We're confused and torn; we feel stuck.

Leading together not only makes us wiser together when many options are on the table but also helps us to move carefully forward, one step at a time, into a situation in which we're not even sure there's one good option. As Proverbs 11:14 says, "In an abundance of counselors there is safety."

6. More Support from the Church

Because elders are first and foremost sheep, not shepherds, they are "of the people." This office is different from that of apostle, as those who represent the chief shepherd in a more significant sense. We might say that while the apostles are "of God," the elders are "of the people."

The elders are from the people and among the people, and having a plurality of elders among the people helps the elders to both listen to the people and win congregational support for decisions before and after the fact. A single leader is not able to hear out, influence, gain support, and deal with individual circumstances nearly so strongly as a team working together.

7. Less Sting from Unjust Criticism

Flying solo in leadership means all the sting lands squarely on the lone pastor. But when we lead as a team, and make and own decisions as a team, we're less exposed to unjust criticism for those decisions. We still feel the sting, but not nearly so sharply when we take it together, which connects, then, to our ability to encourage one another in difficulty.

8. More Encouragement in Difficulty

All leadership in a fallen world involves severe difficulty sooner or later. It's just a matter of time. And perhaps all the more in Christian leadership, because so much is at stake, and because there is a genuine enemy with schemes against us.

Trials will come, but when we lead together, we're in much better condition to walk in those trials without losing hope. Together we strengthen each other to continue truly, deeply, continually rejoicing, even as we experience great sorrow. Having peers in leadership proves to be a priceless encouragement in trouble. And encouragement to do the right thing. Elders are called to protect the flock, to take initiative and lead the church in cases of church discipline, both to spare the flock from theological and moral disease and to call individuals to repentance. Elders must have the courage and love to cut off members who persist in sin, despite being called to repentance, and as a team we're able to challenge each other to not give in out of fear but take the hard step that needs to be taken.

9. More Stable in Transition

Transition comes to every leadership team if the organization is healthy and survives for much duration of time. In particular, when the senior leader transitions, whether to retirement or some other vocation, the plurality contributes greatly to stability during change.

10. More Sanctifying

Not only is there the collective wisdom, but leading together makes us better as individuals. Shared leadership is more sanctifying than leading alone. Leading together, says Strauch,

> exposes our impatience with one another, our stubborn pride, our bull-headedness, our selfish immaturity, our domineering disposition, our lack of love and understanding of one another, and our prayerlessness. It also shows us how underdeveloped and immature we really are in humility, brotherly love, and true servant spirit.[3]

Leading together makes each of us better. "Iron sharpens iron" (Prov. 27:17).

---

3 Strauch, *Biblical Eldership*, 114.

11. Greater Joy Together

Leading together also brings greater joy than going at it alone. "It is much more satisfying . . . to pastor as a team than to be a lone-wolf shepherd."[4] While at times it may feel easier to make all the calls yourself, the joy of leading together, with all its attendant difficulties, far surpasses the simplicity of being the king of the hill.

12. Together under the Chief

Finally, and most significantly, working as a team of undershepherds should remind us continually that there is only one "chief Shepherd" (1 Pet. 5:4). We undershepherds are plural, but there is a singular great "Shepherd and Overseer of your souls" (1 Pet. 2:25), only one "great shepherd of the sheep" (Heb. 13:20). He is the one with shoulders broad enough to roll all our burdens for the flock onto him (1 Pet. 5:7). He is the one who has promised that he will build his church (Matt. 16:18) and that his gospel will go to all the nations (Matt. 24:14) through the church (Eph. 1:22; 3:21).

The reality of plurality reminds us that we are not the lone leader of Christ's church. He is.

―――

Seven Ways to Improve Your Team

As we've seen, Jesus does not mean for his followers to go about their work alone.

He is the one singular leader in his church. No peers. The rest of us follow his example *together*, by laboring in the plural. He alone is "the great shepherd of the sheep" (Heb. 13:20), "the chief

4 Jeremie Rinne, *Church Elders: How to Shepherd God's People Like Jesus* (Wheaton, IL: Crossway, 2014), 95.

Shepherd" (1 Pet. 5:4), "the Shepherd and Overseer" of our souls (1 Pet. 2:25). He means for his undershepherds to work together. He went to Calvary alone. We go through the fire as a team.

During his ministry, Jesus sent his disciples out two by two (Luke 10:1). And throughout the New Testament, leadership in the local church is always plural: first the apostles, then the elder-pastor-overseers (Acts 14:23; 20:17, 28; Eph. 4:11; Phil. 1:1; 1 Tim. 4:14; 5:17; Titus 1:5; James 5:14; 1 Pet. 5:1, 5). Living, leading, and laboring as a team is vitally important both in principle and in practice in the life of the church.

Following are seven ways, among others, for ministry teams (and especially team leaders) to pursue health and fitness in team dynamics.

1. Actively Cultivate and Protect Trust

Effective teams run on trust, and it comes at a premium. Trust is slowly gained and quickly lost. It's worth investing significant time and energy in building trust and taking care not to lose it.

Trust is built by treating those closest to us (our teammates) with the most care and respect rather than the least. As with our families, the temptation can be to presume on the relationships around us and give our best energy and attention to those outside. If such an instinct goes unchecked, we will soon find trust eroded with those that matter most.

In a local church setting, trust among leaders is paradigmatic for the whole congregation. What's true of the leaders will soon be true of the people. Dissent among the pastors leads to factions in the flock. For the church to live the unified vision of Philippians 1:27–28 in the long run—"standing firm in one spirit, with one mind striving side by side for the faith of the gospel, and not frightened in anything by your opponents"—there will need to be evident trust among the leaders.

2. Carefully Monitor Team Size (and Communication)

Humans are finite. God made us this way. He sanctified finitude in creation, and doubly sanctified it when Jesus joined us in human flesh. Finitude is not a flaw but something to be acknowledged and not neglected.

As nice as it would be to include as many people as possible on the team, the larger the group gets, the more difficult it is to keep everyone on the same page. The *lines of communication*, as Larry Osborne observes in the book *Sticky Teams*, increase exponentially with each new member.[5] Many teams trend toward unhealthiness simply because they are too large.

With each addition to your elder counsel, pastoral team, or other ministry crew, assess the team dynamics and survey team members. Keep in mind that adding members doesn't always add effectiveness.

3. Generously Invest Time into Your Team

Healthy teams take time. In a fallen world, they don't simply happen, even among Christians. You can't skimp on time together (quality or quantity) and think everything will be okay in the long haul. Relationships within the team are worth your investment. Focusing "inward" like this won't necessarily detract from your mission together as long as you're careful not to become ingrown, but learn to enjoy life *together* on mission.

It may feel like slowing down to spend quality time with your leadership team, but it's a good slowing down, one that keeps

---

5 Larry Osborne, *Sticky Teams: Keeping Your Leadership Team and Staff on the Same Page* (Grand Rapids, MI: Zondervan, 2010).

you from out-advancing the supply lines. As Osborne points out, "Whenever a group of people increase the amount of time they spend together, there is a corresponding increase in their regard and appreciation for one another."[6] It sounds like common sense, but unfortunately it's not common practice.

4. Humbly Pursue Unity in All Areas

When a ministry team is deeply united around a clear, shared vision of who God is, how he has revealed himself in Jesus and the Scriptures, what he is doing in the world, and how our mission relates to his, it is amazing the kind of camaraderie and team health that can emerge. It is worth working years to get the team on the same page theologically. It is beautiful, rich, and invaluable to be deeply united about the most important truths in the universe.

There's also important unity to pursue beyond doctrine. In the team setting, it is beneficial to be united in philosophy and in friendship as well. Teams are not just cognitive; they must be practical. They take initiatives and act together in the world, which means they must make decisions about methodology, how to go about fleshing out their vision of God in everyday life and ministry.

So respect and friendship are vital. It is good for friends, not just associates, to lead together. Ministry teams should not be cliquish, but it is a gain to the whole church when leaders are genuinely friends and enjoy being together.

5. Boldly Keep Short Accounts

Aggressively have the conversations you don't want to have. For the long-term health of your team, be willing to talk today about

6   Osborne, *Sticky Teams*, 40.

what's unpleasant and potentially controversial. Typically the most important topics to tackle are the ones we fear. They reveal tensions that we'd all like to have go away.

The topics we neglect will not go away with neglect. If you suspect someone is getting frustrated or feeling marginalized or acting arrogantly, tackle it head on now. Speak the truth in love as soon as possible. Don't let it go.

Unless someone takes the initiative to have the awkward conversation, assume the tension will get worse, not better. And when it goes underground, it will likely grow and fester and return to the surface worse than it was before. Negligence of tensions among teammates can signal the destruction of a team. It's just a matter of time.

6. Lovingly Guard the Gate

It's worth the extra time and care to vet prospective leaders thoroughly before adding them to the team. In the long run, it is much easier, and better, not to bring someone on than to remove him later. Ask the hard theological and philosophical questions you can think of up front.

Ask the tough questions about the rough spots in their past. What led to their leaving a previous church or team? What struggles have they had with team members in the past? What steps have they taken, if any, to address their part in it?

Think of your ministry team as one on which every member always plays—no one on the bench. Assume Satan will try to attack through the weakest player. Don't compromise at the gate.

7. Joyfully Lean on the Team's Wisdom

Learn to enjoy not getting your own way. God puts us in teams and has us minister together because it goes better for us and for those we serve. It can be easy to acknowledge this in theory but difficult to embrace when the collective wisdom of the team goes against our own preference on an issue. Ask God for help in these moments to believe in the wisdom of the team above your own. How miserable if everything in ministry went the way you wanted—with all of your own weaknesses and blind spots.

It may seem like a strange joy to cultivate, but it is a great mark of Christian maturity. Even when our personal opinion on some ministry decision is different, we have the opportunity to step back, try to see the wisdom in how God is leading the others on our team, and thank him for them—and for not leaving us alone to navigate these decisions.

Appendix 3

What Is Anointing with Oil?

RECENTLY THE ELDERS of our church gathered after the Sunday morning service to pray over a member who had received a difficult medical diagnosis. Complicating her condition was her upcoming travel to Haiti to work as a nurse on a short-term mission. After hearing the heavy word from the doctor, she still felt the desire to go, but now new concerns were in view: she would be in a foreign place, and quality medical help would be difficult to come by if her own unpredictable condition were to become problematic.

We sent word around to the elders to gather with her and her family after the service. As I'd done before, I picked through my wife's collection of small vials and grabbed the one essential oil for leadership in the local church: the frankincense we use for anointing.

One Passage in James

This was not the first time we'd gathered as elders to pray together for and anoint a member in unusual circumstances, nor will it be the last.

Such a practice may be strange to many of us who grew up in mainstream evangelical churches. Mark 6:13 mentions Jesus's disciples anointing "with oil many who were sick," but James 5:14–15 is the one passage that plainly prescribes this practice in the life of the church:

> Is anyone among you sick? Let him call for the elders of the church, and let them pray over him, anointing him with oil in the name of the Lord. And the prayer of faith will save the one who is sick, and the Lord will raise him up. And if he has committed sins, he will be forgiven.

Five important points make this Christian anointing of the sick distinct from every other anointing.

1. Who Should Call?

James 5:15 makes plain that "sick" in 5:14 is not a common cold or stomach flu. We may be quicker today to consider ourselves sick than they were in the first century. Elder prayer is for those in some serious circumstance and unusually difficult straits. One commentator surmises that "this sick person is bedridden and potentially helpless even to pray for him- or herself."[1] Another provides five pointers in the text that the situation is serious: the elders are called *to* the sick person; the elders do all the praying; the person is said to be "worn out" or "exhausted" (the meaning of "sick" in v. 15); the elders' faith is in view, not the sick person's; and the elders pray *over* the (bedridden) person.[2] (Note here,

---

1 Craig L. Blomberg and Mariam J. Kamell, *James*, Zondervan Exegetical Commentary on the New Testament (Grand Rapids, MI: Zondervan Academic, 2008), 242.
2 J. A. Motyer, *The Message of James*, The Bible Speaks Today (Downers Grove, IL: InterVarsity Press, 1985), 194).

contra so-called prosperity-gospel claims, this prayer of faith is not offered by the sick person but by the elders.)

Calling for the elders is not the Christian's first recourse with any form of sickness or discomfort. However, Christians do have a backstop *within the local church* for help with escalating and dire physical conditions. Such support is not in lieu of medical help but an appeal to God in, alongside, and over it.

2. Who Should Come?

James 5:14 specifically mentions *the elders* of the church. The New Testament consistently and pervasively attributes formal leadership in the local church to a plurality of elders (Acts 14:23; 20:17; 21:18; 1 Tim. 4:14; 5:17; Titus 1:5; 1 Pet. 5:1, 5). It's not *elder* (singular)—not one-man ministry—but *elders* (plural), a team of pastor-elders leading the church together.

As we've noted already, elder is the same office often called "pastor" today (based on the noun *pastor* or *shepherd* in Eph. 4:11 and its verb forms in Acts 20:28 and 1 Pet. 5:2). The same office is also twice called "overseer" in four texts (Acts 20:28; Phil. 1:1; 1 Tim. 3:1–2; Titus 1:7). These are the formal leaders in the local church who don't have authority or wield power on their own but serve in a God-appointed, church-affirmed role in which they represent Christ to his church (to the degree they are faithful to Christ's word) and the church to Christ.

Calling for the elders is the sick person's way of coming to the church to ask for collective prayer.

3. What Should the Elders Do?

The elders should pray. The emphasis in the passage is on prayer, not anointing. "Let them pray over him, anointing . . ." The grammar of the passage communicates that the central reason the elders have come is to pray. Prayer is primary; anointing is secondary. Anointing, as we'll see, accompanies prayer. The power is not in the oil but in the God to whom we pray.

Note here that (unlike the Roman Catholic sacrament of extreme unction, which claims its cues from James 5) the prayer for and aim of anointing is restoration to life, not consecration for death.

4. Why Anoint with Oil?

Anointing with oil is the part that can seem strange to some today. The problem is that we may never have considered the place of oil and the act of anointing throughout the Scriptures.

Throughout the Bible, anointing with oil symbolizes consecration to God (as in Ex. 28:41; Luke 4:18; Acts 4:27; 10:38; 2 Cor. 1:21; Heb. 1:9). The act of anointing does not, as some claim, automatically confer grace and remit sin. Rather, it can be a means of grace, which accompanies prayer, for those who believe. Like fasting, anointing is a kind of handmaid of prayer, or an intensifier of prayer—a way to reach beyond our daily patterns in unusual circumstances.

Anointing with oil is an external act of the body that accompanies and gives expression to the internal desire and disposition of faith to dedicate someone to God in a special way. It is not here simply medicinal, as some have claimed, with our application today being to apply modern medicine along with prayer. Such a view overlooks the wealth of theology across the Scriptures about the symbolism and significance of anointing.

In fact, anointing is so significant that God's long-promised King, whom we eventually learn is God's own eternal Son, is called *Messiah* in Hebrew, *Christ* in Greek, which means "anointed."

Christ himself is the greatest manifestation of consecration to God in his perfect human life, sacrificial human death, and victorious human resurrection from the grave.

So here in James 5, as Douglas Moo writes, "As the elders pray, they are to anoint the sick person in order to symbolize that that person is being set apart for God's special attention and care."[3] Anointing is not automatic in producing healing but serves as a prayerful expression and intensifier of our plea, asking God and waiting for him to heal.

If you ask, then, what kind of oil should we use, my answer is, in light of the theology of anointing: not cheap oil. The very point of the oil is to symbolize the gravity and urgency of the occasion through lavishness and (appropriate) expense. This is not the place to go on the cheap end. The specialness of the act is tied to the preciousness of the oil.

5. How Should They Pray?

Finally, we have specific and important clarity about how the elders should pray: "in the name of the Lord" (James 5:14). The power is not in the oil or in the elders or even in their prayers but in God, in the name of Jesus Christ. When God answers with healing, he does so not decisively because of the oil or the elders, but because of the work of his Son, Jesus.

This means that the elders can pray boldly and with confidence. Where two or three elders are gathered for special prayer, there they should be expectant that God will move. The "prayer of faith" in verse 15 is simply the prayer of the elders from verse 14: the prayer offered in faith that can and often does heal.

3 Douglas Moo, *The Letter of James*, Pillar New Testament Commentary (Grand Rapids, MI: Eerdmans, 2000), 242.

Appendix 4

What Is the Laying On of Hands?

WHAT DOES THE BIBLE TEACH about "the laying on of hands," and how should this ancient ritual function, or not, in the church today?

Like anointing with oil, much confusion often surrounds these outward signs about which the New Testament has very little (but something) to say.

Like fasting, the laying on of hands and anointing with oil go hand in hand with prayer. Because of the way God has made the world and wired our own hearts, on certain special occasions we reach for something tangible, physical, and visible to complement, or serve as a sign of, what is happening invisibly and what we're capturing with invisible words.

Before turning to what the New Testament teaches about the laying on of hands today, let's first get our bearings by looking at how this practice arose, functioned, and developed in the story of God's people.

Old-Covenant Foundations

Throughout the Bible, we find both positive and negative senses of the laying on of hands, as well as general (everyday) or special (ceremonial). In the Old Testament, the *general* use is most often negative: to "lay hands" on someone is to inflict harm (Gen. 22:12; 37:22; Ex. 7:4; Neh. 13:21; Est. 2:21; 3:6; 6:2; 8:7), or in Leviticus 24:14 to visibly lay God's curse on the person who will bear it. We also find a *special* use, especially in Leviticus (1:4; 3:2, 8, 13; 4:4, 15, 24, 29, 33; 16:21; also Ex. 29:10, 15, 19; Num. 8:12), where the duly appointed priests "lay hands" on a sacrifice to ceremonially place God's righteous curse on the animal instead of on the sinful people. For instance, on the Day of Atonement, the climactic day of the Jewish year, the high priest

> shall lay both his hands on the head of the live goat, and confess over it all the iniquities of the people of Israel, and all their transgressions, all their sins. And he shall put them on the head of the goat and send it away into the wilderness. (Lev. 16:21)

This special (or ceremonial) laying on of hands is likely what Hebrews 6:1 refers to when mentioning six teachings, among others, in the old covenant ("the elementary doctrine of Christ") that prepared God's people for the new covenant: "repentance from dead works and of faith toward God, and of instruction about washings, *the laying on of hands*, the resurrection of the dead, and eternal judgment" (Heb. 6:1–2).

While the majority of Old Testament mentions involve priests and old-covenant ceremonies (passing the curse to the substitute), two texts in particular (both in Numbers) anticipate how "the laying on of hands" would come to be used in the church age (passing a blessing to a formally recognized leader). In Numbers 8:10 God's people lay their hands on the priests to officially commission them as their representatives before God, and in Numbers 27:18 God instructs Moses to lay his hands on Joshua to commission him formally as the new leader of the nation.

Jesus's Hands and His Apostles

When we come to the Gospels and Acts, we find a noticeable shift in the typical use of the laying on of hands. A small sampling still conveys the general/negative sense (to harm or seize, related to the scribes and priests seeking to arrest Jesus, Luke 20:19; 21:12; 22:53), but now with the Son of God himself among us, we find a new positive use of the phrase, as Jesus lays his hands on people to bless and to heal.

Jesus's most common practice in healing is touch, often described as "laying his hands on" the one to be healed (Matt. 9:18; Mark 5:23; 6:5; 7:32; 8:22–25; Luke 13:13). Jesus also lays his hands on the little children who come to him, to bless them (Matt. 19:13–15; Mark 10:16).

In Acts, once Jesus has ascended into heaven, his apostles (in effect) become his hands. Now they, like their Lord, heal with touch. Ananias "lays his hands" on Paul, three days after the Damascus road encounter, to restore his sight (Acts 9:12, 17). And Paul's hands, in turn, become channels of extraordinary miracles (Acts 14:3; 19:11), including the laying of his hands on a sick man on Malta to heal him (Acts 28:8).

What's new in the *Gospels* is Jesus's healing through the laying on of hands, but what's new in *Acts* is the giving and receiving of the Holy Spirit through the laying on of hands. As the gospel makes progress from Jerusalem and Judea, to Samaria, and then beyond, to the ends of the earth (Acts 1:8), God is pleased to use the apostles' laying on of hands as a visible marker and means of the coming of the Spirit among new people and places—first in Samaria (Acts 8:17) and then beyond, in Ephesus (19:6).

In the Church Today

Finally, in the New Testament Epistles, as we begin to see what is normative in the church today, we find two remaining uses from Acts that echo the two mentions above in Numbers (8:10 and 27:18), and set the course for Paul's references in 1 and 2 Timothy.

In Acts 6:6, when the church has chosen seven men to serve as official assistants to the apostles, "these they set before the apostles, and they prayed and laid their hands on them." Here again, as in Numbers, we find a kind of commissioning ceremony. The visible sign of the laying on of hands publicly marks the beginning of a new formal ministry for these seven, recognizing them before the people and asking for God's blessing on their labors.

So also the church responds to the Spirit's directive, "Set apart for me Barnabas and Saul for the work to which I have called them," and then "after fasting and praying they laid their hands on them and sent them off" (Acts 13:2–3). Like Acts 6:6 this is a formal commission performed in public, with the collective request for God's blessing on it.

Commission to Ministry

In 1 Timothy 4:14, Paul charges Timothy, his official delegate in Ephesus:

> Do not neglect the gift you have, which was given you by prophecy when the council of elders laid their hands on you.

For our purposes here, the point is not precisely what gift Timothy received (though both the previous and following verses mention teaching), but how the elders commissioned him into his formal role. Timothy was sent off for this specific assignment with the public recognition of the recognized leaders—not only by their words, but through the visible, tangible, memorable laying on of their hands. This public ceremony may be what Paul refers to in 2 Timothy 1:6 when he mentions a gift of God in Timothy "through the laying on of my hands."

The last key text, and perhaps most instructive, is also in 1 Timothy. Again Paul writes:

> Do not be hasty in the laying on of hands, nor take part in the sins of others; keep yourself pure. (1 Tim. 5:22)

Now the subject is not Timothy's own commissioning but his part in commissioning others. The charge from Paul comes in a section about elders, honoring the good and disciplining the bad (1 Tim. 5:17–25). When leaders like Paul, Timothy, and others in the church formally lay their hands on someone for a particular new ministry calling, they put their seal of approval on the candidate and share, in some sense, in the fruitfulness and failures to come.

Laying on of hands, then, is the opposite of washing one's hands like Pilate did. When the elders lay their hands on a candidate for ministry, they both *commission him* to a particular role of service and they *commend him* to those among whom he will serve.

God Gives the Grace

With both the laying on of hands and anointing with oil, the elders come before God in special circumstances with a spirit of prayer and particular requests, but whereas anointing with oil asks for healing, the laying on of hands asks for blessing on forthcoming ministry. Anointing with oil in James 5:14 privately commends the sick to God for healing; the laying on of hands in 1 Timothy 5:22 publicly commends the candidate to the church for an official ministry. Anointing sets the sick apart and expresses the need for God's special care. Laying on of hands sets apart a qualified leader for specific ministry and signals fitness to bless others.

Laying on of hands, then—like anointing or fasting or other external rituals for the church—is not magic and does not, as some claim, automatically confer grace. Rather, it is a *means* of grace and accompanies words of commendation and corporate prayer, for those who believe. Like baptism, the laying on of hands is a kind of inaugural sign and ceremony, an initiating rite—a way of making an invisible reality visible, public, and memorable, both for the candidate and for the congregation, and then through the candidate and congregation to the world.

It serves as a means of grace to the candidate in *affirming* God's call through the church and in *providing* a tangible, physical moment to remember when ministry gets hard. It's also a means of God's grace to the commissioning leaders, who extend and expand their heart and work through a faithful candidate. And it's a means of God's grace to the congregation and beyond in clarifying the identity of the official leaders to whom they will seek to submit (Heb. 13:7, 17).

And in it all, the giver and blesser is God. He extends and expands the ministry of the leaders. He calls, sustains, and makes fruitful the ministry of the candidate. And he enriches, matures, and catalyzes the congregation to love and good works, to minister to each other, and beyond, served by the teaching, wisdom, and faithful leadership of the newly appointed elder, deacon, or missionary.

Appendix 5

How Old Should Elders Be?

The Hebrew Roots of Church Leadership

THE TERM ELDERS can sound strange to modern ears. For those not raised in the church or not raised in churches with elders, it can be a perplexing term. *Who are these "elders" I hear about? Do they meet in secret?*

To the unfamiliar, "elders" may sound sectarian or even cultish. Modern people intuit that the term *elders* belongs to a bygone era, to more *traditional* times. More broadly, the term can have negative connotations in a society that increasingly prizes the strength and beauty of youth over the wisdom and grace of age. And *elderly* is something we all want to avoid.

Who Are the Elders?

Elders is one of three main terms in the New Testament for the leading office in the local church. In the narratives of Acts, as Christianity grew and spread in Jewish soil, the elders were the plurality of formal leaders in individual churches (Acts 14:23; 20:17). Paul wrote to his protégé

Timothy about church leaders as "elders" (1 Tim. 4:14; 5:17, 19; so also in Titus 1:5). Both James and Peter refer to local-church leaders as a team of elders (James 5:14; 1 Pet. 5:1, 5). In other contexts, Paul refers to leaders in this same office as overseers (Acts 20:28; Phil. 1:1; 1 Tim. 3:1–2; Titus 1:7). Less commonly, but no less significantly, those in this same lead office are also called "pastors" (noun in Eph. 4:11; verb in Acts 20:28; 1 Pet. 5:2), drawing on the great Old Testament theme of the shepherd as the leader of God's flock.

Pastors is the most common term today, even though it appears least in the New Testament. *Overseers* likely is used least today. And then most common in the New Testament and now experiencing a comeback in some circles is *elders*.

Why Call Them "Elders"?

Odd as it might sound today, *elders* was not a foreign term in ancient Israel and beyond. At least since the days of Moses and even before the exodus from Egypt, Israel recognized elders (Ex. 3:16, 18; 4:29; 12:21). Egypt too had elders (Gen. 50:7). So did Midian and Moab (Num. 22:4, 7), Gibeon (Josh. 9:11), Gebal (Ezek. 27:9), and other surrounding nations.

In Hebrew, the word for *elder* (*zaqen*) comes from the word for *beard* (*zaqan*). Elders, as one might expect, were not young men but those old enough (in general) to have a full beard. This should not be confused with *elderly*. Having a *full* beard is not the same as having a *gray* beard. In this sense, *elder* was an approximate term in Israel, not strictly linked to a particular age—though a case can be made for an old-covenant minimum. Cornelis Van Dam says we get "the impression that the age of thirty was the minimum. However, Scripture gives no specifically prescribed age for this office."[1]

---

1 Cornelis Van Dam, *The Elder* (Phillipsburg, NJ: P&R, 2009), 29.

Van Dam mentions *office*, which is important. "The elders of Israel" were not simply all the older men of Israel, but *officially recognized* authority figures, whether appointed formally by providence or chosen by the people (as in Deut. 1:13–16).

Given the term's longtime use among God's first-covenant people for officers who were not prophets, priests, or kings, *elders* was a natural name for formally recognized leaders in local churches as they first formed in Jerusalem and spread out from there.

What Did Hebrew Elders Do?

But what did the elders of Israel do in those centuries before the coming of Christ? What were their tasks? Ask any veteran reader of the Bible that question, and you might get a puzzled look. The Old Testament mentions elders with some frequency, but *what they did* is not nearly as plain as we might expect.

Remember, these were the days of *prophets* like Moses and Samuel, *priests* like Aaron and Phinehas, *statesmen* like Joshua and Nehemiah, and *kings* like David and Solomon. And as the nation spiraled downward in royal depravity, God sent major and minor prophets as his mouthpieces to call the nation back to himself. Van Dam summarizes the task of the elders in such times to be "preserving and nurturing life in covenant with God."[2] That's not very specific.

Jim Hamilton adds that the elders were responsible for "the regulation of society at large—judging cases and enforcing the law."[3] They exercised their leadership, and office, in particular through providing wisdom and counsel and rendering judgments on disputes.

2 Van Dam, *Elder*, 8.
3 James M. Hamilton Jr., "Did the Church Borrow Leadership Structures from the Old Testament or Synagogue?," in *Shepherding God's Flock*, ed. Benjamin L. Merkle and Thomas R. Schreiner (Grand Rapids, MI: Kregel, 2014), 31.

What Do Church Elders Do?

More important than what Hebrew elders *did* is what church elders *do* under the terms of the new covenant.

Hamilton asks, "Is there a relationship between the leadership structure of the nation of Israel, the synagogue, and the church?" His answer is yes and no, but he clarifies: "Less yes than no."[4] In other words, even given what (little) we know about the responsibilities of the elders of Israel (under the direction of prophets, priests, and kings), we find "more discontinuity than continuity between the old and new covenant elders."[5] In fact, according to Hamilton, "the similarities basically end with the fact of leadership and the use of the term."[6] Benjamin Merkle agrees: the New Testament office of elder is "an almost entirely new position."[7]

What's not new is that church elders are charged with leading and ruling, or governing (1 Thess. 5:12; 1 Tim. 2:12; 3:4; 5:17; Heb. 13:17). They still judge disputes and provide counsel. They still preserve and nurture life in covenant with God. However, now, under Christ, without earthly kings and prophets over them, more governing weight rests on the elders' shoulders. But most striking of all is how new-covenant elders relate to the absence, or fulfillment, of the priesthood.

Elders Lead and Feed

In the Old Testament, the priests in particular were charged to *teach* the nation. God spoke to Aaron, the first high priest, "You

4 Hamilton, "Leadership Structures," 13.
5 Hamilton, "Leadership Structures," 16.
6 Hamilton, "Leadership Structures," 13–14.
7 Benjamin L. Merkle, *The Elder and Overseer: One Office in the Early Church* (New York: Peter Lang, 2003), 65.

are to *teach* the people of Israel all the statutes that the LORD has spoken to them by Moses" (Lev. 10:11). Memorably, the priest Ezra, in line with the calling of his office, "set his heart to study the Law of the LORD, and to do it and to *teach* his statutes and rules in Israel" (Ezra 7:10). It was Ezra and his fellow priests who, after the completion of the wall under Nehemiah, "read from the book, from the Law of God, clearly, and they gave the sense, so that the people understood the reading" (Neh. 8:8). The priests were teachers.

But now Christ, the great teacher and our great high priest, has come. He not only taught God's word but is himself the Word (John 1:1–3; Heb. 1:1–2). And he speaks to his church today in the word he gave us through his apostles and prophets—and not only when that word is read by individuals but when it is *taught by the elders*, the pastor-teachers (Eph. 4:11), in the life of the church.

Therefore, two fundamental differences between the elders of Israel and the elders of the church are (1) the constitution of God's people as born again, from all nations, rather than focused on the Jewish ethnicity, and (2) the calling of the elders to take up the word of Christ and "feed my sheep," as Jesus said to Peter (John 21:15–17).

In sum, says Hamilton, "the teaching of the Scriptures to the people of God is specifically entrusted to the elders in a way that we do not see in the Old Testament."[8] Even though "oversight of the church is more than simply teaching and preaching," as Don Carson writes, "a substantial part of the ruling/oversight function is discharged *through the preaching and teaching of the Word of God. This is where a great deal of the best leadership is exercised.*"[9]

---

8 Hamilton, "Leadership Structures," 25.

9 D. A. Carson, "Some Reflections on Pastoral Leadership," *Themelios* 40.2 (2015): 197; emphasis added.

Must Elders Be Old?

One final question about church *elders* and their relationship to Hebrew *elders* is, How old should a man be to serve as an elder in the church? In brief, he should be sufficiently *mature* for spiritual leadership, with that maturity being discerned relative to the congregation and in the context of the life of the church. For instance, a wise team of elders will discern when they are aging as a council and need to bring on younger men, in the safety of an experienced team, to begin investing in the next generation of leaders for when the older generation is gone.

Remember, even under the terms of the old covenant, "the elders of Israel" was an office, whether by the providence of God or the choice of the people, not a simple collective of old men, and the general minimum age of thirty was perhaps surprisingly low for what we today might assume for the word *elder*. Now, in the church age, among a body of regenerate saints, the emphasis will be even less on mere physical age, though it's not irrelevant as it relates to a man's spiritual and emotional maturity.

Wise councils also will consider stage-of-life details with a young potential elder. While marriage is not required to be an elder, it may be prudent to wait for a season if the man is unmarried and desires to be married soon, or if he is engaged or a newlywed. Also, as the median age for marriage continues to rise, some otherwise qualified men may need more time to get their feet underneath them as young fathers before adding the additional responsibilities of eldership.

However focused on spiritual maturity new-covenant eldership must be, there is no escaping the wisdom of some modest passage of time in order that elders might "not be hasty in the laying on of hands" (1 Tim. 5:22). As with deacons (the assisting office), so all the more with pastor-elders (the lead office), "let them also be tested first" (1 Tim. 3:10). And as with the other elder qualifications, spiritual maturity will be evaluated in context. Younger congregations, perhaps especially church plants, will often have younger leaders, for good reason, while older, more established churches may fittingly have more elders who are indeed older men.

However strange it may sound to modern ears, *elder* is a term worth keeping and worth teaching with patience and care, not assuming our churches are familiar with it. Alongside *pastor* and *overseer*, this is one (and the most common) way the New Testament refers to formal leaders in the local church, and we at least want our churches to read their Bibles with more understanding. And perhaps *elder* has a new day coming for it, as the church relearns how our forebears thought and spoke about spiritual leadership.

Study Questions

Preface

1. If you do an Internet search of leadership traits, you will find lists that include integrity, gratitude, and trustworthiness, along with traits such as positivity, self-confidence, curiosity, and a good sense of humor. Think of some popular contemporary leaders. Create a list of leadership traits that best define these leaders. Circle any Christian characteristics on your list. Check any characteristics that describe you. Summarize your conclusions.

2. Defend the statement, "In the Christian life and in spiritual leadership the pursuit of joy is not peripheral" (p. 20).

3. Both Christian and non-Christian leaders pursue joy. Draw a two-column chart to analyze the differences. In one column define Christian joy. In the other, write a contemporary definition of joy. Explain how the pursuit of each kind of joy might look similar and different. Apply your analysis to your own pursuit of joy to discover the kind of joy you seek.

4. Pastor Mike genuinely enjoys watching his congregation grow in knowledge of God's word and in obedience to God. He looks forward to one day presenting them mature in Christ. Explain how the experience of submitting to a worker like Pastor Mike is different from submission to grudging or self-serving leaders.

Introduction

1. "The church is a creature of the word" (p. 31). Explain how this truth should impact Christian leaders.

2. You are the creative genius behind your advertising agency's phenomenal success. Compose an advertisement to persuade one-pastor churches of the truth that Christ means for pastoral ministry to be teamwork.

3. The elders all agreed that a long-standing church ministry had become ineffective. Their spokesperson presented the elders' unanimous decision to replace the ineffective ministry with a new one. The members strongly opposed this redirection just as they had most other elder-led initiatives. List reasons why the church's members may be resistant to the elders' proposals. Keeping 1 Peter 5:1–5 in mind, circle the reasons that may be leadership related. Propose solutions to the reasons you circled.

4. Use biblical texts to prove the equation elder = pastor = overseer.

5. Perhaps you are in the process of preparing to be a pastor-elder, or perhaps you are already serving in that role. Or perhaps you are in a pastor-like role as a husband, parent, coach, or group leader,

or as an unofficial advisor to a friend. Draw an outline of a tree with both hanging fruit and falling leaves. Refer to the positive and negative pastor-elder qualities discussed in the introduction. Fill in the trunk and limbs with qualities you desire to structure your character. Fill in the fruit on the tree with positive qualities you are currently nourishing. Fill in the falling leaves with negative qualities you want to be rid of.

Chapter 1: How Christ Appoints His Pastors

1. Bob, a high school senior, Caleb, a high school coach, and Dimitri, a motivational speaker, all attend New Life Church. Bob has expressed a strong desire for pastoral ministry. Coach Caleb, who, for the last four years, has led the young men's Bible study because no one else was available, has been nominated as an elder candidate. Due to Dimitri's outstanding oratory skills, several New Life members have encouraged him to consider pastoral ministry. Create a flowchart with yes/no or if/then options that will help these men at New Life discern whether or not they are being called to serve as a pastor-elder. Use the flowchart to help you discern your own calling and your progress in it.

2. Add examples to support the statement: "The call to pastoral office is not shaped mainly by the internal desires of our hearts but by external needs of the church" (p. 48).

3. Use words and/or drawings to illustrate the process God used to plant the holy desire in you, or in someone you know, to become a pastor-elder.

4. Bob, a longtime member of New Hope Church, has accused Elder Ezra of lying about the condition of a truck he sold to Bob in a private transaction. Bob insists that Ezra covered up the fact that the transmission was leaking when he sold the truck. Ezra denies the accusation. About a year ago, Clyde, another New Hope member, had bought a lawnmower from Ezra and had accused Ezra of lying about the lawnmower's condition. No witnesses were present during either transaction. Based on 1 Timothy 5:17–25, explain how New Hope's elders should proceed.

5. You are part of the team charged with constructing a policies and procedures manual for Narrow Way, a new church plant. It is your job to write a procedural statement for the section of the manual entitled "Elder and Deacon Ordination." Write your procedural statement based on biblical texts relating to the laying on of hands.

Chapter 2: Not a Novice—or Arrogant

1. List reasons why a recent convert appointed to the office of pastor-elder might become puffed up with conceit. Circle any reasons that fuel your own self-admiration.

2. If you walk into Cornerstone Church, you will see a small congregation consisting mainly of college-age singles and young families. Many of these members are struggling to understand and effectively apply the gospel to situations in their lives. Currently there is one very tired pastor-elder who is overwhelmed by the need to disciple these members. The church is in dire need of another pastor-elder, but the available candidates are all under the age of thirty and many

of these men are single. Prioritize the biblical criteria that should be applied when choosing elders for Cornerstone.

3. Jaxon and Emerson are both newly nominated elder candidates in your church. During the screening process, it is brought to your attention that Jaxon is often rude and inconsiderate toward some church members, an indication of arrogance. You also discover that while Emerson is consistently kind and considerate, he often inserts carefully constructed, self-elevating comments into his conversations. You begin to suspect he is conceited. Describe the possible effects Jaxon's and Emerson's leadership might have on the church if they are elected to the office of elder.

4. Design a questionnaire you would use to determine if a pastor-elder or elder candidate is consistently manifesting the characteristic of humility. Administer the questionnaire to yourself to discover evidence of your own humility. Summarize your findings.

5. Describe or illustrate God's role in the process of *humbling*. Explain how understanding God's role affects any pride you have in your progress toward humility and your hope of progressing further.

Chapter 3: Pastors Are Teachers

1. You are writing a book that explains why church elders should teach proficiently. You believe witty chapter titles would entice elders to read your book. List the chapter titles you would include in your book.

2. "The societal pressure today is extraordinary for pastor-elders to practice and be proficient at just about anything else other than teaching" (p. 79). Provide contemporary examples that support this statement. Compose a rebuttal to those who put this kind of misdirected pressure on a pastor-elder.

3. Pastor Finlay interacts with multiple church members over the course of any given day. Everyone agrees his people skills and his administrative skills are outstanding. However, they also agree his teaching competencies are minimal at best. Use concrete examples to illustrate how Finlay's limited teaching capacity might affect the church, even if he rarely steps behind the pulpit or leads a small group.

4. After the last song, the worship team left the stage. Madeline retrieved her worship guide and a pen and settled herself on the third row of chairs in the sanctuary at Crossway's north campus. A screen came down, a live feed clicked on, and the face of the main campus pastor appeared. After she filled in the sermon points on her worship guide, Madeline read the announcement at the bottom of the page. She noted that a pastor based at Crossway's east campus would be bringing the next week's message. If the apostle Paul were sitting by Madeline, what comments do you suspect he might make about Crossway's teaching approach?

5. Add concrete examples to expand the statement: Elder Griffin is a good teacher.

Chapter 4: Pastors Keep Their Head in a Conflicted World

1. You are an FBI profiler. It is your job to compose a profile of a sober-minded Christian. Agents will use your profile to easily recognize and distinguish a sober-minded Christian from one who is not. Create your profile. Determine if agents, using the profile, would identify you as a sober-minded Christian.

2. Create a diagram that demonstrates the interactive process of cultivating sober-mindedness. Label the ultimate source of sober-mindedness. Identify where you are in the process.

3. Describe a situation in which your hope in Christ was temporarily shaken and you lost your head. Explain how the situation may have ended differently if you had remained sober-minded. Describe what steps you can take now to prevent losing your head in the future.

4. You are an illustrator, world-renowned for your illustrations of stickmen with voice bubbles. Create a series of stickmen illustrations that portray a group of elderly pastors discussing the need to transition younger men onto the team. Use voice bubbles to reveal the elders' hopes and fears.

5. Create a profit and loss chart to weigh the advantages and disadvantages of having an elder team whose members are all in the same age cohort. Create four columns, two for profit and two for loss. In one profit column, include the benefits of having wise, younger men on the elder team; in the other, include the benefits of having wise, older men on the elder team. In one loss column, include the

disadvantages of having only older men on the team; in the other, include the disadvantages of having only younger men on the team. Summarize your data.

Chapter 5: Self-Control and the Power of Christ

1. Create a "concept web" to develop the term *Christian self-control*: write "Christian self-control" in the center of your writing space. Then draw lines to connect the word *self-control* to biblically related words and phrases. Combine the information on your concept web and write your own definition of Christian self-control. Then apply your concept by using the definition to determine if you have the characteristic of self-control.

2. Identify a Christian brother or sister who, controlled by the love of Christ, consistently exercises self-control. Recall a situation in which you observed this person respond in a way that demonstrated Christian self-control. Describe the results.

3. Describe a situation in which you have failed to exercise Christian self-control. List reasons for your failure. Circle the ultimate, underlying reason.

4. Provide reasons to support the statement: "The elders *as a team* need to exercise a kind of collective self-control" (p. 118).

5. Aleksandr Solzhenitsyn's nonfiction *The Gulag Archipelago* tells the story of the horrific treatment of millions of Soviet citizens by Stalin's government. In his novel, Solzhenitsyn develops the theme that when a few people have unlimited power, the result is

always cruelty. Describe a church-related scenario that either supports or contradicts Solzhenitsyn's theme.

Chapter 6: The World Needs More One-Woman Men

1. Add information to explain this statement: The attribute "one-woman man" is subjective, rather than black and white.

2. You are designing a dating application for singles. Using answers to carefully crafted questions, your app generates a score that will predict an individual's probability of future marital fidelity. Design questions for the app that will predict low, medium, and high probabilities of future fidelity. Answer the questions to ponder your own trajectory of future fidelity.

3. You are a private detective. A suspicious wife hired you to determine if her husband is being faithful to her. You have not caught the husband in outright adultery, yet there are behavioral clues that suggest he may be being unfaithful. You must report your findings to the wife today. Write your report, including the indicators that lead you to question his faithfulness. Circle any indicators that an independent observer might notice in your interactions with women.

4. You are on the elder team at Grace Church. You have just received the results of a men's survey taken by men ages eighteen and up, all members of Grace. You had suspected a small number of men might be viewing porn, but you are shocked to find that regular use is prolific. Almost a quarter of men over thirty years old and over 50 percent of men in their twenties reported ongoing porn use. Propose an initiative to the elder team that will address this issue.

5. Throughout high school and college, Colton was known as a multiwoman man. Now, he is the husband of Caroline and the father of two young boys. He has been caught in sexual sin for the second time since his marriage. As before, he is repentant and wants to salvage his marriage. Colton is coming to you for counsel this afternoon. You want to be prepared. After spending time in prayer and reflection on Scripture, you decide to jot down some notes. What would you write?

Chapter 7: Does Drinking Disqualify a Pastor?

1. You are designing a commercial for a new boutique winery. The commercial will target the Christian market. You research scripture that supports the drinking of wine and begin creating your commercial. Describe or illustrate your commercial.

2. Under the Fair Packaging and Labeling Act, you must create a warning label for the alcoholic drinks your company distributes. Consider scripture related to the misuse of alcohol and design your label.

3. Pastor Ralf had been discipling Matt for over a year. Typically, they meet at a local coffee shop, but occasionally they meet for dinner and a glass of wine to celebrate Matt's spiritual victories. Wednesday evening, for the first time, Matt was able to attend the Bible study Pastor Ralf was leading at a member's home. Matt felt a little uncomfortable when the host asked if anyone would like a glass of wine. He felt even more uncomfortable when Pastor Ralf accepted a refill, and others followed his lead. Determine why Matt might feel uncomfortable and if Matt's discomfort is justified.

4. Add details to support this statement: The dangers of misusing alcohol "are real for all of God's people and yet, in some sense, even more so for leaders" (p. 147).

5. On Friday night, George's family joined Joe's family at Pepperoni Palace for pizza. Since Joe is a recovering alcoholic, George refrained from ordering his favorite draft beer. On the way home, George mentioned how thankful he was for Joe's ongoing sobriety and for his friendship with Joe. Describe situations in which abstaining or not abstaining from alcohol has affected your Christian joy.

6. As Elder Nathan relaxes with a glass of wine each night, he consoles himself by saying, "It's only one glass." What he doesn't acknowledge is that the amount of wine in the glass has slowly progressed from 2 ounces to 16. Last Saturday night, he uncharacteristically overindulged at his niece's wedding. News about the DUI Elder Nathan received on his way home spread through the church and community like wildfire. Describe the actions, if any, that the elder team could have taken before Elder Nathan overindulged at the wedding. Describe the actions the elder team should take now. State your grounds for these actions.

Chapter 8: Does Your Pastor Love God or Money?

1. Add examples to support the statement, "How Christians handle money . . . is one of our greatest opportunities to show ourselves distinct from the world, or just like it" (p. 153).

2. Develop the concept of *money lover* as follows:

- Write some words or phrases Scripture associates with *money lover*.
- Write some biblically inspired words or phrases that mean the opposite of *money lover*.
- Formulate some examples of a money lover.
- Create an image that represents a *money lover*.
- Compose a definition for *money lover*.

Now apply the concept. Would anyone in your life be able to identify you as a *money lover*?

3. Think of someone who is "rich toward God" (Luke 12:21). Explain how this person's handling of money shows that God, not money, is his or her greatest treasure. Describe any positive effects you have observed of this person's generosity.

4. Imagine that your credit card statements along with your bank accounts and investment portfolios are mirrors that accurately reflect your soul's bent toward generosity or selfishness. Describe the image you see. Explain what your reflected image implies about your belief and trust in God.

5. Examine your church's budget or find a church budget online. Consider whether it reflects a local church leadership, and congregation, of cheerful givers. What adjustments, if any, might you suggest for better management of God's resources, flowing from a generous heart?

Chapter 9: The Tragedy of Distracted Dads

1. Xavier manages his own small business. He believes his success is due to his proactivity in finding solutions for anticipated problems and his responsiveness to his clients' evolving needs. When asked what motivates him to maintain the level of awareness required to be proactive, Xavier said, "I juggle a lot of balls. My business fails if I drop one. Distraction is out of the question." Compare Xavier's management of his small business to your management of your household. Explain how you succeed or why you fail in overcoming distractions.

2. Your spouse and your children, and/or those you are responsible for, have been given unlimited resources to get your full attention through your favorite media outlets. Identify the media they would use. Illustrate the messages each would send. Compose your reply to the messages.

3. Zane and Zoey have five children, ages three to thirteen. As a homeschool mom, in addition to her household duties, Zoey struggles with developing each child's interests, meeting each child's academic needs, and addressing each child's behavioral problems, while fostering each child's love for God and others. At the end of the day, she falls into bed exhausted. Zane struggles to meet his family's basic financial needs. In addition to working a full-time job, he picks up extra work when he can. Often that means working on his day off and sometimes late into the night. Though he and Zoey rarely have time to talk, Zane believes Zoey is doing a great job as a comanager of the household, but he is struggling to understand his role as household manager and has come to you for

help. Based on your understanding of 1 Timothy 3:4–5, describe what it would look like for Zane to manage his family well during a typical week in his current situation.

4. Pastor Yuri's church is in an economically depressed metro area. Many of his members are former gang members, former addicts, and victims of physical and sexual abuse. Yuri's homelife is constantly interrupted by members in crisis situations who demand both his and his wife's counsel. Meanwhile, his fourteen-year-old son spends long, unmonitored hours playing socially interactive video games. One of the men on Yuri's elder team was informed of a video chat Yuri's son had engaged in and was shocked by the conversation's content and language. The elder met with Yuri and expressed concern over Yuri's homelife. Frustrated and tired, Yuri said, "You tell me how I am supposed to take care of this church and my family." Consider the relationship between the phrases "managing his own household" and "managing God's church" written about in 1 Timothy 3:4–5 and compose your answer to Yuri.

5. "One of the greatest needs wives and children have—and all the more in our relentlessly distracting age—is dad's countercultural attentiveness" (p. 163). Describe what countercultural attentiveness looks like in your life or in the life of a father you admire.

Chapter 10: The First Requirement for Christian Leaders

1. Defend the view that "above reproach" is a summary trait or umbrella term for all other elder qualifications.

2. Your job is to design an observational checklist that will be used to determine if a pastor or elder candidate is above reproach. Add specific actions to the list that can be verified through direct observation. Determine if independent observers who use your checklist would consider you to be above reproach.

3. Thousands of church members and nonmembers alike follow megachurch pastor Rick Lessly on several social media platforms. Recently, followers have noticed that his posts have become more abrasive and politically divisive. Furthermore, Pastor Lessly's likes and shares of certain "insensitive" posts have raised eyebrows among some followers and biting comments from others. Pastor Lessly's swift replies to these comments are often callous and sarcastic. Explain why and how the elder team should approach Pastor Rick.

4. Think of a church leader you know and complete this sentence: "Be like him except . . ." Describe how the exceptions you identified might negatively impact the church.

5. Add examples to support the statement, "We sinners cannot yet be perfect, but we can be blameless" (p. 190).

Chapter 11: How Pastors Win (and Lose) Respect

1. Under the subhead "Why Is It Necessary?" are three questions that pastors can ask about elder candidates as well as about themselves. Modify these questions and/or add others based on your understanding of Paul's use of the word *respectable* in 1 Timothy 3:2. Answer your questions to determine if you have the quality of respectability.

2. Add information to develop this statement: Respectability is a "genuine external expression of inner maturity—not hollow or faked" (p. 195).

3. Create a two-column chart to help you answer the question, "What does it mean for a father to keep his children submissive 'with all dignity'?" (p. 198). Label one column "Dignified Behavior" and the other "Undignified Behavior." Based on the chapter and your experience, identify dignified and undignified ways that dads or church leaders exercise authority in the home or the church. List these behaviors in the appropriate column. Then combine your data to create a portrait of a father who keeps his children submissive "with all dignity." Apply your answer by circling the behaviors in each column that characterize you and then determining if your exercise of authority is mostly dignified or undignified.

4. Examine the history of your social media feed, or that of a church leader you follow. Based on your understanding of the relationship between speech and respectability, identify any posts that strengthen personal respectability. Identify those that do not. If you plan to create future posts, describe how you will use your analysis.

5. You are a famous fashion designer, known for creating pastor-elder apparel that screams respectability. Describe or identify online images of clothing ensembles your models will display on the runway at this year's Pastor-Elder Fashion Week. Explain why you chose these styles.

Chapter 12: Love for Strangers and the Great Commission

1. Defend the statement, "It matters tremendously how the elders orient toward 'outsiders' and those who are 'strangers'" (p. 211).

2. Analyze your practice of hospitality by identifying people who typically visit your home for conversation, a study, a meal, or perhaps for a multiday visit. Place the people you identified into four categories: "Christians I know," "Christians I'm trying to know," "Unbelievers I know," and "Unbelievers I'm trying to know." Apply your findings by explaining how your results inform your hospitality goals for the upcoming months.

3. When Elder Keegan began his sermon on hospitality, Tobias crossed his arms and smiled smugly. After all, hospitality was his thing. As a real estate broker, he knew the value of generating contacts. His motto: "Everyone is a potential buyer or seller." Honestly state all your motivations for inviting people into your home or for taking them out for coffee or a meal. Cross out any self-centered motivations. Circle motivations that are biblically endorsed. Check motivations related to evangelism. Compile your data and state your conclusions.

4. Elder Mike regularly invites unbelievers into his life. If you ask him why, he will repeat his paraphrase of Romans 5:8: "God showed his love to me by sending Jesus to die for me while I was in the midst of rebelling against him." Paraphrase a scriptural truth that motivates you to invite unbelievers into your life.

5. Describe how teaching potential elders to understand and apply Scripture looks in your current context. Suggest ways to improve these discipleship efforts.

Chapter 13: The Strongest Men Are Gentle

1. Explain or create a drawing to illustrate the biblical relationship between strength and gentleness. Create another illustration to portray the relationship between strength and gentleness in you. Compare the illustrations.

2. Identify a Christian leader in the home or in church who has the virtue of gentleness, someone who exercises his power and strength in a life-giving, Christlike way. Describe how gentleness is manifested in this person's life in everyday situations. State any positive outcomes you've noticed due to this person's exercise of gentleness.

3. In chapter 13, the father-daughter and shepherd-sheep relationships serve as analogies to illustrate gentle leadership. Create your own relationship analogy to illustrate the leadership attribute of gentleness. Determine if someone could use your life as an analogy to demonstrate this attribute.

4. After administering the Lord's Supper and closing the service at Journey Church, a new church plant, Emily approached Pastor Rocky and said, "I couldn't participate in Communion because I have a gluten allergy. I don't understand why you don't offer a gluten-free option." A few minutes later, Bill approached Pastor Rocky and said, "I don't think you should offer wine during Communion since children are present. It's no different than of-

fering alcohol to a minor." During Pastor Rocky's much-needed Sunday afternoon nap, he was awakened by a call from Frances, who sternly admonished, "After all our discussions, I am appalled that you continue to serve leavened bread for Communion." As Frances continued her criticism, Pastor Rocky's blood pressure rose. Imagine you could intervene at this moment in Pastor Rocky's life. Describe the short- and long-term actions you would take.

5. Recount a situation in which, instead of exercising your strength in a gentle manner, you showcased your strength in a negative or threatening way. Describe the results.

Chapter 14: How Do Pastors Pick Their Fights?

1. New Vision Church, a melting pot of members and regular attenders from various theological backgrounds, requires elder candidates to go through rigorous theological training. The church also requires the candidates to take a temperament test prior to confirmation. It was quite a surprise when test results confirmed that Liam fell into the "disputer" category since some negative tendencies of this temperament type include easily angered, ill-tempered, stubborn, and contentious. Despite these results, and the church's serious consideration of Paul's warning that overseers should not be quarrelsome, New Vision suggested Liam as an elder. How might New Vision defend its decision to confirm Liam?

2. When any kind of controversy or conflict arose in his church, Elder Jacob shrunk back. His modus operandi was passivity; he had zero desire to be an arbitrator. When confronted by the elder team for consistently avoiding conflicts that needed to be resolved for the

health of the church, he said, "I don't see anything in Scripture that commands me to engage in conflict resolution, but I do see Paul's warnings to avoid foolish controversies and quarreling." Compose your reply to Jacob.

3. Over the years, Tom had become more and more domineering in his relationship with his wife, Julie. Furthermore, in his public and private interactions with her, his responses were often insensitive, condescending, and even harsh. To everyone's surprise, quiet, mild-mannered, subdued Julie began flirting with several men in Fairview Church. When Julie was confronted and refused to repent, the elders decided that she must be disciplined. In their effort to do so, many members became defensive of Julie. They insisted that if Julie was going to be disciplined, Tom should be too. Suppose you are a nonquarrelsome, proactive elder at Fairview. Describe how you would intervene in this situation.

4. Describe a time when you or someone you know stepped into a conflict and exited with a positive outcome. Identify any underlying factors (attitudes, virtues, qualities) you suspect led to the positive outcome.

5. Describe a conflict that emerged in your home or church that could have been solved, or totally avoided, with nonquarrelsome, gentle, biblical teaching.

Chapter 15: Why Christians Care What Outsiders Think

1. Reconcile Paul's words in Galatians 1:10, "If I were still trying to please man, I would not be a servant of Christ," with his words in

1 Corinthians 10:33, "I try to please everyone in everything I do." Explain how Paul's attempts to please God and man relate to his exhortation in 1 Timothy 3:2, 7: "An overseer . . . must be well thought of by outsiders."

2. Create a two-column chart to identify actions that either build up or tear down Christ's reputation in your community. Label one column "The Christian Builds Up" and the other "The Christian Tears Down." Complete the chart by adding examples of everyday interactions from within the wider community where believers work, shop, play, etc., that might result in either building up or tearing down Christ's reputation. Then apply your findings by circling any behaviors you've engaged in. Based on the examples you circled, determine whether your overall reputation in the community builds up or tears down Christ's reputation.

3. Three elders from your church walk into a busy coffee shop, order their coffee, sit down together, and open their Bibles. Gossipy onlookers who know the elders' reputations begin to whisper among themselves. Compose the dialogue of these gossipy onlookers. Add additional dialogue that occurs when you join the elders. Summarize your takeaway.

4. You are a reporter for the local newspaper and known for your intriguing headlines. Your series of stories divulging the activities of some church leaders in your community have just been released. One series of stories reflects well on the reputation of these leaders. The other series reflects badly. Compose headlines for stories in both series. Add a headline for a special report that examined your own reputation in the community.

Conclusion

1. Based on the comparison between celebrities and leaders in this section, identify someone who identifies as a Christian leader but best fits into the celebrity category. Name the celebrity-related characteristics of that person. Circle any characteristics that describe you.

2. Based on what you know about the differences between celebrities and leaders, honestly determine if your current desire is to be a celebrity or a true leader.

3. The most fundamental identity of Christian leaders is "being sheep of the good shepherd, not in being his undershepherds" (pp. 252–53). Describe how identifying more as a sheep and less as an undershepherd might affect leadership style.

4. Consider your local church and community context and hypothesize what biblical truths leaders might be most tempted to withhold. Reflect on your interactions with people in your church and community and identify truths that you have softened or failed to declare. Identify underlying reasons for your failure.

5. Pastor Greyson knew he would be stepping on some toes as he prepared his sermon on the final few verses of Romans 1 entitled, "God Gave Them Up." However, as he studied and prayed in the privacy of his office, his courage rose. He resolved not to shrink back from declaring the whole counsel of God. Sunday morning, however, his courage began to fail when, just before the service began, he noticed that a homosexual couple, neighbors of one of the elders on his team; the editor of the local newspaper, known

for his scathing articles; and the outspoken chairperson of the local LGBTQ organization were all sitting in the congregation for the first time. Imagine you are given the opportunity to encourage Pastor Greyson at this moment in his life. Compose your message to him.

6. "True Christian leadership is fundamentally self-sacrificial in the pursuit of greater, deeper, longer-lasting joy" (p. 259). Relate this assertion to the theme that pastors who are joyful in Christ are the best laborers for the joy of their people.

General Index

Scripture Index

✳ desiringGod

Everyone wants to be happy. Our website was born and built for happiness. We want people everywhere to understand, embrace, and apply the truth that *God is most glorified in us when we are most satisfied in him*. We provide a daily stream of new written, audio, and video resources to help you find truth, purpose, and satisfaction that never end. We've also collected more than forty years of John Piper's speaking and writing, including translations into almost fifty languages. And it's all available free of charge, thanks to the generosity of those who've been blessed by the ministry.

If you want more resources for true happiness, or if you want to learn more about our work at Desiring God, we invite you to visit us at desiringGod.org.

desiringGod.org

Also Available from David Mathis

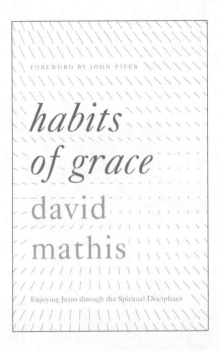

"This book is about grace-empowered *habits*, and Spirit-empowered *disciplines*. These are the means God has given for drinking at the fountain of life. We all need inspiration and instruction for how to drink—again and again. Habitually. If you have never read a book on 'habits of grace' or 'spiritual disciplines,' start with this one. If you are a veteran lover of the river of God, but, for some reason, have recently been wandering aimlessly in the desert, this book will be a good way back."

JOHN PIPER, Founder and Teacher, desiringGod.org

For more information, visit **crossway.org**.